A Boat to Take You There

Gayle M. Goertzen

Tellwell Talent
www.tellwell.ca

ISBN
978-0-2288-7134-7 (Hardcover)
978-0-2288-7135-4 (Paperback)
978-0-2288-7133-0 (eBook)

For you, Dad

TABLE OF CONTENTS

PART I: BEFORE

PART II: I REMEMBER

PART III: THE SUMMER YEARS

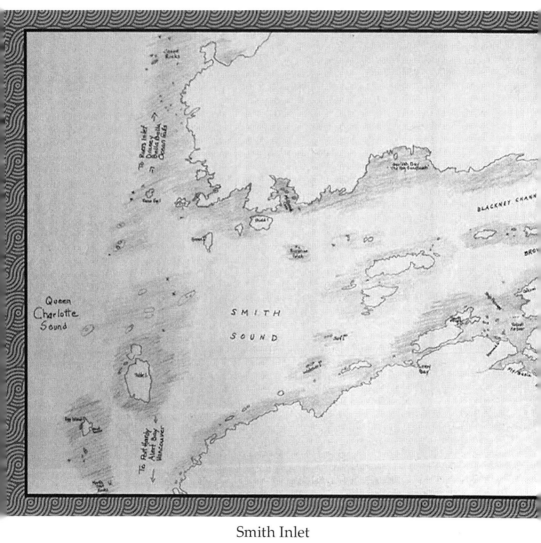

Smith Inlet

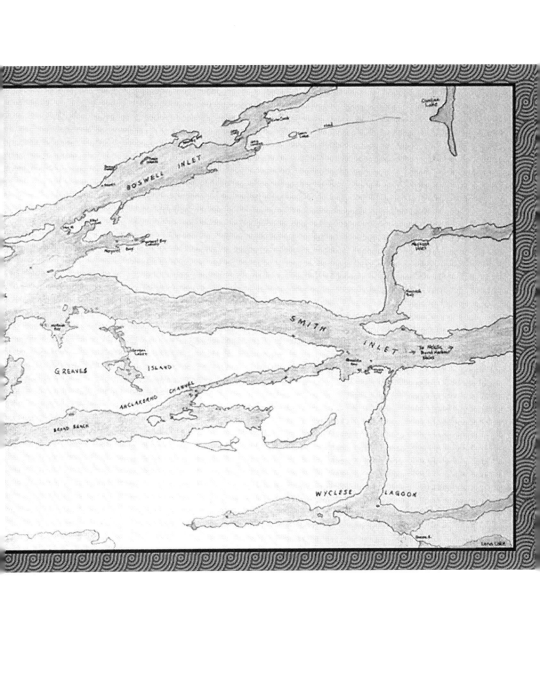

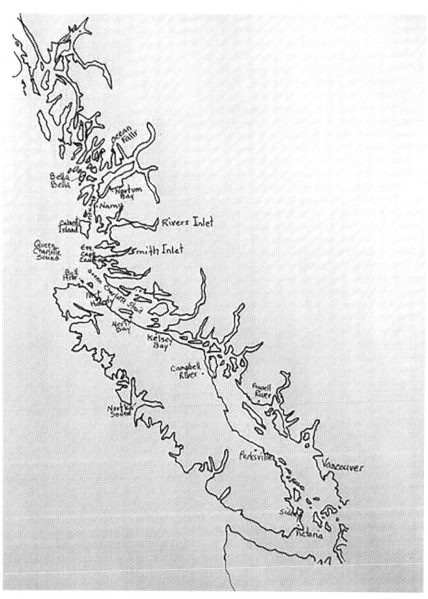

Coastline of BC

ACKNOWLEDGEMENTS

Many people wrote this book with me in the form of manuscripts, logbooks, stories, diaries and letters. In fact, my brother Roland wrote so many great stories he should probably be called a co-author! But it all began with Dad. He held out that box of old logbooks and said, "I guess these aren't good for anything anymore, are they?" I opened history when I opened those yellowed pages, and I promised Dad I would use them to write a book.

Special thanks to Ada Johnson and granddaughter Rosie for the use of Ada's manuscript which so clearly describes the events in Takush from 1950 to 1954. Thanks also to Gloria and daughter Helen for the use of Gloria's diary. Thanks to Lance, Lloyd, Dennis, Ken and Roland, without whom there would be very limited early history or logging info in this book—particularly Lance, who answered my questions about the early GMG years on a daily basis. Thanks to all of my GMG family for remembering with me. Thanks to James Walkus and everyone else from Smith Inlet whom I pestered for information. It's our story, not just mine! I hope it takes you home for a little while.

Thanks to my geologist cousin, Bruce Rafuse, for the ancient story of the inlets. Thanks to Greg and Lee Kier for the hours of work with images, diagrams and old photos. Thanks to all the Smith Inlet families who shared their photos for this book—I wish I could have used every one.

Of course, you wouldn't be reading this book if not for the Tellwell crew, who took care of the technically mysterious details of publishing a book. I am especially grateful to my editor, Darin, for liking my story, and for kindly and skillfully helping me make everything better.

Last, thanks to my husband Jeff who made writing this book possible and always believed I could do it even when I didn't. That's huge.

Prologue

The Biography of an Inlet

About thirteen thousand years ago—thousands of years before the Roman Empire and the Egyptian pyramids—two adults and a child walked a narrow strip of beach on Calvert Island. To the west was water, to the east, ice. Their footprints were found in 2018 and changed scientists' ideas about when humankind arrived on the Northwest Coast.

The footprints were gathered around a focal point. Probably a fire. I hope this small family was roasting a fish over that fire for their dinner and rejoicing over the receding ice.

"Remember this day, child, and tell it to your children so they will know the danger of the moving ice."

Legends of ice are born.

My family gathered around a fire here, too, balancing cheese sandwiches on forked sticks over the flames on a Saturday afternoon.

"Mind your sandwich, child. Isn't this a beautiful, lonely place? Maybe we are the first people to ever step foot on this shore!"

My family feels like we've lived here forever. But the ancestors of that small family might have lived here even before the ice, when the inlets were river valleys, fault-lines. Did they watch with alarm the ice growing thicker and descending lower, moving slowly through the valleys, rasping out the bottoms into deep U-shapes, weighing heavy on the land, moving out into the inside passage, pushing them to the outer shores of Calvert Island? Or could it be they more recently arrived from another continent while searching for sea mammals along the ice edge?

In 1794, when Captain George Vancouver charted Glacier Bay, Alaska (which is actually an inlet with several arms), there was no inlet, merely an indentation in the shoreline. The massive glacier was more than four thousand feet thick in places. Eighty-five years later, naturalist John Muir discovered that the ice had retreated about forty miles, forming a bay. In 2022, the glacier has retreated sixty-five miles to the heads of its inlets, even exposing pieces of Canadian shoreline!

Earlier, farther south, our inlet emptied of ice in a similar way, its shape gradually revealed as deeply cut valleys filled with water, and lagoons and lakes with narrow connecting channels or skookumchucks (strong waters) such as the Bull Run between the Ahcklakerho and Takush Harbour, and the Wyclese Lagoon and Long Lake Toksi (narrows). When the ice began to melt, ice dams were formed in places such as these and water built up behind them until they suddenly burst out into violent floods. All this ice melt caused the ocean waters to rise, creating a new shoreline.

Legends of floods are born.

With the ice gone, the inlet became alive and a giver of life with a head, a mouth and moods. Its tributaries and waters were the life source for creatures of sea and land, and for the dense forest of trees growing green and thick on the steep hillsides, exposing their bony ankles at the waterline. Salmon filled the waters, beautiful and plenteous. They swam out of the lakes and down the rivers, into the inlets, out to the sea and back again to spawn.

They were food for all, and all searched them out to live from and beside them.

Legends of creation are born.

I wish the child walking on Calvert Island—I'm going to say she was a daughter, a keeper of the history—lived to see this re-creation story; the opening up of the inlet, the land emerging as the weight of the ice was removed, the return of vegetation, animals and fish. And I wish she could sit with us at our bonfire on the big golden sand beach on the north side of our inlet and sing us her wail song.

PART I

Before

Chapter 1

Olive Point

Ron is our skipper for the day and meets us at the water taxi. It was Lloyd's boat previously, and Lloyd says this is the first time he has been a passenger and not the skipper on this boat. As Ron motors out of Hardy Bay, Lloyd recounts hair-raising tales of storms and rescues.

"It was December," says Lloyd. "A forty-five-foot longliner ran into weather about a mile and a half off Storm Islands and swamped. When I found them, there was a young man in the water holding an older man who was wearing only underwear, and there was a third man treading water nearby, still in his rain gear."

Lloyd tried rescuing the two first by manoeuvring his boat, throwing a line and reaching for them, but in the end a huge wave simply washed them both onto the back of the boat. When Lloyd turned to rescue the man in the rain gear, he was gone. The young man shouted and cried, and they looked for a long time, but he was gone.

I look at the deck of the boat, where the men would have washed aboard, and shudder as my body remembers the fury of the sea. The climbing of the watery mountains, the pause, the nosedive into the valley, green water washing over.

Lloyd's voice is quieter than I remember, tired.

"My boat was loaded with freight," he says, "including a giant Santa, a giant snowman and a candelabra. When the older man woke up, the first thing he saw was Santa Claus's face and he started screaming. He thought he was in hell."

Dennis's and Helen's voices are loud and escalating. They are having a disagreement about whether their Grandma McGill was born in Scotland or not.

Ron shouts, "WAIT!" as he fishes around in his pockets for his earplugs and puts them in. "OK, carry on! I came prepared."

Everyone laughs, and in the end Helen wins by saying, "Hey, this is be-nice-to-Helen day!"

Darby Gildersleeve and his daughter sit behind me. Others of our children are with us too—Helen's two daughters and Ryan, and Dennis's son. But Lance, the big brother to us all, is conspicuously missing, and Helen's feelings are hurt.

It's calm but foggy. Somewhere a foghorn moans. Rocks loom on either side of us, but it's the modern age of instruments and Ron is watching them; he knows the rocks are there and speeds between them. He says when the fog is gone, there is wind, and he prefers fog. Lloyd says he knows where Captain Vancouver hit a rock nearby, in the fog, on his way to survey Smith Inlet. The rock is on our right, just northeast of Ghost Island, a perfect name for rocks that make ghosts, I think.

By the time we round the corner into Smith Sound, the fog has lifted and we can see Surf Isle and Watcher Isle clearly. We pause to remember their namesakes and take photos. On the north side of Smith Sound is the sliver of gold that is the Big Sand Beach. On our right, hidden, is Takush Harbour, once the home of the Gwa'sala people. We float quietly, mists rising, water gurgling around the rocks, and Darby says, "Feels kind of magical, doesn't it, to come back home."

We pass Frank Rocks where the Japanese sub sank in 1945. Later, a US ship came and picked it up with its big pincer-like arms and dumped it in a deep hole so no one could find it. But we don't know why. No one knows about it except us—we exchange smiles of delicious mystery.

At Olive Point, Dennis recommends a particular landing site (against Lloyd's advice), and we slowly pick our way up the treacherous non-trail to the top of the hill. Darby is carrying a pickaxe and a shovel. And Ryan is in a box, carried by his dad.

Breaking through the brush into the open, I pause in reverence. There is a breeze stirring the high clouds, stretching them out over the water as far as I can see until they blend into the horizon. Sound is hushed by thick moss under my feet, climbing the gravestones, the trees. I look at the stones: Lucy George—a large abalone shell rests on her grave; her husband Chief George— his cross is rotted away; Ethel Johnson—precious lost daughter; Charles Sanden—the trapper who died of a broken heart; Don Goertzen; Harold Goertzen; Alvin McGill; Gloria McGill.

"I was here for every one of these burials!" Lloyd says.

We trip over mossy lumps. Pulling at the moss, we see the rectangular grey of a tombstone. And another, and another! There are tombstones everywhere under our feet and more lumpy areas where crosses have rotted away—so many Gwa'sala names and small, nameless spaces all hidden under the thick moss blanket. Lloyd says there were so many funerals when he was a boy that he and Cousin Heather used to play funeral. I imagine it.

"It's your turn to be the dead guy this time."

"No! I don't wanna be the dead guy, I wanna be the preacher!"

And what did they use for a coffin? Did they row to shore, dig a hole somewhere and bury each other?

I pause at Uncle Don's stone: Donald Ervine Goertzen, 1924–1952, *He Lies Where His Heart Lived*. Oh, what a hole this man left behind! I feel the pain of his loss rising up from the ancient ground. His presence was so vital to so many! He loved the Gwa'sala people, and they loved him—needed him. And they lost him. Aunt Claire lost her loving husband. Harold, Rosalie Ann and baby Donnie lost their dad.

And there is Harold's stone beside his dad's. He died of a glioblastoma five years later. Everyone is on the hill by now, and we struggle through this "why"—only one of the many why's on this hill.

Today there is another "why." The reason we're here is still ahead of us. Ryan's sisters hang on to each other. The boys take turns digging a hole beside Uncle Alvin, Ryan's precious papa. Ryan's sister wraps his box in a bag from her purse, I don't know why, and Helen kneels and places the box in the hole.

"My son, my son, my baby boy…"

Her grief twists my gut, makes me know why Lance is not here. Who can relive the death of a son? No one can withstand watching the grief of a mother losing her son, another son gone too soon. We take turns placing dirt over the box that holds Ryan, filling in a hole that cannot be filled.

There is nothing else now. But everyone agrees there needs to be a work bee to clear the hill or no one will be able to find their loved ones up here anymore. Helen and I find a place to pee in the woods. Just like the old days.

Back on the boat, we eat salmon sandwiches and pickle and cheese sandwiches, old childhood favourites that Dennis made for us. Well, really for his sister Helen.

We speed past Hazel Island (named after Mom, I always liked to think) and the hillside where my big sister Marcia first whistle-punked with Dennis. We pass the black pilings that were once Boswell Cannery, and the old fuel dock path where my brother Roland chopped Dennis's head. I see the opening to Security Bay—GMG's first logging show in the wake of the war, and there is Coho Valley on the right—their final logging show. Straight ahead, before we turn our corner, is a hill covered in tall hemlock, balsam, spruce and cedar; it's the hill across from camp that was once a logging slash, and Dad told me it would be all grown up by the time I was a grandma.

Now we can see the first floathouses over the strip of protective rocks at high tide—the Alvin McGill house, the church, school, guest house, cookhouse, Roy McGill house, bunkhouse, teacherage, Louis Goertzen house, Ernie Knopp house. Our lifejacketed friends are racing up and down the floats. Ken is spinning doughnuts in his boat in front of camp, and Murray is teasing Otscar with chunks of fish on a string. But only a few of us can see this.

We round our little island, and Ron slows to nose up to its rocky beach because Helen and I want to walk on it again. But before we're even close, Helen strips down to her skivvies and dives into the water! Exposing her aging body means nothing to her.

"*This* is what it feels like!" she yells in joy.

She swims, suspended and weightless just like when she was a kid, to the island. She is the only one brave enough to do what we all want to do—strip to our skivvies and jump in the cold water! Cleanse something! And maybe start again from the beginning.

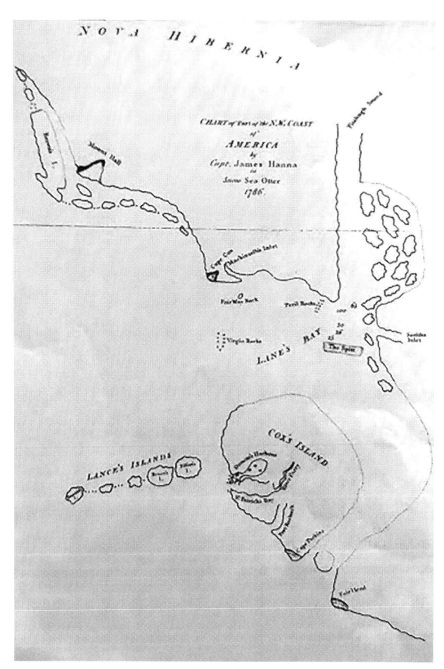

James Hanna's chart of Smiths Inlet, 1786

CHAPTER 2

INLET UNFATHOMED

I n 1786, Mozart premiered *The Marriage of Figaro* in Vienna, my Mennonite ancestors were fleeing Prussia, the French Revolution was brewing, the slave-trade was outlawed in the US, John Molson founded a brewery in Montreal, and Captain James Hanna sailed into Smith Inlet.

Hanna ended up in Smith Inlet because of his own bad luck. What he really wanted was to load up with sea otter pelts in Nootka Sound on the west coast of Vancouver Island, but two ships from Bombay arrived just before he did and bought them all. So he sailed north, hoping to find more locals selling sea otter pelts and perhaps discover the rumoured Northwest Passage while he was at it. Every country and every captain wanted to be the first to find this fabled fast route to Asian trade.

Hanna didn't survey Smith Inlet; he was more interested in finding out where Fitz Hugh Sound went—he had high hopes it would be the Northwest Passage. He waited through more than one gale, then the doldrums, the currents nearly washing him up on the rocks. He decided Fitz Hugh Sound must be a river, noting in his ship log, "I never in the mouth of any River or Inlet, found such large quantities of Timber, and Rubbish, as continually came down here with the Stream."[1] He named the place he waited in Smiths Inlet after no one knows who, although he did have three fellow traders back in China, all three Scottish, all three named George Smith; perhaps he named it after all three of them.

He hung about the area, charting the bottom end of Calvert Island and naming rocks (the Sea Otter Group) for nearly three weeks. He recorded no sightings of local people, but you can be sure the local people saw him; the snow-rigged, 120-ton ship named, hopefully, *Sea Otter* was likely the first sailing ship they had ever seen. Spanish ships had been sailing past at a distance since 1774, trying to establish a Spanish presence, and Captain James Cook did the same in 1776, but they had made a straight shot up the outside from Nootka to Alaska and their ships would have appeared small on the horizon. Hanna finally gave up on entering Fitz Hugh Sound and sailed away, never to return.

Captain George Vancouver arrived at Smith Inlet on August 10, six years after Hanna, in the ten-gun full-rigged survey ship HMS *Discovery* accompanied by the armed tender HMS *Chatham*, a four-gun survey brig captained by Lieutenant William Broughton. Vancouver's mission was, very basically, to establish British presence (as the Brits had problems with the Spanish thinking everywhere was theirs) and to survey the coastline in hopes of finding that elusive Northwest Passage. He had Hanna's sketchy chart and was making his way up Queen Charlotte Strait in the fog, headed for Smith Inlet, when he hit a couple of rocks.

The *Discovery* hit first. Seven hours she lay on her side in what Vancouver referred to in his ship log as "a bed of sunken rocks"[2] just off Ghost Island in Queen Charlotte Strait, almost directly

---

[1]   W. Kaye Lamb & Tomas Bartroli, James Hanna and Henrey Cox: "The First Maritime Fur Trader and His Sponsor," (B.C. Studies no 84, Winter 1989-98)

[2]   Ed. W. Kaye Lamb, *The Voyage of George Vancouver 1791-1795, Volume II,* (p 641-655) Hakluyt Society, Cambridge: University Press, 1984

across the strait from the present town of Port Hardy. The high tide and some serious rowing released them, but soon after they were underway again, it fell calm, and the ships became vulnerable to the pull of the tide drawing them towards more rocks.

About two miles past the *Discovery's* rock, the *Chatham* was halted by another. A second long night lay before them as they waited out another tide. Two ships, two tiring nights of heaving and ho-ing, casting off of stores and shoring up of hulls with spars and topmasts. Finally, they were freed to sail north. The *Chatham* sustained some damage to her hull but was able to sail.

Vancouver had planned to base out of Smith Inlet and send his boats out from there to survey the area, but when he saw more rock piles in front of Smiths, noting in his log that "detached rocks were again seen to encumber the shore," he didn't want a repeat of his last two nights and changed his mind. Instead, he hugged the steep eastern shore of Calvert Island and ducked into Safety Cove. The cove suited his purposes, so he secured the ships and sent out the boats to explore the area the next morning.

Master James Johnstone and Henrey Humphreys took two cutters north, and Vancouver joined them for a portion of time in the yawl. The weather was squally and unpleasant. In fact, the weather was bad enough that it became a main topic in Vancouver's log, and he repeated phrases like, "thick rainy weather, increased torrents of rain, thick stormy weather." Vancouver was not enjoying himself, and noted the area was "…as desolate inhospitable a country as the most melancholy creature could be desirous of inhabiting," and, "the inclemency of the weather having, on this occasion, been more severely felt than in any of our former expeditions."

Really, George? It's August for Pete's sake!

Back in comfort on the *Discovery*, Vancouver was worried about Lieutenant Peter Puget and Master Joseph Whidby in Smith Inlet, noting in his log, "The weather, though clear at intervals for a short time, continuing very boisterous, filled our minds with much solicitude for the welfare of our friends in the boats; particularly those detached to the S.E who were greatly exposed not only to its inclemency, but to the violence of the sea, which, from an uninterrupted ocean, broke with great fury on the southern shores."

Puget and Whidbey surveyed Smiths and Rivers Inlets for one week and came back exhausted. They reported their findings to Vancouver. "The entrance into Smith's inlet was nearly closed by rocky islets, some producing shrubs and small trees, others none; with innumerable rocks as well beneath as above the surface of the sea, rendering it a very intricate and dangerous navigation for shipping. Within the islets and rocks the northern shore appeared the clearest; but the opposite side could not be approached without some difficulty, not only from the numerous rocks, but from a great oceanic swell occasioned by the prevailing tempestuous weather."[3]

So it seems the explorers had some poor weather and a tough time getting into Takush Harbour. But they described it pretty accurately. They saw a village in Takush Harbour and continued down the inlet. "About three leagues [6.6 km] within the entrance, the rocks and islets ceased to exist, and the inlet contracted to a general width of about half a mile; though, in particular places, it was nearly twice that distance from shore to shore; both of which were formed by high rocky precipices covered with wood."

On August 13, 1792, Puget's and Whidbey's boats were about halfway up the inlet when two cultures met for the first time; the British met the Gwa'sala (People of the North). The Gwa'sala are the northernmost people in a larger group of people called the Kwakwaka'wakw, who all spoke, and many still do, the Kwak'wala language. (The anthropologist Franz Boas mistakenly

---

[3]   Ed. W. Kaye Lamb, *The Voyage of George Vancouver 1791-1795, Volume II,* (p 641-655) Hakluyt Society, Cambridge: University Press, 1984

recorded the Kwakwaka'wakw people as "Kwakiutl" which was the name of the first tribe in a rank-ordered list of about twenty-two Kwakwaka'wakw tribes.) About this encounter, Vancouver entered into his log: "About halfway up the channel a village of the natives was discovered, which our gentlemen supposed might contain two hundred or two hundred and fifty persons. It was built upon a detached rock, connected to the mainland by a platform, and, like those before mentioned, constructed for defence."

This describes the Gwa'sala location at Wyclese (from Gwikilis meaning "whale turned to stone"). The people were positioned here to catch and process the salmon on its way into the lagoon and up to Long Lake (Tse?la). The defence observed would have been against raiding tribes. When tribes raided—and there were several non-Kwakwaka'wakw tribes to their north—they killed men and took food, tools and supplies, canoes, blankets, masks with their associated dances, and slaves. (In fact, there would be a particularly devastating raid on the Gwa'sala by the Heiltsuk of Bella Bella in the 1850s which resulted in a significant reduction in population.)

Puget says they were exploring a small branch on the south shore (thought to be the Ahclakerho, a channel which opens near the location at Wyclese) when:

> we had many new visitors and many more were perceived coming in. I must own their Numbers at first was not altogether pleasant, as those already near the boats behaved in a most daring and insolent manner. Mr. Whidbey and me immediately consulted and we were both of the opinion, the intention of the natives was not friendly. The boats were directly put in a state to act on the defensive, but we were determined not to begin hostilities without their absolutely attempting to take the

boats; seeing us prepared and preparing to resist such an attempt, for a lighted match was close to the swivels, they thought proper to conduct themselves more quietly, though still armed with daggers and other offensive weapons, we continued pulling out in the main branch, they following and dropping off as we came from the cove.[4]

The explorers recorded sightings of three settlements in the inlet: Wyclese, another presumed to be the Takush site, and another somewhere in the Ahclakerho. Vancouver's logbook records one of the encounters:

A great number of its inhabitants, in about thirty canoes, visited our party, and used every endeavour they thought likely to prevail on them to visit their habitations. They offered the skins of the sea-otter and other animals to barter; and beside promises of refreshment, made signs too unequivocal to be misunderstood, that the female part of their society would be very happy in the pleasure of their company. Having no leisure to comply with these repeated solicitations, the civil offers of the Indians were declined. And the party continued their route back, keeping the northern or continental shore on board.

Were the inhabitants friendly and generous as described by Vancouver? Or opportunistic and defensive of their territory as in the incident described by Puget? It's easy to imagine how both could be true; it would certainly seem wise to be cautious of the new people. There is an incident recorded in 1801 that is similar to Puget's story. The American fur trader David Ockington, captain of the 183-ton brig *Belle Savage*, recorded in his ship's log that

---

[4]   Ed. W. Kaye Lamb, *The Voyage of George Vancouver 1791-1795, Volume II*, (p 641-655) Hakluyt Society, Cambridge: University Press, 1984

150 Gwa'sala, under "Chief Wacosh," attacked and captured his vessel, but it was retaken.

If Puget and Whidbey had complied with the friendly solicitations and been prevailed on to stop and "visit their habitations," they would have seen, and perhaps used similar words to describe, what Franz Boas, the anthropologist, saw between 1885 and 1930. They would have said something like this—my condensed version of Boas' lengthy descriptions:

"We were led up the path to the biggest house by men with long, thin faces distinguished by a high and narrow nose which was sometimes markedly hooked. Their skin was light brown, like a suntan. The men wore their hair long, tied in a knot at the back, with a fur headband; for clothing, an apron, supplemented by a blanket with a belt over it if they were cold. The blankets were made of various animals or woven cedar bark. The women wore two braids in their hair, decorated with strings of sea otter teeth, with tassels, an apron and a blanket. The men and women both wore earrings and nose rings of abalone and painted their faces with red and black paint. Women also wore arm rings, wristlets, knee rings, and anklets of mountain goat wool and yellow cedar bark. The children were naked or wore a blanket, and everyone was barefoot. They said "yo" to greet each other but did not shake hands or embrace.

"Unlike the houses in the villages farther south, their houses were "big" rather than "long." They were square, with four families each. Posts and beams were hewn with stone adzes. The walls and roof were planks split with wooden wedges and stone mauls and fastened together with cedar withes and spruce roots.

"Inside the front door, we immediately smelled ammonia from the urine in the large bentwood box at the door. At night, all urine is collected and dumped into this box to make a solution for cleaning hides for blankets. A platform, about two feet high and four or five feet deep, was built against the walls around the interior of the house. Enclosed rooms with doors were built into each corner, like four small houses inside the big house. These were private family bedrooms, which were entered by permission only. Inside the bedroom were beds of cedar branches covered with deerskin, with blankets of mountain goat and bearskin, and pillows of skin filled with bird down.

"Each compartment had a fire in front of it with two or three stones as andirons, and several stone and wood implements. Beside it, a large wooden platform served as a seat for reclining. Above the fire was a rack of poles for drying and smoking food. A stack of bentwood cedar boxes stood by the fire, the largest as big as three feet high and two and a half feet square. Smaller boxes were stacked on it to form a sort of pyramid of boxes. The largest box contained eulachon oil stored in dried kelp tubes stoppered with rounded wood, coiled inside like ropes. The smaller boxes contained dried foods—salmon, clams, hemlock bark sap balls, cakes of berries, seaweed and roots.

"More large boxes were stacked around the walls, storing, among other things, blankets for potlatching, and in the centre of the room was a larger firespace, with adjustable boards in the roof above it and a long pole for moving them. The most important families of the house lived in the two rear compartments."

It was summer, so Puget and Whidbey would have been offered fresh salmon, halibut, flounder, cod, hair-seals, clams, cockles, horse clams and berries. They may have noted a hierarchy, with the slaves serving them. If it had been winter, they would have been offered water, then dried salmon dipped in eulachon grease, then more water, followed by an "after food" of dried hemlock bark sap or roots, perhaps clover roots, steamed in the bentwood box, flattened and put in a dish with eulachon grease on top, to be eaten with the fingers of their right hand. Or perhaps they would have been offered a fresh duck or eagle, fat from feasting on fish.

But, for reasons of haste or caution, Puget and Whidbey did not stop to enjoy the hospitality of the Gwa'sala, and these descriptions of the people and their homes were not recorded until after Boas arrived in 1885. (See chapter sources for more information.) Instead, the explorers pushed on to the head of the inlet and kept to the north shore on their way back out. They nipped into the mouth of Boswell, then out of Smith Inlet to Rivers Inlet, which they surveyed without encountering any of the inhabitants. Then they returned to the ships.

When all the scouting boats returned, Vancouver was done for the summer. He kept Hanna's name for Smith Inlet, which was later used for the sound at the entrance, and for the longer arm of the inlet. Although Vancouver said he wanted to honour the names given by previous explorers, he was pretty sloppy about it—certainly wouldn't have passed my Smith Inlet schoolteacher's muster. On his charts, Smiths Inlet became Smith's Inlet, Peril Rocks became Pearl Rocks, and Fitz Hugh Sound, Fitz Hugh's Sound. And somehow the charts today simply say Smith Sound and Smith Inlet, with no "s" either plural or possessive!

Neither Hanna nor Vancouver paid any attention to the fact that people may have already named everything. It's probable that the Gwa'sala had been there long enough to watch the ice recede and the inlet take shape. They had experienced the powerful floods of bursting ice dams and worried about the rising ocean, and these stories were passed down. They knew every bay and lagoon, every island, arm and skookumchuck. The inlet was their history book, each location and name a chapter. Location names connected them to their origin story, commemorated events, identified their territory or described what could be found there. Each time their canoes passed by, stories were told and history and culture were preserved in the listener.

This kind of history telling has the advantage (or possibly disadvantage) of fluidity; it can be changed to fit the needs of the current generation, which is much more difficult to do with a written history. Some history was permanently recorded, however. At the same time the explorers entered the Gwa'sala into the European history books, the Gwa'sala added a chapter to their own—sailing ships were painted on the cliffs at Long Lake.

Several Gwa'sala names do remain, either on the charts or in local verbiage, and many more are regaining usage. But the meanings of some of these place names have been lost, and there are several different spellings for each word based on how many scholars attempted to spell them. The spellings often contain strange symbols that are not common in the Latin alphabet to represent the clicks and throat sounds. Some examples are:

Kigeh: (gigex, geg ̇ägē) "a place to come." Labelled Indian Island on the marine chart
Takush: (t'̲akus, tā̄g ̇us, takawis) the village site at Kigeh
Gikume Point: (gigame') "big chief"
Wakas Point: (Walkus, Wa'kas) also an important family name
Wyclese Lagoon: (wyclees, waitlas, gwika̲lis, gwikilis) "whale turned to stone." The rock island near the mouth of the lagoon, inhabited as Puget described, and the site in one of the Gwa'sala origin stories
Quascilla Bay: (qwashella, gwasilla, quascila, quashilla) this word is now "Gwa'sala"
Ahclakerho: the channel on the south side of Smith Inlet
Toksi: (Toksee, t'u̲xse', t'u̲xwsa'yi, Docee) "narrow place." A site at the entrance to the short river (now called the Docee River) between Wyclese Lagoon and Long Lake
Tse?la: Long Lake

History is fluid, spelling is fluid, whateva'! We shall remember this fluid-spelling concept as we read our story! Thankfully, the U'mista Cultural Society, whose mandate is to ensure the survival of all aspects of the cultural heritage of the Kwakwa̲ka'wakw peoples, has recently developed an orthography for the Kwak'wala language. But the world, including the producers of the marine charts, has not yet caught up.

Back in Smiths Inlet in 1792, only the British were spelling things. After Vancouver's visit, he recorded in his log: "Smith's Inlet, and many other channels of this kind that we had examined, afforded no soundings in the middle with 80 fathoms of line..."

Fathom means to encircle with outstretched arms, to embrace. To measure the depth of, take a sounding of. To comprehend, understand. None of the explorers could fathom the inlet in any sense of the word. They did not embrace or love it; they could not sound its depths—they would have needed a 195 fathom (356 metre) line at low tide to reach the deeper parts of the inlet—and neither did they understand it. They hadn't the line, the time or the heart to fathom our inlet. Their lack of appreciation allowed Smith Inlet and its people to remain undisturbed a little while longer.

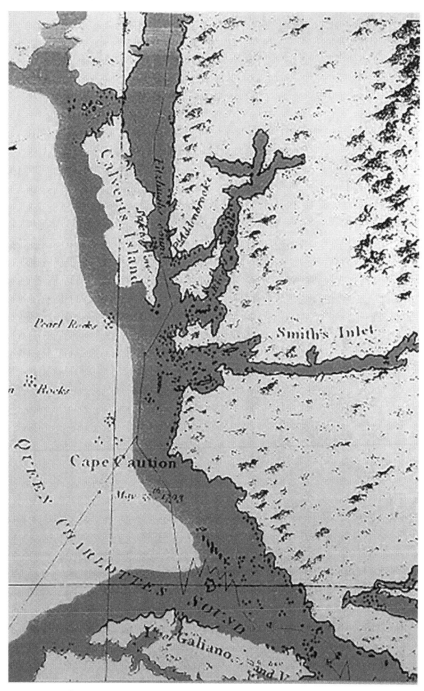

George Vancouver's chart of Smith Inlet, 1792

CHAPTER 3

LOVE AND WAR

In 1936, Canada's Great Depression was in full swing. Alvin was sixteen years old and lived with his family in White Rock, BC. He was the third of six siblings, five of them boys.

"My dad simply couldn't feed us," says Alvin when he tells his story.

He and some friends decided to relieve their poverty-stricken families by boarding a ship to Australia, but he couldn't bear to hurt his mother by not saying goodbye, so when he told her he was leaving, she put a quick end to his plans.

"You put that bike away and get in the house right now, young man. You are going to school!"

But he was still restless, and in less than a year, he and his friend had devised a new plan.

"Every weekend my mom went to work at Woodward's in Vancouver. With both Mom and Dad gone to work, my friend Lloyd and I took our bikes on the bus, and we met my mom at work. She couldn't stop me from going because she was at work, and I could still say goodbye. She was upset. She said, 'You get right back on that bus!' But I said, 'Not this time, Mom,' and hugged her goodbye."

The boys began their long bike ride to Penticton. In the evening, it became dark and they saw a storm coming. They found a barn to sleep in and sneaked into the hayloft, agreeing to wake and be gone before the milkers arrived so no one would know they'd been there. Instead, they woke to the sound of milk swishing into a pail.

"What shall we do now?" Lloyd whispered.

They decided to go down the ladder and show themselves. Two hired hands were milking the cows, and they advised the boys to ask the farmer for breakfast.

"Well, we couldn't bring ourselves to beg for food, but we had a couple dollars between us, so we went to the farmhouse and asked the lady if we could buy a loaf of bread. The farmer's wife said she would have none of that and insisted on feeding us a breakfast fit for kings! She fed us venison and strawberries! For breakfast!"

The boys couldn't believe their good luck. For two hungry boys this was an ultimate act of kindness. And their luck continued. The farmer offered them a job haying for a few days for free room and board plus a few cents a day. They stayed on for two weeks.

When the haying was done, they got back on their bikes and finished their journey to Penticton.

"We got involved with the rail bums," remembers Alvin. "These were mostly young men who rode the trains here and there looking for work and adventure. The first ride, I was so cold and shivering so hard I thought I would die and fall off. I was so frozen I couldn't remove myself from the roof of the train. My new friends dragged me off and fed me two cups of coffee.

"Another time, we were going up the corkscrew tunnel, and I was so cold I decided to run up the corkscrew, jumping from one level to the other. At the end, I jumped back on the train but in a different spot. My friends thought I was a goner—thought I hadn't laid low enough and I'd got swiped off."

The boys eventually found work on a farm in Alberta when Canada joined the war in September 1939. Canada, under Liberal Prime Minister Mackenzie King, vetoed conscription for overseas service. All men could be drafted for military training and home guard duties, but only volunteers would be sent overseas.

Consistent with the beliefs of his family's church, Alvin registered as a conscientious objector (CO), which meant he refused military training for moral or religious reasons. By 1940, the government decided COs would be required to perform alternative service for four months, the same length of time as standard military training. In May 1941, Alvin was sent to a camp near Banff to trailblaze the park for fire prevention and in preparation for post-war tourism.

"A truck picked me up in Banff and took me to camp. The driver showed me to a tent, gave me a scratchy army-issue blanket and a tick. 'Fill your tick here,' he said, and pointed to a pile of straw."

Work—hard physical labour like felling trees, running a sawmill, slashing trail, building bridges, fixing roads and clearing brush—started early in the morning. The men were paid fifty cents per day (military pay was $1.30 per day) plus room and board, clothing not provided.

The boss, Charles Crook, was Scottish. When he learned Alvin's name, he said, "With a name like McGill, you shouldn't have to work." He gave Alvin the job of driving truck, and Alvin drove the boss around at work and made runs to town to pick up new crew, mail and supplies.

The townspeople had just sent their men off to war to fight for their country, as all courageous men should do in their opinion, and they didn't always hide their disapproval of the COs. They called the COs "yellow bellies" (cowards), "zombies" and "conchies." One day when Alvin made a trip to town to pick up mail and new crew, a woman approached him.

"What are all these men doing in civvies?" she demanded.

Alvin explained that they were conscientious objectors; men who felt it morally wrong to bear arms.

"Well, I should take a gun and shoot every one of you! Shame on you! Why aren't you fighting for your country?"

And she unleashed a lengthy tirade of verbiage to shame them.

Sobered, Alvin returned to camp with his crew. Most of the crew were Mennonites—pacifists with a long history of fleeing countries to avoid military duties. They were hard workers who were glad to fulfill their alternative service requirement in exchange for military exemption, but here they all were, in perfect safety, blazing trails in a park. They were unable to provide for their families on only fifty cents a day, and they were homesick. In many cases, their families were left to struggle for survival without them, running the farm alone or taking jobs wherever they could. The accusations of cowardliness and laziness hit home.

There were rumours of being "frozen" into their present position for the duration of the war, and the men responsible for families at home were very concerned they'd be unable to provide for them for such an indefinite period. Because Alvin rode with the boss, the men in camp pumped him for information at the end of every day. One night Alvin came in and flopped onto his bunk.

"Ah bunk, old buddy, we're together for the long haul now." *Sigh*. "And I had big plans. Stupid war. Ah well, I have you, bunk, old buddy."

The men were silent. The man in the bunk across from Alvin sat up and put his face in his hands and sobbed out loud, tears falling. Alvin immediately regretted his joke. (In April 1942, after Alvin and his friends were gone, the camps *were* "frozen," and others had to experience what this group only feared.)

Eventually, Alvin won the friendship of the Mennonite boys.

"One of them was sick, and there was an obnoxious guy who kept picking on the sick boy, he being the only one there weaker than himself," Alvin says. "Finally, I stood up and grabbed him by the shirt, looked into his eyes and said, 'You pick on him one more time and you'll have me to contend with!'"

This was a significant threat because Alvin had taken up boxing while at the camp and was good at it.

When Alvin's four months were over, he went back to White Rock. Logging was an essential service in WWII, providing both paper and airplanes, and the logging camps were continually replacing loggers gone to war. His older brother Roy was working for a logging company up the coast, so Alvin looked on the big board in the Vancouver Employment Office, saw a post for a job at Gildersleeve logging camp in Smith Inlet and caught the steamship north.

When he arrived at Margaret Bay Cannery that autumn day in 1941, Willis (Bill) Gildersleeve's floating camp was situated in Boswell Inlet, off of Smith Inlet, and Bill was at Margaret Bay to pick up his freight. Alvin walked the wharf asking likely looking people, "Are there any logging jobs around here?"

"Ask that guy over there," was the reply, with a point towards a tall, handsome man packing boxes onto his boat.

"I hear you have a job available," Alvin asked Bill.

"Well, can ya swing an axe? All right then."

Alvin went home with Bill.

In June, Bill's daughter Gloria came home from her sister Genevieve's house in Oregon, where she had just graduated from high school. Gloria was, just like in the romance novels, a dark-eyed, raven-haired beauty who played the piano and sang. She planned to spend her last summer at home, then return to college, get her teaching certificate and choose from among the many suitors pursuing her—all of them the singing evangelist types. But when she met Alvin, she forgot all of it. She thought he was the most beautiful blue-eyed, blonde-haired man she had ever seen. He had a magnetic personality and a good sense of humour. He made her heart skip a beat from the moment she saw him, and she immediately began flirting with him.

There were rowboat rides in the path of the moon, hikes in the woods, long talks in the evening. Alvin began collecting logs to build a float for a house, and Gloria's parents began to worry. They had goals for their daughter; they wanted her to become a teacher and marry one of her singing evangelists. Sister Genevieve learned of the new romance and wrote a scathing letter to Gloria asking her what she was thinking. Did she really want to throw her life away as the wife of an uneducated logger?

Gloria was torn between love, and loyalty to her parents and her own dreams. Finally, when it was almost time for her to return to college, she made her decision and told Alvin she needed to go back to school; her parents wanted her to go to college and she would honour their wishes. Maybe she hoped Alvin would say, "No, please stay! I love you!" But he wisely did not. Instead, he sold his float and made reservations on the steamship. He could not stop her dreams, and he could not stay there.

But Gloria's brother Clyde liked Alvin. When he heard the loggers chatting at work—"Poor Alvin, he's not building a house on that float anymore, and he was gonna ask her to marry him, too!"—he immediately went to Gloria.

"You are making a terrible mistake!" he said to her. "You will never find a better man than Alvin. Alvin was going to build a house on that float and ask you to marry him! What are you doing?"

That's all it took for Gloria to ditch loyalty to parents and her previous dreams. Now she knew Alvin really did love her. She ran to the bunkhouse and invited him for a boat ride, so he took her out on the water and let her do the talking. Gloria proposed to Alvin, and that romantic boat ride brought them back to camp engaged!

In a romance novel, that would be the beautiful ride-into-the-sunset-in-a-boat ending. But the real story is more complicated than that. Gloria began receiving letters from disappointed suitors, and her beloved sister Genevieve begged her to reconsider. But Gloria was in love, and the camp folk helped her plan a grand affair in the cookhouse for her wedding day. The day before the wedding, word came that the minister of Indian Affairs, who was to perform the ceremony, could not make it to camp. Gloria was distraught.

"Let's go to Vancouver and get married," Alvin suggested. "We'll catch the steamer at the end of the week."

So Gloria packed her bags. They arrived at Margaret Bay in plenty of time, excited to make the beautiful trip to Vancouver on the *Cardena* and get married. But the ship was late. They waited all afternoon, all night, all the next day, and into the next night before word came that the Union steamship *Cardena* had hit a rock and would not be arriving. They returned home unmarried. Disappointed, they looked at their options.

"Captains are authorized to perform marriages at sea," said Gloria. "Let's ask Charlie Anderson!"

Charlie didn't want to perform a marriage, so they phoned a minister in Vancouver and asked him to marry them over the radiophone.

"I can't do that," said the minister. "It's not legal."

In an act of desperation, Alvin offered his friend Frank Anderson forty dollars to take them to Ocean Falls in his little gas boat to get married.

"All right," said Frank, "but you'll have to pump the boat along the way; she's been taking on water."

For about sixteen hours, Alvin sat at the stern pumping the lever up and down, up and down, in a rainy southeaster while Frank steered and Gloria sat in the bow with Frank's wife Dorothy. They finally arrived, wet and cold, in Ocean Falls and went straight to see Judge Hill to get a marriage license.

"I can give you a license," the judge told them. "But because Gloria is not yet twenty-one, it requires her father's signature before you can marry."

This was too much for Gloria and she burst into tears, sobbing her disappointing wedding experiences to the judge.

"There, there," said the judge. "Don't cry. I think we can fix it up somehow."

And the kind-hearted judge, made more kind by inebriation, tried to comfort her with hugs and kisses and eventually conceded to obtaining her father's signature at a later date. With the license in order, the judge took them to meet the minister. The minister said he had never performed a wedding for a white couple before, but he supposed it couldn't be much different from the ones he performed for the villagers.

By this time, Alvin and Gloria didn't care a whit about the details of the wedding service or the lack of wedding dress, bridesmaids, groomsmen, special music or fancy vows. They were married on October 24, 1942, approximately two months after their planned wedding date. The bride wore a black skirt with a turquoise blouse, black hat and black shoes.

Their "honeymoon" night was spent in a room at the old Martin Inn. There was a single bed, cockroaches crawling up the walls and a toilet down the hall. But Alvin took Gloria in his arms and danced her around the room singing, "You're mine, you're mine, you're mine." Life was perfect.

The next day, Alvin bought a new oil stove for Gloria and put it on Frank's boat. They repeated the miserable ride home, arriving late. Everybody was tired and wanted to crawl straight into their beds, but Alvin insisted on taking the stove off the boat and putting it on the float before they went to bed. The next morning the boat was underwater, hanging by the cleats, but the stove was safe and dry. This seemed a good sign after all their trials.

All was happiness until a Saturday morning not long after when Gloria found Alvin lounging about instead of getting ready for church.

"Hurry Alvin, it's almost time to go."

"Nah, you go. I don't want to."

"But you have to—we have to go to church."

"No, I don't have to. It's your church not mine. I don't belong to any church; I don't have to go."

Gloria was stricken. She felt deceived. She was sure Alvin believed the same as she did! Her mind probably flashed to the singing evangelist suitors she had rejected and the warnings and the difficulties she encountered trying to marry Alvin. But what was she to do about it? And there was a baby on the way!

Well before the due date, Alvin and Gloria went to Vancouver to stay with relatives and wait for the baby. Alvin's mom and his sister Myrn came to the hospital with them for the delivery. When it was time to deliver, the doctor saw the umbilical cord wrapped around the baby's neck twice and acted quickly to save the baby from strangulation. In his desperate efforts to remove the cord from around the neck, he broke the baby's jaw and an ankle. He thought the baby was dead and left him at the foot of the bed, turning his attention in alarm to Gloria, who was hemorrhaging. Grandma and Auntie took the baby and began dipping him alternately in cold and hot water, hoping to bring him to life.

At this point Alvin went outside. I'm sure he was feeling pretty sorry for anything bad he had ever done, and he prayed a sincere and desperate prayer.

"God, if you save my wife and baby, I will commit myself to you, and I will join Gloria's church."

Baby Lance finally took a breath and turned pink while the doctor brought Gloria's hemorrhage under control. Alvin kept his promise for the rest of his life. If ever confronted or questioned on this loyalty, he simply answers, "I made a promise to God. And I keep my promises."

And Gloria was happy.

Alvin and Gloria

CHAPTER 4

GILDERSLEEVES

C lyde Gildersleeve was two years old when his parents, Willis (Bill) and Alice moved to Nootum Bay in 1920. Nootum Bay, with its lovely sand beach, is just north of Fitz Hugh Sound as you enter Burke Channel and just before Restoration Bay where Vancouver beached his ship for repairs in 1793. Clyde's uncle George (Doc) had been in Nootum Bay since 1916, along with Doc's brothers-in-law Almon and Lloyd Owens. The Gildersleeve and Owens brothers were loggers from Oregon, where opportunities were declining, and BC's logging opportunities seemed endless.

In the beginning, the Gildersleeve and Owens brothers hand-logged up the Nootum River; they felled and bucked the trees, then floated them down the river to the beach where they split them into cord-wood for the nearby canneries. Because the BC inlets provided sheltered water and steep shorelines, hand-logging was unique to BC. No power equipment was required, or even allowed, with a hand-logging license. Gravity was the hand-logger's most valuable tool; all he needed was a forty-five-degree slope, a "misery whip" (saw), a Gilchrist jack to assist the movement of stubborn logs that refused to slide down the hill on their own, a peavey, and his own skill and strength. Trees were carefully selected for the desired market because falling a tree was a lot of work. It required two men with a misery whip sawing in rhythm back and forth on little springboards stuck into the tree high above the ground. There were also hours of filing in the evenings to keep the saw sharp.

Eventually, the Gildersleeves and Owens would log for Pacific Mills Ltd. of Ocean Falls and progress to A-frame logging with a steam donkey, truck logging and even rail logging. They towed their camp, built on log floats cabled together into a towable unit, wherever their new logging claim was situated. In 1922, the Owens and Gildersleeve camps split up, and in 1927, Doc and Bill split into separate camps as well. (Even later, Lloyd Owens logged in Alaska, as did some of Doc's and Bill's sons.)

The Doc and Bill Gildersleeve families were large, and people often confused them with each other. Doc and Amy's family was made up of Elsie, Richard, Ella Mae, Frank, Pearl and Keaton. Bill and Alice had Genevieve, Gerald, Clyde, Wayne, Gloria, Roger, Claire and Murray. Their history on the BC coast is a pioneer story of hardship and courage that can be read about in the book *Afloat in Time* by James Sirois, Doc's grandson.

When Clyde was twelve, a new schoolteacher was hired for the Bill Gildersleeve camp. The night Nancy Craig arrived was dark and stormy. Bill's camp was situated in Nascall Bay, off Dean Channel, and the channel was rough. The Union steamship *Cardena* whistled its arrival, and the camp boat *Alice C.G.* pulled up close, the two boats rocking up and down in the waves. Nancy assumed the terrifying transfer from one boat to another was impossible, but it was nothing unusual for the *Cardena* or the *Alice C.G.* Nancy was lifted from the hold of the *Cardena* by crane and lowered to the heaving deck of the *Alice C.G.*, where Bill Gildersleeve and Stanley Sargeant, Genevieve's husband, awaited her.

Nancy was eighteen years old, and this was her first teaching assignment; a real adventure for a city girl from Victoria! Though

Nancy grew up in Victoria, she narrowly missed a ride on the *Titanic* and so was born in Scotland. Nancy's mother, from Largs, Scotland, wanted her unborn child to be born in Canada, but there was a coal strike in Britain at the time which restricted normal sea travel except for that one fated ship. So Mrs. Craig made a special trip to Glasgow to get tickets for the *Titanic*. When she arrived, she was told they had sold out two hours before, so Nancy was born in Largs and arrived in Canada as a baby in 1913.

Nancy became a beloved teacher in the Gildersleeve camp. She and Gerald, the boss's eldest son, fell in love and planned to marry. In the summer of 1933, Nancy went to Victoria for summer school and Gerald stayed to log for the summer before going away to school. The camp was in Elcho Harbour, off Dean Channel, and the crew was Bill, Stanley, Gerald, Clyde and Wayne; a family affair. One day they were cold-decking (piling a very large pile of logs at the bottom of a spar tree to be swung from there into the water). Gerald was on top of the pile when the whole pile started rolling, and he was killed in a mass of rolling logs. He was just twenty-one. Everyone was heartbroken. Nancy did not return to camp; instead, she accepted a job in the Peace River area.

At camp, Clyde assumed the role of eldest son. The Gildersleeves missed their teacher and kept in communication with her. Two or three years after Gerald's death, Clyde wrote to Nancy and suggested that she come back and again fill the teaching position. Nancy returned, and Clyde fell in love with his former teacher.

In 1937, Bill towed his camp all the way to the head of Smith Inlet at the Nekite River. Here the Gildersleeve family met the Gwa'sala. Before logging a new claim, Bill always went to the village and asked permission of the chief. He invited the Gwa'sala over to visit and sing. Bill played the fiddle, Alice played the piano, and the whole family loved to sing. The Gwa'sala loved to sing too. Alice fed them salmon sandwiches and taught the ladies how to make bread, macaroni and tomato casserole, and gluten steaks.

Not many of the Gwa'sala could speak English, resulting in an often-told funny story. Clyde had a great, knee-slapping sense of humour, and I can imagine him telling it.

"Paul Sissons was the Bullcook for Dad's camp, you know, when we were at the Nekite. And you know he was a vegetarian. But the grub was getting low so he decided to go duck hunting up the Nekite. Not for himself, of course. For the crew."

Clyde grins in anticipation.

"Well, while he was off hunting, his boat went high and dry on the flats."

Chuckle.

"And now he had to wait for the tide, and he was getting pretty hungry. So he went over to see Happy Boone—Happy had a cabin up the river—and it so happened that Happy was cooking up a big pot of wonderful-smelling stew. And of course, Happy offered some to Paul."

Another chuckle.

"*My that smells good*, Paul thought. *I think I will forgo my vegetarian diet just this once for some duck stew with bannock*. It was delicious, and Paul filled himself up with stew. Then he lay back on the bench, rubbing his tummy."

Clyde rubs his tummy and begins laughing.

"Paul didn't know duck was so tasty. Happy couldn't speak much English, you know, so Paul rubs his tummy and says to Happy, 'Quack quack?' And Happy shakes his head and he says, 'No. Bow-wow,' he says."

By this time Clyde is rocking with laughter and slapping his knees.

"'Bow-wow,' he says!"

And his listeners, after gasping at the thought of a vegetarian eating a dog, join in.

Clyde and Nancy were married at the mouth of the Nekite River on August 15, 1938, by Reverend Peter Kelly, the first captain of the United Church mission boat *Thomas Crosby IV.* Previously named Cle-alls, the Rev. Peter Kelly was the son of a Haida chief. He was baptised by the Rev. Thomas Crosby and became the first Haida child to receive formal schooling and become an ordained minister. Author Alan Morley tells his story in the book *Roar of the Breakers.* The Haida were known to be a warring tribe; I wonder if the Gwa'sala found it strange that the son of a Haida chief, whom they once would have built defenses against, such as Puget and Whidbey saw at Wyclese, was now ministering to them from the *Thomas Crosby IV.*

Clyde and Nancy planned to do something similar to what Rev. Kelly was doing on the coast with the *Thomas Crosby IV.* The inlets are vast, and the mission boat could only visit the communities about once a year, so the newlyweds felt there needed to be another mission boat. When Canada joined the war, they moved to California, where Clyde attended school to become a minister. Heather was born there in 1941. And then the US joined the war. World War II was a horror in Europe, a game changer for everyone in Canada, even to the remotest inlets—a killer of young men, a postponer of dreams. Clyde went back to Smith Inlet to log for his dad.

CHAPTER 5

GOERTZEN BROTHERS

W hen Canada declared war in 1939, Alvin McGill was working on a farm in Alberta, Clyde was logging for his dad in Smith Inlet, and Louis was living in Winnipeg, keeping bees with his brother Herb. Herb had over one hundred hives, and Louis had gradually built his own up to forty. In winter the brothers cut firewood for a dollar a cord ("You can't get rich *that* way," says Louis), and Louis finished grade ten by correspondence. By this time, Louis's parents had sold their last quarter section in Flat Valley, Saskatchewan.

Years later, Louis tells me and my tape recorder his story.

"We must not have been very good farmers," Louis says to me and the microphone, "because every year, my dad sold another quarter section, and by the time the war came, my folks had moved to Langley Prairie, BC. Only Don was left at home to move with them."

Louis's parents were Dietrich Goertzen and Eva Neufeld. Their families were Mennonites whose ancestors experienced over four hundred years of discrimination due to their pacifist beliefs. During the Reformation, they immigrated from Friesland to Prussia to avoid persecution. There they remained for 250 years, blending their native tongue with German to form a language unique to the Mennonites called Plautdietsch, or Low German. (This was Louis's first language, which he was not allowed to speak at school for fear of punishment.)

When the Mennonites began to experience discrimination and high taxes for military exemption in Prussia, they immigrated to Russia at the invitation of Catherine the Great, who wanted to settle the Volga River region. But one hundred years later, politics had changed and forced another immigration, and Dietrich's parents (Jacob Heinrich Goertzen and Maria Willems Goertzen) and Eva's parents (Dietrich and Maria Neufeld) were part of that great Mennonite move to the Americas, arriving in New York between 1873 and 1875. It's strange that the life of a peacekeeper should be so at odds with the world, but the world does not embrace the pacifist.

The homesteading opportunity in Saskatchewan drew the families north, and Dietrich and Eva Goertzen began their family in Waldheim, Saskatchewan, the town Eva's parents, Dietrich and Maria Neufeld, had begun and named in memory of their home village in "the old country." Dietrich and Eva (so many Dietrichs!) had a large family: Bill, Mary, Herb, Diedrich (died as a boy), Reuben, John and Frank (twins), Louis and Leona (twins, Leona died as a baby), Clarence and Don. In Saskatchewan, the young Goertzen family joined a new church while maintaining their pacifist beliefs, so in WWII the Goertzen brothers registered as conscientious objectors.

Louis's brothers Clarence and Frank found work in BC at a logging camp owned by Toriachi Tanaka.

"Clarence wrote me a letter saying logging was considered an essential service, and if I would come work with him as a faller, I could get postponement," says Louis. "I got a bus ticket from Winnipeg to Langley Prairie, it was called then. The ticket was ten dollars, and the trip took about five days. Don was there at our folks' going to school, and Clarence met me there and we went right up to Reed Island. We worked there all summer, and since we were making a little money, we could afford to go to school. Clarence wanted to be a church minister, and I wanted to be a medical doctor."

So in the fall of 1941, brothers Reuben, Louis, Clarence and Don all attended boarding school at Canadian Junior College (CJC) in Alberta. It was the first time Louis had attended school since his fifth-grade year at the little Carson Community School before his family made their journey by covered wagon to a homestead near Goodsoil, Flat Valley. (The story of that journey could fill its own book!) In those early Flat Valley years, there was no school, and all the Goertzen boys were caught in a simple struggle for survival. So Louis thoroughly enjoyed both the classes and the social life at CJC and made the best of every moment. He met a pretty girl who took his fancy—Alice Berg.

On December 7, 1941, while the boys were enjoying their school year, Pearl Harbour was bombed. The Japanese on the BC coast were then considered a possible threat. On December 10, just three days later, the Fishermen's Reserve (Gumboot Navy) began confiscating Japanese boats, and they were happy to do so. There was definite prejudice against the Japanese in BC; they were smart, worked hard and consistently caught more fish than anyone else. They also kept to themselves and spoke their own language—how suspicious!

By late summer 1942, all the Japanese had been removed from the one-hundred-mile zone off the BC coast. This relocation program was funded partly by the sale of their property, which included fishing boats, motor vehicles, houses and personal belongings. Toriachi Tanaka and his family were offered refuge at CJC. So Mr. Toriachi worked on the CJC farm, his wife Mitsuyo in the cafeteria, their children attended school, and they often invited the Goertzen boys to their home. But Tanaka's logging company was no longer in operation; they would not be allowed to return to the BC coast until 1949, four years after the war ended. The Goertzen boys had to find somewhere else to work for the summer.

They had heard of another logging camp where they would not be asked to work on their Sabbath—Gildersleeve Logging in Smith Inlet. After school let out for summer, the boys first attended a weekend camp meeting in Burnaby Park, and in a seemingly insignificant moment, Don and Louis met their future brother-in-law, friend and business partner. Marian (Myrn) McGill spotted them there and said to her brother, "Hey, I know those guys from CJC! They're the Goertzen brothers!" Myrn called to them and introduced Reuben, Louis, Clarence and Don to her brother Alvin.

Days later the Goertzen brothers boarded the steamship in Vancouver and were happily surprised to find their new acquaintance, Alvin McGill, on board—also headed for Gildersleeve logging camp.

"We were pretty happy about all working together," Louis remembers, "but then we realized we were working at different logging camps. We were disappointed because we were at Doc Gildersleeve's camp and he operated on Saturdays, and Alvin was at Bill Gildersleeve's camp and his camp shut down for Sabbath. So on Saturdays we'd hike over the hill from Draney Inlet to Boswell Inlet to go to church at Bill's camp."

Eventually the Goertzen boys moved from Doc's camp to Bill's camp and became acquainted with Clyde and Nancy, Alvin and Gloria and Claire and all the rest. Alvin and Don were falling partners, and it also happened that they both loved the boss's daughters; Alvin was married to Gloria, and Don fell in love with Claire. Alvin and Don became the best of friends.

At the end of the summer of 1942, there wasn't enough money for all the Goertzen boys to go back to school, so Louis and

Don encouraged Clarence to go back without them; they would support him and take their turns later. So Clarence returned to school alone. Louis had been writing to Alice Berg, and he asked Clarence to keep an eye on her for him. Well, he did. Maybe a little too close of an eye because it turned out that Clarence fancied Alice just as Louis had, and Alice fancied Clarence! Louis and Clarence were particularly close as brothers; their love for each other prevented any rift such a thing might have caused, and later, I had a lovely aunt Alice!

In Smith Inlet, it was hard to tell a war was going on. Everybody went to work every day, and with hunting and fishing there was enough food for everyone. But the Gumboot Navy—fishing boats fitted with guns that patrolled the coast for Japanese boats and submarines—occasionally showed up. They had meetings with the loggers, gave them guns and instructed them how to respond in the event of an attack.

In Europe, the Canadian boys were dying. In November 1944, the Canadian Army incurred heavy losses in the Scheldt Campaign, and conscription became mandatory; reinforcements were needed and there were no more volunteers, so the loggers were required to register in Vancouver. They boarded the steamship, unsure of their destiny. Alvin left behind Gloria, little Lance and another baby on the way. Don said goodbye to Claire, whom he intended to marry as soon as possible. A few of the Gwa'sala went, though they were not required to do so. The army must have seemed a very foreign place to them; Alfred Johnny stayed the longest, making it to Halifax before going AWOL.

Alvin had decided not to be a CO anymore, but he failed his physical examination due to a foot defect and returned to Smith Inlet on the next steamship. The steamship captain derided him for not going to war, saying, "All the men dying in Europe for our freedom ... only cowards left here ... and here you are, looking healthy and strong." A man couldn't help but feel guilty for not dying in Europe. Of course, Alvin's return was one of the happiest days of Gloria's life.

Bill Gildersleeve wrote a letter describing how essential his son Clyde was to his logging operation, reminding whomever it may concern that the Ocean Falls mill needed the wood to continue their war-related industries. So Clyde stayed in camp with his wife Nancy and daughter Heather.

The rest of the COs had a choice: join the army or work in an alternative service. Louis, Don and their brother Reuben (who also took his wife Pat) went to work at the mill in Ocean Falls.

CHAPTER 6

LOVE LETTERS FROM OCEAN FALLS

Ocean Falls was a remote mill town on the central BC coast and the hub of civilization for anyone living between Vancouver Island and Prince Rupert. It serviced logging camps such as the Gildersleeve's, tribal villages, fishermen, canneries and travellers. When the Goertzen brothers arrived in 1944, Ocean Falls had a police station and courthouse, a post office, a hospital, clinic and dentist, three churches, an elementary school and a high school, an inn with a cafeteria and pub, a variety of housing, a company store, a swimming pool, a theatre and a selection of sports and clubs.

The mill at Ocean Falls was running five paper machines that made a variety of paper and a sixth machine that made pulp which was converted to wadding for artillery shells. The sawmill cut clear-grained Sitka spruce from old growth timber on the Queen Charlotte Islands (now Haida Gwaii) for the frames and struts of Britain's famous de Havilland DH.98 Mosquito bomber, one of the fastest operational aircraft in the world at the time, and versatile in war. Its wood frame construction won it the nickname "Wooden Wonder" or "Mossie."

Louis worked in the machine shop, which was converted into a foundry to make pump and engine parts for Park ships and Fort ships—merchant steamships built in Canada. Park ships were named after local and national parks of Canada and operated by the Canadian Merchant Navy, and Fort ships were built for operation by the British Merchant Navy. These were the equivalent of America's Liberty ships; their purpose was to replace merchant vessels lost to U-boat attacks and thus keep the supply line to Europe.

Though Ocean Falls played an important role in the war effort, the town suffered from a labour shortage. Around four hundred Japanese workers had been removed after the bombing of Pearl Harbour, and many workers were deployed as the demand for troops increased. Women and COs filled this gap. In 1944 and 1945, the Goertzen boys were three of about one thousand workers in the Ocean Falls mill.

The men were allowed to take leaves, often boarding the steamship to Vancouver. Louis took a leave to attend the first Seventh Day Adventist camp meeting in Hope, BC. How could he know that it would possibly be the most terrible week in the history of the world and also the sweet beginnings of his own family? On August 6 and 9, nuclear bombs were detonated above Hiroshima and Nagasaki, beginning the end of the war. Oblivious, Louis and Hazel Ritchey were rowing on the lake, hiking up a mountain and falling in love. It doesn't take long to fall in love—after Hazel was introduced to the handsome Louis, who was wearing his new brown suit that he bought from "Goldie" (Ted Goldbloom) the travelling salesman, she went to her mother's tent and told her she had met the man she was going to marry. They were together only five days before Louis had to go back to Ocean Falls. By the time he got there, a letter was waiting for him, and he answered immediately.

Ocean Falls, BC
August 15, 1945

Dear Hazel,

Arrived Ocean Falls last night and today is VJ day. Happy day!! Waiting to welcome us were our Ocean Falls friends and also your most welcome letter. Really, it was good to hear from you.

… Claire is awful inquisitive, and she's been plying me with questions ever since she saw me read that letter. About all I can say is that you're really swell and she can't help but believe so. I told her you were twenty years old, and I want you to tell me how far wrong I am. I'm afraid I'm a bit older than you perhaps thought. Make a guess and I'll tell you how far wrong you are. You say it doesn't make any difference, but it wouldn't be fair to you. Best to get things straight before you unite with a guy entirely unsuitable.

Claire and Don packed the boat [*Stewart K*] today with provisions enough to last for two weeks and left for a vacation as well as honeymoon. They married June 26 but haven't had a chance to get away yet. They looked pretty happy about it. I'm going to live in their suite until they come back. For company I have three guitars, one piano, one clarinet, one radio and one record player. I really star with the radio and record player.

… Well, the war is over. So long I have waited for this day, that now that it has come, I'm at wits' end. It should not be long before we hear from our chief down below. That means I'll do one of six things. The whole thing seems a bit confusing.

You mention college, but I'm almost afraid of going back now. When Clarence and I decided to go through college his aim was ministerial and mine the medical. Here they are trying to persuade me to get into a logging enterprise. That's really where money comes easy these days. As far as that goes, the mills want to keep us but I've had about enough. It's been too tough. The whole thing is perplexing to say the least, but it's nice to think of someone interested in my affairs.

When Louis received Hazel's letter and the announcement of the end of the war within the same twenty-four hours, it seemed like things were lining up at last. With the war over, he hoped it wouldn't be long before he would be released from his essential service job and be free to make his own plans.

The Union steamship delivered the mail once a week on Fridays. Every Friday Louis sent a letter out on the boat and received one from Hazel. Hazel carefully saved every letter, but Louis lost his after a time, and so this letter story is one-sided. The most important words of all must have been spoken by wire, however, because sometime between that first letter in August and a letter dated October 9, a wedding proposal had been made. On October 9, Louis wrote Hazel to convince her to scrap her plans of a wedding with friends and family in Kelowna and come up to Ocean Falls on the steamer.

"The thing is would you want to come up?" Louis writes. "We could get married in the United Church. Claire says she's dying for a chance to wear her formal. And Pat says her place is wide open for any such occasion. In other words, we and me would welcome you with open arms. It's an opportunity for us to get started, and I thought I'd pass it on and get your opinion of the thing."

His argument, and he was pretty pleased with himself about it, was that he found a good deal on a chesterfield, dining set and bedroom suite, and perhaps an apartment. Almost as an aside, he mentioned he was still under strict orders to stay put because the government refused to allow COs to go home until the last man returned from overseas.

> Ocean Falls, BC
> Oct 15, 1945
>
> Oh yes, you want to know how old my sisters are. Well, Claire is nineteen and Pat twenty-two. We've a bad reputation for cradle robbing. Don is pretty much a kid himself. Claire was a Gildersleeve at one time but no relation to the "Great Gildersleeve." Her sister Gloria married Alvin McGill, and her brother Clyde Gildersleeve is logging with McGill. They want Don and me to go in with them and start a little company. They're a good bunch, and we'd have lots of fun.
>
> Love from me to you,
> Louis
> Xxxxx

Hazel packed her wedding dress and boarded the *Princess Adelaide* in Vancouver for her twenty-four-hour trip to Ocean Falls. She boarded at the pier in Vancouver, up the gangplank and then down to the purser's office to be assigned a cabin. After stowing her things, she went back up on the deck to watch the ship pull out of the harbour and the lights of Vancouver fading away. There was no turning back now. At bedtime, the dining room served a light buffet then she went to her cabin and slept to the rocking of the boat and the sound of the motor—if a woman who is on her first trip at sea and leaving home to marry a near stranger in an unknown, remote land *can* sleep.

By breakfast, the boat had already gone through the treacherous Seymour Narrows. A few stops were made—Campbell River, Port McNeil, Alert Bay. Unfortunately for Hazel, lunch was about the same time the *Princess Adelaide* entered the Queen Charlotte Sound, and the ship was known for its gyrations in the big swells of the sound. It took about four hours to cross the sound. She passed Egg Island and Table Island at the entrance of Smith Sound, but she was too sick to leave her bunk and look out at her new home.

When they were out of the swells, around Namu, a steward walked the cabin corridors and played some notes on a little hand-held xylophone to announce dinner, and the ship served dinner in great style. One can only hope that Hazel had recovered enough to enjoy this luxury.

At the top of Fitzhugh Sound, the water is divided by King Island, creating a Y. Fisher Channel is to the north and Burke Channel to the east—all named by Captain Vancouver in 1792. The *Princess Adelaide* chose Fisher Channel and kept left at Cousins Inlet. Cousins Inlet takes a sharp corner at the very end, so Hazel, watching for her destination, thought she was steaming straight into a mountain when Ocean Falls suddenly appeared like a giant, spectacularly lit Christmas tree on the dark hills. She was tense with excitement to see Louie again, and she searched for his face in the crowd gathered on the dock. Seeing him would be a reassurance that she was doing the right thing.

But Louie wasn't waiting for her! Unimaginable! Instead, Claire, Don, Pat and Reuben met her at the boat. They watched the gangplank for the face in the photograph Louis had shown them. Don assured Hazel that Louis was doing something very important—he was making arrangements for their new home in Security Bay.

Her soon-to-be brothers- and sisters-in-law walked her to their apartment. They walked past the government buildings and hospital, the Martin Inn and the general store that sold everything, past little shops and houses cozied up to the wooden streets. Apartments and houses stretched around the bay behind her and up the rocky hill, connected by wooden streets, ramps and stairs, all the way to the dam. Across the river were an impressive number of structures housing power and mill equipment as well as the machine shop where Louis had worked for the past two years. She recognized things from Louis's letters as they were pointed out to her. The town was different than anything she'd ever seen, and the air smelled like rotten eggs. But Hazel was mostly just thinking about meeting Louis. How should she greet him? A hug? A kiss? She'd spent only five chaste days with him, and now, not quite three months later, they were going to be married.

Louis and Hazel were married on Saturday, November 10, in the United Church of Ocean Falls. Don and Claire were their attendants, and a small celebration at Pat and Reuben's apartment followed. They stayed together in an apartment that night, and the next morning, so the story goes, Louis said to Hazel, "Aren't you going to get up and start the fire? My first wife always did." Hazel may have gone along with this bit of Louie-style humour, but still, she walked to Don and Claire's apartment to verify that there had been no previous wife.

The COs had just been liberated from duty, so the next day Don, Claire, Louis and Hazel loaded the *Stewart K* with groceries and belongings and made the trip to Security Bay in Boswell Inlet. Hazel's second boat ride was significantly less elegant than her first; Queen Charlotte Sound felt even worse in the *Stewart K*. If she noticed or cared, future familiar places began sliding by—the big golden sand beach, Hazel Island, Boswell Cannery—until they finally arrived in Security Bay. Hazel stepped over the gunnel onto her new yard—a raft made of cedar logs covered in cedar planks with her house in the middle. And there, inside the little house, was the chesterfield, dining set, bedroom suite and rugs that Louis had so proudly found for them in Ocean Falls.

Alvin, Gloria, their boys Lance and Lloyd, as well as Clyde, Nancy and Heather were all there to greet them. Gloria invited everyone over for dinner, and the four families were together for the first time. They talked about weddings and babies, logging and the future. I can see them gathered around the table, Alvin telling one of his favourite stories in his slow, distinct voice. "Well, I was talking about starting a little logging company, you know, with Don and Claire and Clyde and Nancy, and then Louie here asks me if he can join. Says he and Don have a boat to contribute. I thought, *How bold!*"

Alvin chuckles and his pale blue eyes are smiling. He has a dimple in his chin.

"I figured we probably had enough guys already, so I tell him it's only for married folk. And he says to me, 'What if I find a wife?'"

Another chuckle.

"I say, 'Sure,' and I think to myself, *That's not likely to happen.* But the next thing you know, Louie shows up with this young blonde!"

There is much laughter, Clyde slapping his knees, Louis grinning sheepishly, Hazel blushing.

In January 1946, GMG Logging Company was formed by Clyde Gildersleeve, Alvin McGill, Don Goertzen and Louis Goertzen. And just as Louis said, they were a good bunch, and they had a lot of fun!

GMG, 1947. Left to right, back row: Don holding
Harold, Louis, Alvin, Clyde. Middle row: Claire, Hazel,
Gloria, Nancy. Front row: Lloyd, Lance, Heather

Louis and Hazel

CHAPTER 7

FISH! SMITH INLET AND THE SALMON RUSH

By the time GMG started logging in 1946, the Central Coast that Vancouver described in 1792 "as desolate inhospitable a country as the most melancholy creature could be desirous of inhabiting" was filled with creatures of all sorts, melancholy and otherwise—British, German, Scottish, Norwegian, Japanese, Chinese, American, Canadian and, of course, the local tribes who'd been there since who knows when.

After the otters that Captain Hanna and future fur traders sought were gone, somebody found gold on the Fraser River. The gold rush of 1858 triggered a steady stream of immigration and colonization as people saw the resources of the coast.

The first market for salmon began in the fur trading years. Local tribes were fishing and selling salmon to the Hudson's Bay Company (HBC) for food, and HBC soon found a way to profit from the plentiful salmon. The HBC had been shipping furs directly to China via Hawaii (the Sandwich Islands) and employed many Hawaiians who had developed a taste for salmon. In the 1830s, HBC began shipping barrels of salted spring salmon to Hawaii, making Hawaii the first market for BC salmon.

As canning techniques improved, the canning of salmon began. Starting on the Fraser River and spreading north, the 1870s saw salmon canneries pop up everywhere there was a sockeye run. Federal fishing regulations and licenses were introduced, and timberlands were leased. The first logging up the coast seemed to be primarily for the canneries: cordwood for steam power and timbers for construction of canneries and boats.

Salmon are anadromous, which means they hatch in freshwater lakes and streams and migrate to salt water where they eat like crazy then return to freshwater to spawn and die. This is a four-year cycle for the sockeye, valued for its bright red colour and firm flesh, and it was the only fish those first canneries wanted. It was soon discovered that the Fraser sockeye had a unique cycle. A year of good returns followed by a year of fewer returning sockeye, then two years of poor returns. So canning companies began looking for other sockeye runs, and canneries were soon built in the Skeena and Naas rivers, and in Rivers Inlet and Smith Inlet. Smith Inlet had a total of five, and Rivers Inlet fourteen, though not all at the same time. The great salmon rush had begun!

Each cannery, set into the crevices of the wilderness, was its own mini-society, with rank and racism, opium and alcohol, love, work and war. Enormous buildings on pilings were constructed for the cannery lines, net-lofts and can fabrication. There were offices, a store and a power house, and crammed onto the edges of this, the cannery owner built separate living quarters for each ethnicity of workers. There was a Japanese camp of small shacks, a China house (large bunkhouse built to their specifications), another camp of small shacks for the local tribe, a bunkhouse for summer students and workers, a cookhouse, and bigger houses up on the hill for the management. This huge outlay of resources that occurred before anyone knew the strength or cycle of a salmon run was one of the reasons for a lot of bankrupt and abandoned canneries.

The segregation of ethnicities seems odd now but was normal at the time and was actually requested by the workers themselves. Each group became valued for their areas of expertise. The local tribes were very important, not only as fishermen, but for their wives and children who worked the slime line, cleaning the fish and rinsing them, and the cutting and filling lines, packing the fish into the cans. They were also valued for net mending. Entire villages would go to "their" cannery for the summer and live there until the season was over.

The Chinese, who came over for the construction of the Canadian Pacific Railway, began working in the canneries when railway construction was finished. They arrived at the canneries early every season to make cans. Though they worked many places in the cannery, their specialty was the skilled butcher. With eight strokes of a knife, the butcher could remove the head, tail and fins, slit open the belly and scrape out the entrails.

The Japanese men were highly valued for their production as fishermen. It was said that they fished twenty-six hours a day and consistently brought in more fish than everyone else. Their families joined the slime, cutting and filling lines, and were excellent net menders. But of course, the Japanese were all removed from the coast after the bombing of Pearl Harbour, which left a significant labour gap.

Without refrigeration or ice, everyone in the canneries worked long hours into the night to get the fish into cans as quickly as possible. The canning line changed over the years with the invention of an automatic butchering machine, cutting and filling machines, and the "steam retort," a giant pressure cooker which replaced the huge cooking kettles of boiling water.

Until the canneries, the Gwa'sala in Smith Inlet had been bypassed by missionaries, neglected by the government and generally left alone. The formidable Queen Charlotte Sound had succeeded in maintaining their isolation. Smith Inlet had a huge sockeye run, however, and everything was about to change.

In 1883, Messrs R.P. Rithet and J.A. Laidlaw of Victoria built the Quashela Packing Company cannery beside the entrance to Wyclese Lagoon to process the very run of sockeye the Gwa'sala were processing when Puget and Whidbey found them on the rock Wyclese at the entrance to Wyclese Lagoon in 1792. The Quashela Packing Co. employed the Gwa'sala to catch the fish, and the Gwa'sala used their ancient techniques to do so. The Quashela Packing Co. was granted exclusive drag-seine fishing rights on Quascila Creek, the path to Wyclese Lagoon.

Drag-seining was prohibited elsewhere (for good reason), with a couple of exceptions such as the Nimpkish River. It was very efficient (thought to be too efficient), providing the cannery with large quantities of fish at a very low cost. One end of the drag-seine net was secured in shallow water, the other end let out in a circle with the net sweeping the bottom, encircling and trapping the fish.

For even better efficiency, the canneries and fishermen broke the regulation "unlawful obstruction of streams," as John Williams, Inspector of Fisheries for BC District #2 (Rivers and Smith inlets), reported (words in parenthesis by Edward Higginbottom):

> To enable (the Indian seine crews) to catch more salmon for which they were paid five cents each, by the canners, they obtain a piece of gill net and make it fast across the creek (some 100 yards upstream from the mouth) from one side to the other, being a deep net and the creek shallow, it drags the bottom with an overlap, upon which they pile rocks and brush making a barricade that no mature salmon can pass through; the fish finding the creek impassable generally turn back, but some

persist in descending the creek and get gilled in the net; those that return to the mouth of the creek swim round and round until they are eventually caught by the Indians in their drag-seines.[5]

For some unknown reason, the Quashela cannery was dismantled after its first year and moved to Wannuck (also spelled Wannock and Whannock) cannery in Rivers Inlet where the Quashela Packing Company continued to process the Wyclese Sockeye. In 1901, Rithet and Laidlaw transferred the property and fishing rights at Wyclese to their Victoria Canning Company, then sold to the BC Packers Association (BCPA) in 1902. And this is when politics began to affect even remote Smith Inlet and the Wyclese fish stocks.

The drag-seine license the Quashela Packing Company had used before selling to BCPA was given, by Dominion Fisheries, to a company owned by R. Kelly, a provincial Liberal leader. Henry Doyle of the BCPA protested it, but they could not get it back. So the BCPA rebuilt the cannery, naming it Smith's Inlet Cannery, and fished thirty-five gill nets in Wyclese Lagoon. In response, Dominion Fisheries ruled the salt water Wyclese Lagoon a freshwater lake (Quashella Lake) making it off limits, and the only fishing permitted would be the drag-seine, whose license belonged to Kelly.

The BCPA charged the fishery officer with unfairness and partiality, and the matter remained unsolved. In 1919, the drag-seine license was cancelled after an incident involving some gill netters who were opposed to exclusive rights and burned the drag-seines. The Smith's Inlet Cannery had two more owners— Wallace Fisheries and BC Fishing and Packing Co.—before closing in 1931 and demolition in 1938.

---

[5]   Edward Higginbottom, "The Changing Geography of Salmon Canning in British Columbia, 1870-1931" (Thesis, Simon Fraser University, 1988), summit.sfu.ca/item/5427

When GMG began logging in Security Bay in 1946, and even when the Gildersleeves arrived in 1937, most of the tumultuous history of the canneries was already over. Mechanization of the canning line, cost of labour and camp upkeep, refrigeration, ice, and bigger, better boats for packing fish all contributed to a more economical solution: closing the small canneries and consolidating. In 1946, Smith Inlet salmon were packed either to Namu Cannery (BCPA) or Goose Bay (Canadian Fishing Company). Margaret Bay, Boswell and Leroy Bay Canneries were now just fish camps that provided supplies, net-mending floats, storage and packers.

The GMG men and many of the early loggers were also fishermen, logging most of the year and joining the fishing fleet for the weeks of the salmon run. The canneries remained a hub of activity in the summers and were maintained by caretakers in the winter. The steamship, and later the freight boat, arrived bi-weekly, monthly or bi-monthly depending on the time of year and the year, and the store was kept open for the locals who lived in the inlet. The cannery had radiophones if needed, fuel and somebody to talk to; a speck of civilization in the wilderness.

Boswell Cannery docks looking towards Security Bay,
with tubs of bluestone on the docks for cleaning and
dying gillnets, GMG logging slash in the distance

CHAPTER 8

A-FRAME LOGGING

Bill Gildersleeve's retirement in 1945 prompted Alvin to start his own logging operation. Pacific Mills sent a man named Jago to manage Bill's camp, and at the end of a year, Alvin swore he would never work for another man again for the rest of his life.

Though Pacific Mills in Ocean Falls pretty much owned the loggers and kept most of Bill's operation, Bill did give Alvin and Clyde his A-frame and a few shacks. But they still needed a yarder. With his wife sick with appendicitis in the Ocean Falls Hospital, and two babies in tow, Alvin arranged a meeting with the manager at Pacific Mills to ask for backing.

"I was really nervous," Alvin remembers. "But the guy just tells me I have to go to Vancouver and ask the head honcho. So I go to Vancouver and present what I want. I told him I wanted $7000 to buy a donkey, and the guy says, 'That's too much, I'll give you this cheaper donkey to get you started.' And he sends it up. It was a 10-10 Lawrence, brand new, 110hp, filled with gas and ready to go." Alvin gives a wry smile. "And with the power of an alarm clock."

With the addition of Don, Louis and their boat the *Stewart K*, GMG Logging Company began logging. Small logging operations such as GMG that worked on a contract basis have the nickname "gyppo" loggers. Most of the gyppo logging camps were, at least at first, A-frame loggers. This is the method GMG used to log the shoreline. Thousands of millions of board feet of timber (logger talk for a lot of timber!) was logged by gyppo loggers this way and made its way to mills and eventually people's houses. My brother Roland explains A-frame logging as follows:

> It all starts with a timber sale, and a timber sale starts with cruising the timber—actually walking through the woods with an axe, giving the occasional tree a whack to determine if it is hollow or rotten, keeping track of the number and size of the trees that might bring a profit.

> Only after the permitting process is complete can the falling and extraction of the logs begin. Once the trees are felled and bucked into lengths, the logs are extracted by attaching the A-frame float to the beach in front of the logging claim and pulling the logs off the hill with the aid of the donkey.

> Think of an old-fashioned clothesline, the kind where your mother climbs up a couple steps and attaches clothes to the line. The line runs through a pulley attached to a pole out in the yard, and when she pulls the string on one side the clothes move away from the house; pulling the string on the other side brings them closer to the house. This simple engineering design with minor variation but on a much grander scale was and still is the basis for almost all the logging done with cables.

> The power used to drive these back-and-forth cables comes from the donkey, a powerful winch with several drums powered by an engine. These were steam in the early days, giving way to gas and

eventually diesel. This machine is securely bolted to two large logs fastened together to form a huge sled. This enables the donkey a primitive form of mobility, as it can drag itself around.

The drums on the donkey are wrapped with cable. The cable from one drum (the haulback) goes out to the back of the logging claim, through two pulleys, called blocks by loggers, then back towards the donkey. At some point it meets the mainline, which is the more powerful line used to drag the logs out of the woods.

Where the haulback and mainline meet there is a series of swivels and chain links that hold the chokers, and this is called the butt rigging. The chokers are a twenty-five- to thirty-foot length of cable hanging from this butt rigging with a quick-connect on the end used to lasso or "choke" the logs. Now the engineer can engage the haulback drum while feeding out the mainline until the chokers are poised over a log. The chokermen quickly choke the log and signal the engineer, who engages the mainline drum while paying out the haulback, and the logs are quickly dragged to the landing where they are unhooked and the process repeated.

Now back to Mom's clothesline. If the pulleys are not high in the air, all the clothes will be dragged through the mud. Loggers call this height "lift," and lift is critical for keeping the cables off the ground, giving an upward pull when dragging the logs so they don't get stuck behind stumps and things.

In A-frame logging this lift is achieved with an A-frame: two large logs fastened in the shape of a huge A, standing upright over one hundred feet in height with blocks at the top that the cables run through. The A-frame is firmly attached to a massive raft or float made of large logs, with cables and guy-lines for added stability. The A-frame float is held off the beach with logs called stiff legs. The donkey is placed at the edge of the float, and the cables run from the drums up through the blocks in the top of the A-frame and then out into the logging claim. For single swing A-frame logging, the haulback blocks are placed about 1500 feet away, high up the hillside, attached to stumps called tail-holds. The lift for the back end of the clothesline is achieved in this manner. The mainline pulls in the logs and they are unhooked into the ocean where they are organized into booms and towed to market.

Once all the logs are dragged out from under the cables, the cables have to be moved to a new location. This is called changing roads and is done by moving the haulback blocks to new tail-holds. Since the donkey remains in place, every time roads are changed the cables are moved around the A-frame like slices of a pie. Once the pie is logged, there are two options: You can move the entire A-frame system down the inlet to the next logging site or you can move the donkey off the float and 1500 feet up the hillside to where the initial logging ended and log the next 1500-foot pie. Sometimes this is repeated a third time.

Moving a donkey is an epic enterprise. A large cable is run out in the desired direction and attached to one or more stumps. This often doesn't provide the power needed, and more blocks and cables are added for more power. This huge machine, as long as fifty feet in length, can travel through creeks and small rivers, over ravines, up and down small cliffs and sidehills so steep they sometimes lose oil pressure even though they have specially built deep oil pans. A donkey will go where nothing else can.

Stories are told and retold of harrowing experiences encountered while moving the donkey. Imagine this behemoth of a machine, engine roaring, smoke belching, the donkey puncher clinging to the machine so he doesn't fall off. He has a grim but determined look on his face, all his weight thrown against the friction lever that keeps the drum turning, the donkey grinding slowly along. He can't see where he's going, so there is a guy perched precariously on the front of the sled, often hanging on for dear life, yelling directions.

At this second site up the hill there is no A-frame, so lift is achieved by rigging a spar tree. The spar tree accomplishes the same task as the A-frame, but since it can be anchored to the ground it needs only one tree; again with the guy-lines for stability and the blocks at the top for the cable to run through. This most basic form of cable logging, where the lift is obtained by the cables going through the top of the A-frame, spar tree or nowadays a steel tower, is called high lead logging or high leading.

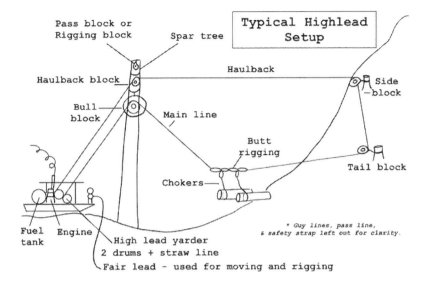

Typical high lead set-up. For even more lift, a "scabline"—a short cable going from the butt rigging to a block on the haulback—was used

Gyppo loggers with only one donkey have no choice but to move their donkey up to the spar tree and log the entire 1500-foot pie, creating a huge and dangerous pile of logs called a cold deck, then move the donkey back down to the A-frame float and "swing" the entire pile of logs, a few at a time, into the chuck.

Swinging all these logs is much more easily accomplished with a method called skylining. This method provides even more lift. Let's go back to Mom's clothesline. Say she washes a lot of heavy pants, so heavy that they are dragging in the mud. She needs more lift. A skyline would be similar to Mom having Dad, on his day off, fasten another line above the clothesline, higher up on the pole that holds the pulley, pull it nice and tight and then place a trolley on it with a rope from the trolley down to the clothesline directly above the heavy pants. Now as Mom pulls the pants out to dry or back in to fold, the trolley slides back and forth along the skyline taking the weight off the clothesline so it won't sag into the mud.

In logging, the skyline takes a lot of stress and weight, so it is the heaviest cable of all. The trolley is called a carriage, and it rolls back and forth above the butt rigging with enough lift to hold the logs (heavy pants) entirely in the air if you so desire.

Simple, right?

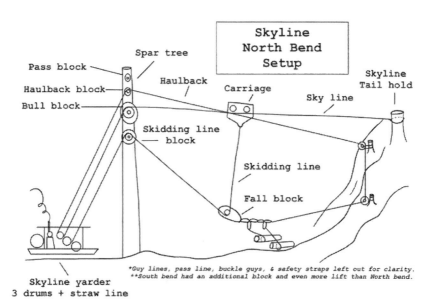

Skyline set-up

Ideally, when you move the donkey to log the next claim there is an appropriate tree in the right spot that can be topped, rigged and used for a spar tree. But what if there is no tree standing that will work?

Again, the answer is simple: You find a good tree, fall it, cut it off at about 120 feet long and use your donkey engine to drag this behemoth that weighs many tons to the appropriate spot. Then you raise it, rig it and get to the main event, logging.

To explain it, we need something smaller than a huge tree, something easier to relate to. Let's grab an imaginary broomstick, lay it on the floor and fasten the end closest to the donkey (you will be the donkey in this example, the butt end) firmly to the floor. The butt of the tree needs to be firmly fastened to a strong stump or it will slide instead of rise.

If you fasten a string to the top end then go back to the butt end and pull on the string from ground level, nothing good will happen. Perhaps the string will break, but the stick certainly will not rise; you need some height advantage. This was achieved in two different ways: either the top of the tree was raised (imagine resting the stick on a chair and then pulling on the string) or the pulling point was raised (imagine pulling on the string from knee or waist height). The first example, raising the top, was common especially when your equipment was alongside a logging road; you could place the top on a pile of logs or rocks with some additional equipment you might have—a cat or loader, for example. Twelve feet was all the height advantage you would need to allow the powerful donkey engine to pull up the spar tree.

In the woods with only a donkey engine to assist you, it was more common to raise the pulling point. If a steep hillside was nearby, this could be done by fastening a pulley (block) to a stump up on the hillside then running the cable through that and then to the top of the tree. If you had no hillside nearby you had to use a gin pole. Gin poles are trees that are much too small or of the wrong species to be a spar tree; they are basically a mini spar tree with guy-lines and a block attached part-way up to run the pulling cable through and thus give the needed height advantage. There were two types of gin pole. The easiest to rig was a tree already standing (it had to be marked so the fallers would leave it), and the other type, used where there was no tree standing, no nearby hillside, and no way to raise the top up, was a flying gin pole.

Depending on how it was rigged, the flying gin pole was raised like a mini spar tree, though much more easily because of its size. Sometimes the flying gin pole and the spar tree were raised together, the pole coming up first because it was so much smaller. When it came up against the guy-lines and stopped, then the spar tree would begin to rise. The spar tree was so much taller that as it approached a vertical position, the gin pole would rise off the ground and appear to fly.

Obviously, there is a lot more going on here than just pulling up the spar tree. Most trees were at least partially rigged on the ground—much easier to do on the ground than when it's 120 feet in the air. Rigging includes adding all the guy-lines, tree plates, buckle guys, blocks and straps including the pass block, haulback block, bull block, skidding block, safety straps and so on.

If you simply pulled up the tree it would, of course, fall over sideways at some point, so a tripod of lines was usually used. The more powerful mainline that pulled the tree up formed one leg of the tripod, and the two other legs ran from the top of the tree out to stumps at appropriate angles then back to two additional drums on the donkey. As the mainline pulled up the tree, these other drums slowly paid out cable so the tree wouldn't fall over. Once it was upright, additional guy-lines were attached, and finally everything was stable and you could start breathing again.

All these things are much easier to say than do. It's easy to write things like "attach the block to a stump on the hillside and run the mainline through it," but it's actually very difficult. Moving blocks alone could weigh several hundred pounds. The straps that anchored them to the stump were about all a man could handle, and the mainline is so big and heavy a man can only drag a short piece of it for a short way.

All these tasks were accomplished by first dragging the small cable (called the strawline, or haywire in some areas) and a small block called a snatch-block out to where you needed the big stuff. Then the donkey engine would engage the strawline, which would drag out the heavy blocks and cables that had to be wrestled into position. Guy-lines had to be wrapped around stumps and anchored with railroad spikes driven in with sledgehammers. And these jobs had to be repeated over and over until everything was in position. It was difficult work.

Alvin, Louis, Don and Clyde—or any other logger on their way home from work—would never have thought of the word "simple" to describe what they did that day! The men extended themselves every day and were fit and strong, coming in the door hungry and smelling of trees.

Booming: in front of boom winch, left
to right: Alvin, Louis, Don

GMG men, 1946–1948, left to right: Clyde, Louis, Alvin, Don

CHAPTER 9

A WHISTLER AND HIS LOG

As a newlywed, Hazel (the mom of the clothesline and the heavy pants) was introduced to A-frame logging as a whistle punk and wrote a story about it—lucky for us. Her little story, written soon after she arrived in Smith Inlet as a new bride and recently rediscovered in a box in the attic as a clipping from an unidentified newspaper, is a trip to GMG, 1946.

A Whistler and His Log
By Hazel I. Goertzen

What an abnormally beautiful day! One of those days after a weekly deluge; or a deluge lasting a week, so common in this northern British Columbia region.

The sunrays danced through the leaves and limbs of the overhanging trees and mirrored dainty filigree patterns on the crystal-clear waters below. Kingfishers chattered and fished in bird-like ecstasy. Even the staidest of the staid must surely have felt they had a new lease on life. I'm sure I did anyway, but then I probably wouldn't be classed as so very staid.

Such a day, I mused, must be spent profitably. Bake bread? Not at all interesting. Iron? Lands no— that least of all. Bake cookies? With me that rates second to ironing. Well then, how about writing a story? Maybe go rowing and watch the baby seals flip about by that flat rock around the point and perhaps sneak up on long-legs Heron and get a few pointers on fishing.

These thoughts had no sooner chased each other through my head and out again when my better half bounced in and with great alacrity strode about the kitchen—a little nervously I thought.

"Uh," he began, "Dear, could you possibly come whistle-punking today? We're on the sidehill now, and it's almost impossible to manage without some help."

At my look of surprise and hesitation he continued, "Please, we need you awfully bad. With only the four of us, it gets pretty hard at times."

"But I don't know a thing about it," I said timorously, and I almost wished that I could be "tied down with some children" as some women wish they weren't. However, a quite new marriage prevented me from asserting myself too strongly.

"Nothing to it, nothing at all. Don your slacks and come, the men are waiting," he said, and with a reassuring, all-will-be-well grin, he went out.

Thus my problem was solved, my day planned for me; and now if you who read will climb with me up that boulder-strewn hill yonder, we will get a fine view of the day's activities from the whistler's observatory, a moss-covered log.

As I sit here on the hillside in this logging country of northern British Columbia, I can see the sunbeams with their early morning radiance penetrating into every corner of the little floating village below me. I say little because the village consists of only the four families of the four shareholders forming the company. I hear the barking of the dogs; a Pomeranian and a Labrador retriever, the pets of the children whose shrieks of joyous laughter echo and re-echo through the hills as they play feverishly against time.

The drumming of a woodpecker, the saucy chatter of a blue jay, the hoarse cry of the raven and the rusty creak of the heron remind me that here there is much scope for bird study.

As I sit here today on an old moss-covered log, I am not an ornithologist, neither a logger nor any of a number of things I might have been; I am just a lowly whistle punk, or what might sound more dignified, a signal control man. My job for today is to hasten logging operations by squeezing the bug.

This bug, or whistle, when squeezed sends in the signals to a machine operator at the foot of the hill. My signals register in the Buddha, which is on a sort of raft or float. Now the Buddha is not an idol such as some people worship. It is a donkey, which in turn is not an animal but a powerful machine equipped with engine, levers and all the whatnots necessary for pulling logs off a hillside. The donkey puncher is at the controls.

An A-frame is built on the same float on which the donkey sits on skids or runners, so that it may be pulled off onto another float if necessary, or even up the hill. The A-frame describes itself. Two big logs stick up into the air about 120 feet in the shape of a letter A. At the top of this A-frame are big iron blocks or pulleys through which cables pass to a spar tree also about 120 feet high and situated about one thousand feet off the beach up the hillside.

The top of the spar tree is also rigged with blocks. Cables are passed through these blocks then fastened at different angles to well-rooted stumps, so that the strain on the tree will not be too great. These cables are called guy-lines.

There is a heavy block at the top of the spar tree, and it is called a shoe. A two-inch cable is passed through this shoe, then across about one thousand feet to the beach and through another shoe at the top of the A-frame. This cable high in the air is called a skyline. A carriage rides along this line. A line passes through the carriage, which is somewhat like a pulley, and at each end of the line, which is now double, chokers are fastened. These chokers aren't the kind often seen around women's necks; and if they do wrap around the chokerman's neck, there's just a sporting chance there'll be any neck left.

The donkey puncher manipulates the levers, and the carriage moves along the skyline taking the dangling chokers up the hill to where the chokermen await it. The men shout "whoah" when the chokers get near enough to the log in question. The whistler squeezes the bug once, and the resultant toot in the donkey shed tells the operator there that it's far enough, and he stops the lines—until another whistle.

The chokermen have choked a log now and are clambering quickly out of the way. At the all-clear signal the donkey slowly begins to pull. Small trees snap off, and a deep path is gouged into the earth as the huge log goes writhing down the hill. At the bottom there is a big splash, and spray leaps into the air as the log hits the saltchuck. A chaser there unchokes the log and gives the signal for the return of the chokers.

It is an awesome and terrible spectacle to watch a once proud monarch of the forest in whose limbs the fauna and avifauna of the woods once nested go scraping and writhing downhill to a sudden end.

Oh, there has been a mishap. Something seems to be broken. The donkey has stopped roaring, and aside from the rhythmic sound of the bucker's saw, I can hear only the wind whispering high overhead. And I smell that intangible something that comes solely from the green trees of the forest, soft banks of moss sprinkled lightly with pinecones, and that very clean smell of newly hewn timber. To me these smells are reminiscent of bonfires and corn roasts on the old farm, and the fragrant scent of sweet clover and new-mown hay.

Here, the salty tang of the sea air prevails.

All reminiscing aside! The donkey puncher has resumed his punching; the chokermen their choking (of logs); the chaser his chasing; and now

I, the lowly whistle punk, must get back to my moss-covered perch and start squeezing the bug once more.

The GMG ladies all had their turn on the hill as whistle punk. Gloria took Lance and Lloyd with her, Nancy took Heather, Claire went up the hill, too, before she had baby Harold. But Hazel had no children for several years, making her the woman of choice to spend many a day on her "moss-covered log."

GMG camp in Margaret Bay, 1949 summer. A-frame float with A-frame, Buddha donkey, machine shop, and the *Jonah* on its side in front of it; camp houses front to back: Louis, Don (with *Stewart K* docked), Alvin, Clyde (out of view). Tug on left, ready to tow boom. Two landing barges with supplies for rebuilding Egg Island lighthouse after it washed off in November 1948.

CHAPTER 10

STEWART K

T he *Stewart K* was a thirty-foot cabin cruiser. Its first job after Louis and Don purchased it was as Don and Claire's honeymoon cruiser, and then it was the GMG camp boat. It wasn't a gill netter or a tug; the men used the *Jonah,* a little boom-boat, to pull booms and floats, and the *Stewart K* to go places. A few times a year the families took the *Stewart K* to Ocean Falls for business, physical check-ups and dental repairs.

One morning Alvin, Gloria, Lance, Lloyd, Louie and Hazel started out for Ocean Falls in the *Stewart K.* They expected to be there by dinnertime and were looking forward to a nice dinner at the Martin Inn. Instead, a storm blew up and they were forced to take refuge in Port John in Fisher Channel. Today's *Fishery and Oceans Sailing Directions* labels the Port John anchorage as "indifferent quality for small craft." Nevertheless, for several days the *Stewart K* shared Port John with a tug, also stormbound.

For supper they ate the remains of their lunch. They slept in tight quarters, and the next day they found a few tins of canned food on board and gnawed on some hard tack. The storm showed no sign of letting up, and the boys started complaining of hunger. They had a gun on board, so Alvin went ashore to find a deer. He tromped around for hours with no luck. He went out again the next morning but still no success. Finally, Louie said, "OK give me the gun, I'll go get a deer."

Louie had given up hunting after his hunting accident as a teenager in Saskatchewan, but he had always been an excellent hunter. His mother said that if she sent Louie out hunting, she knew she would have something to feed her family for supper. Now Louie couldn't see children going hungry just because of his personal issues, so he rowed to shore to track a deer.

"In half an hour I got two," says a grinning Louie when he tells the story.

He dressed them, and Gloria cooked venison steaks for supper on the little stove and again for every meal for the next couple of days.

Hazel was a vegetarian, so perhaps she remained hungry. In any case, everyone was relieved to finally arrive in Ocean Falls and have dinner at the Martin Inn!

Not long after, the *Stewart K* came to a sudden and frightening end. The event is burned into Lance and Lloyd's memory, and for good reason. Hazel, in a story she wrote about it, recalled it being a "sultry, hot fall day." Clyde had left GMG and gone back to school by now, and Alvin's brother Roy had taken his place. Roy untied the *Stewart K* and stood on the float, holding the line. Alvin, Louis and Don were on board the boat trying to get the engine started. They tried it once. It smelled of gas. They opened the floor hatch over the motor to see inside and opened the front windows and the back door to disperse the fumes. The *Stewart K* had a Graymarine engine—a four-cylinder, 90hp gas engine with the prophetic name of Fireball! Don and Louie looked down into the engine through the floor hatch to see what was wrong, and Alvin, standing by the wheel, again pushed the start button. There was a poof and an explosion of fire.

Roy pushed the boat away from the floats to keep them from catching on fire, and the ladies and kids came running—crying and praying. Flames shot from every opening of the *Stewart K*. They saw one fiery figure, then two, jump from the boat into the water. Where was the third? Roy was helping Louie out of the water before they finally saw the third man jump off the back of the boat. Louie's skin slipped off in Roy's hand, so Roy hauled him out by the armpits. Don was next, then Alvin, who was the most severely burned. In the confusion caused by the explosion, Alvin had run for the back door instead of crawling out the window in front of him. The engine hatch was open, and he fell into the motor, gas fumes rising up his pantlegs and exploding. Stumbling out of the hole, he finally made it to the door and into the water.

The men looked frightening with their burned faces, hair singed off and skin hanging. Louis had an old army surplus radio in the office, but it required a six-volt battery. GMG had three six-volt batteries: one on the donkey, one on the boom winch and one on the *Stewart K*, so now they had two. Don ran along the boom-sticks to the boom winch for the battery so they could call out. Hazel made the call.

"Hello Bull Harbour Radio, Bull Harbour Radio. GMG Logging calling. Mayday, mayday, this is an emergency."

"Hello GMG Logging, Bull Harbour Radio, what's your trouble? Do you need help?"

"Bull Harbour Radio, GMG answering. Our boat is on fire, and three of our men are burned, can you send a plane?"

"GMG Logging, Bull Harbour Radio. Roger, will do. Give exact location."

"Bull Harbour Radio, GMG back. We're in the Ahclakerho off Smith Inlet, on the north side. You'll see the smoke."

Airplanes were still very rare, and it seemed a miracle to all that a private plane was just over the hill in Seymour Inlet. The little two-seater responded to the mayday and arrived in just half an hour. Somehow, they managed to get four men in it and still lift-off. The windows were open, and the skin on their arms flapped in the breeze all the way to Alert Bay. The little plane skimmed the treetops, leaving behind the hushed and worried families and the *Stewart K* still burning in front of them as proof that it really happened.

The men determined the cause later. Roy said he had nailed a gunwale back onto the boat. The nail had gone through and pierced the gas tank, which was full, and gas slowly dripped into the bilge. The motor would not start for lack of oxygen, all the airspace below being consumed with gas fumes. When the men opened everything up, allowing oxygen to the motor, the next attempt to start the motor set the explosion.

The men spent some time in the Alert Bay Hospital and ended up with scars, and Louie forever blamed his lack of hair on the *Stewart K.* But they were OK. The men began looking for another boat and found the *Westpoint.*

Chapter 11

Breakfast at the Queen's Table

Everyone living in the inlet has a narrow-escape story. Or two or three or more. Rocks looming out of the fog, engines stalling in unfortunate places, deadheads hit or nearly missed, beachings, and stories of terrible weather when we truly thought we would most probably drown. Great green walls rising before us, our wee, barely protected selves climbing to the top, diving straight into the valley again and hopefully again, the wave tops violently torn off by the wind and sprayed around like a thousand pressure washers. Most of these stories happen in Queen Charlotte Sound.

Queen Charlotte Sound begins right where Smith Sound ends. So coming out of our inlet, whether going north towards Rivers Inlet, Bella Bella Hospital and Ocean Falls, or south towards Port Hardy, Alert Bay and Vancouver, we're in it! This forty-mile stretch of water is open all the way to Japan, and the chart is sprinkled with appropriate names like God's Pocket, Storm Islands, Cape Caution, Peril Rocks, and Safety Cove. The Gwa'sala might say this is the place where Kumugwe, whose house is under the sea, becomes most angry.

Egg Island and Table Island sit with Queen Charlotte on one side and Smith on the other—sounds so homey, evoking images of sitting at the table eating scrambled eggs with the queen and Mr. Smith. But all hell can break loose around this breakfast!

Scattered about these more obvious islands are the rockpiles charted by James Hanna: Pearl Rocks (Hanna actually named them Peril), Hanna Rocks, Virgin Rocks, Iron Rocks, Egg Rocks. Sometimes the rocks are roaring with spray and sometimes they're deadly invisible.

In his 1792 logbook, Vancouver recorded: "The entrance into Smith's Inlet was nearly closed by rocky islets, some producing shrubs and small trees, others none; with innumerable rocks as well beneath as above the surface of the sea, rendering it a very intricate and dangerous navigation for shipping." He was right. By the 1880s, marine traffic up the BC coast was dramatically increasing. The fishing and cannery traffic accounted for much of it but also logging camps and mines, then the Klondike gold rush. Every time a ship wrecked, the need for navigational aid became more and more obvious, so a series of lighthouses were built to light the watery road from Washington state to Alaska.

Egg Island lighthouse was constructed in 1898 on a west-facing islet connected to the larger egg. The wooden tower with an attached dwelling, fifty feet high and painted white with red trim, was built seventy-two feet above the high tide line. The light was a revolving white catoptric light and flashed every thirty seconds.

The very first winter proved Egg Island to be a storm-battered, unfriendly rock. William Brown was the first keeper, with his three-year-old son and an assistant—his wife had died just weeks before. As the winter storms hit the new lighthouse for the first time, Brown watched mountains of water smash and carry off the boathouse and ways and burst through the lower windows of his home.

A government steamer, the *Quadra*, serviced the lighthouses on the coast in the early years and brought supplies twice a year in March and November. At Egg Island, the transfer of supplies was problematic due to the swells, and people and supplies were often dumped into the sea in the attempt. This nearly eliminated the possibility of friendly boats "dropping by" for a visit, so it was a lonely post.

Brown's assistant escaped as soon as he could, leaving Brown and his three-year-old boy alone for the following winter. A sea wall had been built to blunt the enormous seas but was easily swallowed by the first large winter wave. Later in the winter, when Brown got sick, he hung the flag upside down—the distress signal—and stopped manning the light. The light was out for twenty-seven days before he was rescued!

In 1903, the entire lighthouse was moved sixty-four feet to the top of the islet and onto a thick concrete foundation, reducing the winter fears of being washed away. The foghorn was added in 1906. But the isolation was still very real. In September 1919, William Hartin requested relief at once because his wife had gone crazy. And Arnold Moran quit because the "cruel isolation" affected his wife's health. His brother Thomas Moran was his successor.

On Feb 9, 1934, when the buoy tender and lighthouse supply ship the *Newington* arrived, captain Ormiston decided it was too rough to send a boat in. But Thomas was desperate to get his ill wife to a doctor, and he heroically managed to row her out to the *Newington*. He left his friend Don MacDonald on the island, and Captain Ormiston asked his seventeen-year-old mess boy to go to shore and assist Don while Tom was away.

Weeks later, Captain Dixon, steaming north on the SS *Catala* in the black of night, missed the reassuring rays of the Egg Island light. Concerned, he made his way to the island. All was dark. His first officer, Eric Suffolk, launched a lifeboat with four crewmen as oarsmen. The swells meant to throw the boat onto the rocks, so Suffolk stripped, tied a rope around his waist and swam ashore. Imagine trying to safely land yourself on a rocky beach in the dark, inside the unrelenting surges of an open ocean swell!

Suffolk managed it and found the lighthouse dark and empty. The kitchen table was set for two; the plates had bits of old food on them, but nowhere could he find the two men. From the height of the island, he saw their upturned boat rising and falling in the surf below. The bodies were never found.

By 1948, the winter storms through the years had washed the porch off twice, smashed the windows twice, torn a good portion of the roof off, torn away sections of the walkway, demolished a fence and a steel derrick, and broken in the foghorn building.

In the early hours of November 2, 1948, there was a November-style storm combined with an unusual sea. GMG was tied in Margaret Bay, a protected spot inside the inlet, and it was suffering—floats crashing and grinding, wood on wood, cables straining. But the lighthouse was front and centre of the inlet—entirely exposed to Queen Charlotte and the great Pacific Ocean and everything they had to offer. What happened at the lighthouse that night is a story told and retold by many. I first heard it from my dad, then from an old newspaper clipping my mom kept, later in other books and stories. The story is slightly different every time in minor ways, like the number of days stranded and how they were rescued. Finally, the boy in the story, Dennis Wilkins, told his eyewitness account, trumping the others.

If I had been Robert Laurence Wilkins, or his wife Ada Marie, or their nine-year-old son Dennis Edward in the early hours of November 2, 1948, I would have put my head under the covers to block out the screaming wind, increasing roar of the sea, the hissing spray on the walls. But they were listening to the election results—Truman was beating Dewy—and had gone to bed. The light shone from the top of the tower, the foghorn was blowing, the weather no worse than other November storms. But at 2 a.m., a sea broke through Wilkins' bedroom window and washed both of them, with their mattress, onto a watery floor, and their sunroom fell off the cliff.

The family made to escape out the laundry room door off the kitchen, but the laundry room wasn't there. After several tries, Wilkins managed to smash the kitchen window, and the trio with their little dog Boots escaped. Smokey the cat was left sleeping on a chair. Outside, everything was gone—the trees, grass, outer sheds, the engine for the hoist. The sea was roaring. Their first choice of refuge was the foghorn building, but it was full of water. So they crawled across the broken bridge connecting the lighthouse islet to the main island.

They made their way to the boathouse to find refuge, but the seas had reached the boathouse as well. Wilkins walked back to the bridge to have a look at the lighthouse. He saw the light, still shining, still turning, coming towards him. As he watched, the sea lifted the entire lighthouse off its foundation and tipped it over right in front of him. The Wilkins family ran to the highest point on the island, fearful that the sea would take the entire island.

That was a Tuesday morning. On Thursday, the marine agent in Prince Rupert made an appeal to all shipping in the area to investigate and report on the condition of Egg Island. The fish packer *P.W.* and the tug *Ivanhoe*, sheltering in Takush Harbour fifteen miles away, set out to respond but were turned back by the enormous sea. Other boats, all sailing far out to sea to avoid the rocks, veered in to have a look but were unable to land. They did get close enough to see that the tower and buildings had disappeared.

Finally, on November 7, the Wilkins family was rescued by the fishing vessel *Sonny Boy*. The family had spent five full days and nights in the chicken coop, Wilkins and Ada still in their pajamas. They suffered from exposure and hunger and were taken to see Dr. Darby at the Bella Bella Hospital.

After the Wilkins were rescued and the weather had subsided, some of the more curious GMG folk went to see the destroyed lighthouse.

"I remember seeing the lighthouse lying smashed on its side in the ravine, and pieces of blue china everywhere," says Lloyd. "Dad picked up a couple pieces for Mom."

Wilkins always wondered why the lighthouse washed off and not the foghorn building. When he was sent to help rebuild the lighthouse the following summer (which was reconstructed of concrete), he saw that when the structure had been moved to higher ground, it had never been bolted onto the foundation. The builders never anticipated such a sea—now said to have been a tsunami or rogue wave—which also explains the strain the GMG floats experienced that night.

A couple of years later, the keeper, Laurie Dupuis, received a wire from his wife, who was visiting in Victoria, that seemed to indicate she was not returning but which actually intended to tell him she *was* returning (a story supporting the value of proper punctuation!). Unable to bear life without her, he committed suicide just before she arrived on the steamer. The human mind is not intended for too much isolation. Perhaps this is why, when the weather was very good, the GMG folk went to visit the too-much-isolated lighthouse keepers and their children.

Later in the history of the lighthouse, there were several children living there, and I recall many visits. Mom said we had to visit the folks at the lighthouse because they were lonely and their kids had no one to play with. They couldn't even go to school, like lucky me, she said, and they were "pretty bushed."

"But Mom, I don't know them. Maybe they won't like me."

"Oh my, you're bushed too," Mom said, and off we went.

Sometimes we went in our own boat with Dad, and sometimes the ladies and kids went in Aunt Gloria's boat. There was always a swell from Queen Charlotte Sound, so we accessed the island from the boathouse side facing the inlet, crawled up the rocks to the stairs, then hiked across the island to visit the keepers. There was a little gravesite with a few names on crosses—*Who is buried there?* I wondered—a field, and some little houses shining white against the unending blue sea. The sea was always a brilliant blue—probably because we only went in very good weather!

By the time I was going to school in 1964, the old lighthouse was replaced by homes built on the bigger island, a metal tower at the very top for the light, and a helicopter pad on the foundation of the old lighthouse. The moms in the houses were always so happy to see us. There was a lot of shrieking and hugging, and we were fed sandwiches and pie, then Mom had to scoot me out from behind her to go play with the kids while the ladies visited. Sadly, I did not perform well. Mostly I just followed the kids around while they showed me things—the bushed leading the bushed.

They showed me the garden, and we played on the helicopter pad where the old lighthouse once stood. I listened to their lighthouse stories, and we clambered over the rocks, beachcombing, looking for the lost pieces of other people's lives washed ashore by a moody Queen Charlotte. Or an angry Kumugwe, sweeping the floors of his house under the sea.

Egg Island lighthouse, 1949, newly rebuilt in
higher location. Old location to the right

CHAPTER 12

THE TRAPPER'S GAME AND THE MARGARET BAY TREASURE

T wo old trappers lived in the inlet. They'd been around for so long no one could remember when they got there—probably the twenties. Charlie Sanden lived in a little brown floathouse in Margaret Bay just across the bay from GMG, and Vic Hackrey's cabin was in Wyclese Lagoon. Each had their own trap-lines, targeting mainly marten.

By the time GMG came along, the two had been living alone for so long they were "quite the characters." Charlie and Vic stopped by the camp from time to time and chatted with the men and enjoyed the ladies' baking. The loggers noticed that the two trappers liked to heckle each other, and one day Charlie revealed to them "the game."

Charlie and Vic, perhaps while sharing a drink in front of the fire, made a pact with each other: if either one of them ever saw the other stealing from his trap-line, the poacher would be shot! They shook hands on it. And they did poach from each other's lines—an exciting game for two lonely characters with little entertainment. *Would he really shoot me? Nah! Or would he? Would I really shoot him?*

The game may have been going on for decades, no one knows. But one day, Charlie was in his boat near his trap-line when he saw

Vic coming out of the woods with furs flung over his shoulder. So Charlie stood up in his boat, took aim and fired!

Lance was playing with Harold and Lloyd on the floats and was the first to see Charlie's rowboat surging across the bay. Lance used his cardboard tube telescope to focus on the boat. Charlie was in a hurry, leaving a wake behind him, and in the bow a lumpy bundle covered with a tarp heaved with the rhythm of the oars.

"Gloria, Gloria!" Charlie called as he drew closer. "The game is over, Gloria! The game is over."

Charlie bumped the laden bow up to the floats. Gloria and Claire, the only ladies home, shooed the boys inside. "You boys stay inside the house and do not come out!" Gloria sternly demanded.

Through the window the boys watched their mothers' horrified reaction to what was under the tarp. Then the ladies took action. Gloria and Claire, with baby Rosalie, jumped in the rowboat and rowed off to fetch their husbands, who were falling in Ethel Cove. They left the boys behind to watch their retreating boat through the window and Charlie behind to take care of Vic.

What was going on in Charlie's head as he made his way home with Vic in the bow of his boat? Suddenly his competitor was looking a lot like his only friend. And now he was gone. Was he angry with Vic for forcing him to follow the terms of the pact? Maybe he was angry with himself for his hasty reaction. And what should he do with Vic? It wouldn't be a good idea to leave him outside. Maybe if he brought him in for one last drink by the fire …. Stephen King could write a ghoulish novel just about poor Charlie at this point.

Meanwhile, Alvin and Don were called off the hill and a run was made in the gas boat to Margaret Bay Cannery to call the RCMP. The nearest police station, in Ocean Falls, prepared to dispatch the police boat; a small double-ended scow with a three-cylinder Easthope engine—a putt-putt boat!

Now there was nothing to do but wait. It was a couple of days before the RCMP arrived to begin their investigation, and all this time Vic was still with Charlie. The RCMP interviewed Charlie and the GMG families and Harold Malm, the Margaret Bay Cannery manager, before finally taking the body away with them back to Ocean Falls. But oddly, they didn't take Charlie.

The smoke still rose from Charlie's cabin across the bay, and many quiet discussions took place in GMG.

"We're living across the bay from a murderer."

"What do we tell the children?"

"I wonder if the police are going to come back for him?"

"I wonder how Charlie is doing?"

A few days went by, and then at breakfast one morning Alvin looked out the window and noticed there was no smoke rising from Charlie's chimney. He wondered how long there had been no smoke. He thought about it from time to time all day, and the next morning he decided to go over and investigate. His family didn't want him to go. Charlie shot one friend, maybe he would shoot another. Should he take a gun for self-defence?

Alvin rowed across the bay and nudged his boat onto the shore. Charlie didn't come out to meet him as he usually did, so Alvin knocked on the door.

"Hallo! You home, Charlie?"

No answer, so Alvin opened the door. And there was Charlie sitting in his favourite chair in front of a cold fire, his back to the door. Feeling uneasy, Alvin approached cautiously; Charlie was a murderer, after all.

"Charlie? Charlie, are you OK?"

Then he looked at Charlie's face, slack and grey in the pale light from the window. He didn't need to take a pulse. He stepped back, and back again, out the door, into the daylight and the fresh air.

Then another trip to Margaret Bay Cannery, another phone call to the police, and another wait for the police boat. The RCMP took Charlie's body to Bella Bella Hospital where Dr. Darby saw the body, several days dead, and decided he did not want to do an autopsy. But he knew the story. He wrote on the death certificate, "Died of a broken heart."

Charlie had no family and a lot of money stashed somewhere. But though the RCMP searched thoroughly, and curious others even more, Charlie's stash was never found. It became known as "The Margaret Bay Treasure."

Dressed for church, 1950. Left to right, back row:
Alvin, Clyde, Louis. Middle row: Gloria, Claire,
Genevieve, Nancy, Hazel. Front row: Heather, Rosalie
Ann, Harold, Lance, Lloyd. Don taking photo

CHAPTER 13

THANK YOU, IONOSPHERE

B y 1950, war technology significantly reduced the isolation of the inlet and made life easier in many ways.

"We were quite isolated in the beginning," Louis recalls. "But the boat came in once a month, so we got our supplies that way, and the mail came once a month. There were no airplanes and there were no radiophones, but they came in not too long after, which made quite a difference. And we didn't have our own electricity in the early years, but we always had a good water system because of the mountain streams, and it was quite comfortable."

But now airplanes began servicing the coast and could be summoned on radiophones in an emergency. Outboard motors meant zipping through the Bull Run to the village, Margaret Bay or Boswell in minutes, ending hours of rowing. Large ships installed radar and VHF radiophones. Then the forestry boat installed a phone, and soon after, the *Thomas Crosby IV*. Camps bought light plants to power lights, wringer washers and electric sewing machines!

The ladies felt relatively civilized. Electric lights illuminated the dark mornings and evenings; now kerosene lamps were just a back up when the power plant was shut off. Gas wringer washers were converted to, or replaced by, electric. Woodward's even started selling conversion kits to convert wood-burning stoves to oil-burning stoves, providing better temperature control and eliminating the tedious, never-ending chore of firewood, though it also eliminated Lance's young livelihood. He was paid ten cents a disc to stand on the floats and, using a cross-cut saw, cut thick discs off a log that was tied to the floats, then haul the discs up onto the floats and chop them into firewood. With the new oil stove, he simply pulled a hose and filled the oil barrel outside the house every Friday or so. Now if only the ladies could have a refrigerator!

Of all the modern conveniences, there was a single piece of new technology which made the biggest difference of all: the ten-inch-square steel box that was installed in the office. This single-frequency phone, using frequency 2292, connected GMG to the radio station in Bull Harbour. Previously, Louis's old army surplus radiophone had been very limited. But now family members could be contacted almost any day you liked! In a restricted fashion, at least. Groceries and parts could be ordered immediately and shipped on the next boat, reducing wait times by two weeks or a month in winter when the steamers reduced their schedule to once a month. Theoretically, though it probably never happened, if an item was important enough and needed badly enough to justify the cost, it could be ordered on the phone one day and flown in on an airplane the next!

The adults all learned how to use the radiophone. In an emergency, when you couldn't wait for the "sked," the procedure went like this:

Turn the phone on, press down on the button, CLICK. "Bull Harbour, Bull Harbour, GMG Logging." OFF CLICK.

Say "Bull Harbour" at a higher pitch, then drop your voice for "GMG Logging" and lilt up at the "-ing" sort of like a chant, over and over until Bull Harbour answers.

If it's a life-and-death emergency, use 2318 and repeat, "Mayday, mayday, mayday." So if somebody needed a flight to the hospital right away, this is how it might go:

CLICK. "Bull Harbour, Bull Harbour, GMG Logging." OFF CLICK.

"GMG Logging, Bull Harbour. How can I help?"

CLICK. "Bull Harbour, GMG Logging, we need a plane sent right away for an injured logger, over." OFF CLICK.

And Bull Harbour would sort out the details for you or connect you with an airline.

Though Bull Harbour listened for emergencies twenty-four hours a day, regular messages were sent and received during scheduled hours. GMG turned their battery-powered phone off until the "sked." There was an afternoon sked at 2 p.m. and an evening sked at 7. At these times, folks in Smiths and Rivers inlets turned on their phones and listened as Bull Harbour called out their call-names. When they called "GMG Logging" you answered "nothing" or you answered "traffic." Then Bull Harbour said, "Go ahead GMG Logging," and you read them the message, or "wire," and the address to which it was to be sent—Vancouver Supply Ltd. or Gramma's phone number—and the message was later relayed to them by the Bull Harbour radio station. Of course, everyone on the sked heard the message too, so your neighbours, some you'd never met, knew a lot of interesting things about you, like what kind of equipment your camp had, who was sick with what, and what you eat for breakfast!

The radiophone was a life-changer for everyone, including the villagers in Takush, who often boated over to call an airplane when somebody became ill, or to call their friends in Alert Bay, or to call the hospital in Ocean Falls. Villagers, fishermen, visitors, stranded boaters, GMG folk—every call made was recorded word for word because charges were incurred by the word. In the beginning, every caller had to come to Hazel and Louie's house, walk through the kitchen, the bedroom and then into the tiny room beyond it, which was the GMG office.

The first two entries in the radio logbook, dated January 22, 1950, were to advise of arrivals and departures. It seems everyone was returning after Christmas with family. The third was a grub order for the four GMG families. The messages are recorded like this:

> January 24, 1950
> To Vancouver Supply Ltd. 25 Alexander St.
> Vancouver, BC
> *Please ship following to Boswell Union, Sat:*
> *In case lots:*
> > *Tomatoes 2*
> > *Milk Pacific 3*
> > *Orange juice 1*
> > *Tomato juice 1*
> > *Apple juice 1*
> > *Peaches 1*
> > *Honey 1*
> > *Butter canned 1*
> > *Peanut butter 1*
> > *Brittack 1*
> > *Two drums Trumilk*
> > *Two cases milk, Pacific*
> > *Quaker oats 2*
> > *Raisins 1*
> > *Dates 1*

> *Catelli 1*
> *Yeast 1*
> *Instant Postum 1*
> *White flour 2 sacks 50 lb*
> *Brown flour 2 sacks 50 lb*
> *Peas dried 25 lb*
> *Soy beans 25 lb*
> *One sack carrots*
> *50 lb squash*
> *50 lb sweet potatoes*
> *50 lb cabbage*
> *2 boxes apples, Newton*
> *One case eggs*
> *2 doz celery*
> *No gallon cans*
> GMG Logging Co.

It's a list of long-lasting staples which translated into oatmeal, peanut butter on toast and fruit for breakfast, pancakes on Sundays, bread for fish sandwiches in the lunchboxes, bean soup, pea soup, veggie soup, baked beans, steamed veggies, macaroni and tomato casserole, matrimonial cake, boiled raisin cake, oatmeal cookies, apple pie and Postum with Pacific.

The men's orders reflected the company's regular needs and the needs of their modern, recent acquirements—new light plant, oil stoves, outboard motors, chainsaws, movie projector.

> January 24, 1950
> To T. Eaton Co. Vancouver, BC
> *Please ship COD to Margaret Bay: one propeller for 33hp*
> *Sportwin Model Evinrude. Two crankshaft oil seals on*
> *4 valves for 6 horse 3000 watt Power-Lite Light Plant*
> *serial no. 86300698*
> Don Goertzen

Feb 21, 1950
To Home Oil Ltd. 555 Burrard, Vancouver, BC
Have Dinamac stop in Tacush Harbour next trip.
Require 1000 gal. stove oil
500 gal. white gasoline
Let us know when you come so we can have oil float
anchored out there.
GMG Logging

To Burnett Power Saws and Engineering Co. Ltd.
1616 Pandora St. Vancouver, BC
Ship to Margaret Bay Union Saturday following parts
for Model B6
*   1 chain for 4 ft. blade*
*   1 oil line complete Pt no. B6-58*
*   1 clutch control wire casing Part No. B6-71*
*   2 clutch control wires with nipples part no B6-70*
GMG Logging

Takush Village used the new radiophone for the first time to order potatoes.

April 5, 1950
To Indian Agent Alert Bay
8 sacks of potatoes is not enough. There are thirty families
in this band and are asking for 5 sacks more
Chief G. Walkus/per Charlie G. Walkus

And, of course, there was a continual conversation with E. Patersen (which they later spelled "Petersen"), Northern Pulpwood, Ocean Falls, B.C.

April 28 Received 1
From Ocean Falls to GMG Logging Co.
Please wire Ocean Falls inventory MBM [million board
feet] felled and bucked. Also MBM in water for our fiscal
year ending April 30.

E. Patersen

April 31 Sent 1
To E. Patersen, Northern Pulpwood, Ocean Falls, BC
*Logs in water 700 M. Felled and bucked one million
[board feet]. 22 sections ready for towing. Send 100
chains with tug.*
GMG Logging Co.

May 18, to Northern Pulpwood, Box 879,
Vancouver, BC
*Please have shipped to Margaret Bay Union Monday:
500 ft. ¾ in. steel core mainline, six choker wires 25 ft. 1
in. steel core, 1 doz. Jerrulles 1 inch, 20 lb. choker babbit,
1 sack blacksmith coal, 2 rigging shackles for 1 in. main,
2 fan belts for Lawrence 10-10.*

In June, GMG ordered a sack of potatoes, four crates of strawberries and six watermelons for a Dominion Day picnic at the big sand beach.

Summertime bustled. Every one who could, went to town, otherwise known as "The Big Smoke" or Vancouver, for at least a week. Guests came and went. Fishermen crowded the inlet and stopped by to visit. Summer travellers could catch the SS *Cardena* or call Pacific Coastal Airlines in Alert Bay to reserve seats to Vancouver. (Regular shuttles didn't begin until 1954.) On August 1, Alvin and Gloria came back from Vancouver on the SS *Cardena*, radioing GMG for a pickup at Margaret Bay, and Hazel called August 22 to say she was coming back on the *Sea Gypsy*, Clyde and Nancy's new boat.

It was a time of growth and improvements, with the radiophone as key player. It was also the summer that Chief George made a plea to Don and Claire Goertzen to come live with his people at Takush and teach them.

CHAPTER 14

TWO WORLDS CONNECT

When Chief George asked Don for help, Don knew a request from the heart of a fellow man was a plea he could not refuse. He would give up his living and his life for it. GMG bought him out. To make a living, Don would go fishing in the summers, do some hand-logging and trapping, and GMG would assist when needed. Claire had long been friends with the girls her age in the village, and she supported his decision all the way. They would bring their two children with them, Harold, born the summer of 1946, and Rosalie Ann, born January of 1948.

The chief had observed the Gildersleeve, then the GMG community, and wanted the same quality of life for his people. Don was young, outgoing, friendly and helpful, and everyone liked him. The chief specifically asked Don to teach his people about God and to educate the children. Chief George said he knew educating the children was important for the future of his people, and if Don reopened the school, they would no longer need to send children away to St. Michael's Residential School in Alert Bay to get an education.

Don and George Walkus took the *Westpoint* to Kelsey Bay, then made a road trip to visit the Department of Indian Affairs (DIA) in Victoria to obtain permission to reopen the day school in Takush. George Walkus, son of William Walkus (Gooje), was

Chief George's nephew and had the title of Elected Chief—chosen because he had completed seventh grade at St. Michael's and could read and write. Though the DIA officially employed day schoolteachers, the Indian Act stipulated that a reserve's chief and councillor had the right to determine a teacher's religion. George put his request to the official, and permission was given.

Then Don and Claire went to the Hope Camp Meeting the last weekend of July hoping to convince Frank and Ada Johnson to come teach in the community. Although Don looked for them all week, Frank and Ada were not there as expected. Finally, on the last Friday night of camp meeting, Don got up in front of a huge congregation and pleaded for somebody willing to leave their present comforts and live in a tiny house in a remote, technologically primitive and culturally foreign-to-them village and teach the children there. No one responded.

Frank and Ada arrived later that evening and were told of Don's plea. They knew the call was for them. Ada had a teaching certificate, and Frank was a man of many skills; he had even logged in Smith Inlet for Bill Gildersleeve. Also, Frank had a special place in his heart for the people. He owed his life to a Chinook woman who nursed him as a child when his mother could not. They accepted the invitation.

> August 8, 1950
> Don Goertzen
> *Have been informed by M.S. Todd you know suitable teacher for SI* [Smith Inlet] *Indian School. Please inform by telegram name and address of applicant so I may contact.*
> R.F. Davey, District Inspector BC Indian Schools

Johnson family

On September 4, 1950, Frank and Ada boarded the SS *Cardena* in Vancouver with their children Frank Junior, Donnie and Ethel to change their lives forever. Don told them to disembark at Margaret Bay, about a three-day journey on the *Cardena*, where he would pick them up. The *Cardena* stopped at every little community on the way—one long, two short, and one long blast on the whistle announced their arrival at all times of day or night. The ship serviced different communities weekly, bi-weekly and monthly, and it so happened that this was NOT the week for Margaret Bay's stop. Instead, they were dropped at a place they had never heard of, in Rivers Inlet. They stood on the dock beside all their belongings under the giant letters WADHAMS, feeling stranded and alone. Mrs. McKetty came to greet them.

"Of course I know where GMG is," she said. "It's the only logging camp in Smith Inlet. But it's in the Ahclakerho, five hours away! Come. You'll have to wait for the sked."

Mrs. McKetty kindly fed them supper and found them a cabin to sleep in.

At precisely seven o'clock that evening, Don sat with Alvin and Louis in the GMG office and turned on the radiophone to listen to the sked. After Bull Harbour gave and received messages, the locals could talk to each other if they had something to say. It was a rare evening that anyone missed the sked, and that night Wadhams had a message for GMG.

Don responded and caught the morning tide through the Bull Run. He pulled up to Wadhams in the *Westpoint* just before breakfast and picked up his passengers. The tide was wrong for the Bull Run on the way back, so they hugged the mainland shore around the corner into Smith Sound, motored through Tye Pass and Shield Pass, across Blackney and Browning channels, east into Smith Inlet, around Cape Anne, west through the Ahclakerho Channel and Broad Reach before finally turning into the narrow passage near Takush River. The Johnsons spotted GMG's float camp in a secluded cove of Greaves Island—Fly Basin. (Officially, Fly Basin is in Takush Harbour, but the locals referred to all the shallow bowls and flats around the Bull Run as Fly Basin.)

As they pulled into camp, coho and dog salmon were jumping around the floathouses, waiting to go up the Takush River. Everyone came out to meet the new family. Ada was tall and fair-haired in contrast to her husband who was dark and slight. They both had a quiet and kindly manner. Their three children were happy to meet the GMG kids, and the boys were soon trying to catch the jumpers with a salmon hook and the lid of a tin can.

The next day was Friday, September 8. Gloria and Claire's sister, Genevieve, was at camp for a visit, and as they were chatting and preparing dinner for their guests the Johnsons, Gloria glanced out the window and saw someone rowing a skiff towards camp.

"I wonder who would be coming to camp at this time of day," she said.

As the little black flat-bottomed skiff drew closer, she recognized the rower. It was Lily Johnny, Chief George's daughter who was married to Alfred Johnny, Chief Johnny's son. *Twice a princess*, Gloria liked to think. Lily pulled up to the floats, exhausted, and helping hands took the rope and lifted her from the water-filled boat. She had rowed about five miles to the camp from Takush Village with a badly broken oar in a leaky boat.

"Come quick," she said. "My kids are sick. Alfred is gone."

Don had built a beautiful little boat with an outboard on it, named the *Wakini*, probably the first speed-boat in the inlet.

"If we hurry, we can make the tide," he said.

The ladies quickly assembled sulfa (sulfonamide), Aspirin, mustard, buckets, towels and cloths of all sorts and loaded them into the *Wakini*. Then Don, Claire, Gloria, Genevieve and Lily climbed in. By this time, it was getting dark and the tide was rapidly going out through the Bull Run, the boulders baring themselves as the tide roared. At half tide, the Bull Run would be dry and impassable, but Don manoeuvred the *Wakini* through before the water dropped low enough for the kicker to hit bottom.

With only the beams of their flashlights to guide them, they tied the boat up at the Takush dock and climbed the steep bank to Lily's house. Her house had no ceiling or partitions, no running water, and a wood-burning barrel stove struggled to keep the place warm. They heard whimpering, harsh breathing and coughing from Geraldine, Alfred, Douglas and Judith. But baby Judy was the most seriously ill.

Don built up a good fire and put water on to heat. When it was hot, they began applying hot and cold fomentations and mustard plasters. I imagine a lot of wailing going on because fomentations and plasters are no fun—there's a reason they are nearly obsolete! But without antibiotics, these were the healing methods for bronchitis and pneumonia. The idea was that the heat would kill the "bugs," increase blood circulation for healing and loosen up mucus for coughing up.

While they worked, they showed Lily how to do it. First, lay a cloth on the chest of the patient to protect the skin. Then dip a cloth of wool or flannel (called a fomentation cloth or a compress) in the boiling water, wring it out and fold it into an appropriately sized square and place it on the dry cloth. A dry towel goes on top of the wet compress, followed by a blanket. Replace the wet compress with a newly hot one every few minutes when the old one begins to feel cool, and about every fourth compress switch the hot compress with a cold one. If you have ice, soak the cold compress in ice water. When the patient begins sweating, wipe their face with a cool, wet cloth and be sure to keep a damp, cool cloth on the forehead. After about twenty or thirty minutes of this, rub the skin briskly with a cold washcloth, then allow the patient to rest for an hour or two before repeating.

If the patient is sick enough, and strong enough to withstand it, use the mustard plaster. Mix four tablespoons of flour with two tablespoons of mustard powder and enough water to make a thick paste. Spread the paste on half of a clean flour sack towel (or other thin cloth such as flannel) and fold it up. Protect the skin with petroleum jelly and a layer of cloth. Apply the mustard plaster, another towel and a blanket. Leave on for up to twenty minutes but keep checking the skin for blistering. Keep the face and forehead cool as with the hot and cold fomentations. For pneumonia, apply to both chest and back.

Yes, getting sick in the 1950s was pretty miserable! And heaven forbid you should get a sore throat because then your mom would make you wear a wet wool sock around your neck all night, sometimes with the addition of Vicks VapoRub. During the day, you had to carry a diaper around, even to school, doused in eucalyptus for sniffing.

The team may have administered sulfa as well. The white powder for wounds or tablets for ingestion had been a staple in first aid kits since the war and worked as an antibiotic. Soon it fell out of favour due to unpleasant side effects and the fact that bacteria developed resistant strains after exposure to the drug. And then, of course, penicillin became more readily available. But on that night in Smith Inlet in 1950, sulfa and Aspirin were their only pharmaceutical defenses.

The little medical team worked through the night and hoped to catch the next tide through the Bull Run back to camp. Though the older children were resting more easily, baby Judy still gave cause for concern, so Lily gave permission for them to take Judy with them to continue treating her.

Gloria collected all the laundry she could find, Genevieve gathered up little Judith, and they headed for the Bull Run. This time it was so shallow Don had to jump out of the *Wakini* into the cold water and pull the boat through. But they made it home in time to rest a little before church.

The first church service the Johnson family attended in Smith Inlet was in the Louis Goertzen home. The children had Sabbath School in the bedroom, and everyone came together in the living room for the church service. It was all very unusual for the Johnsons. Frank Junior remembers, "It was as worshipful as in any church … Louis Goertzen presented a message on the love of God and the Sabbath. The message touched me more deeply than just about any Sabbath presentation I had heard before or since."

The Johnson family moved into a converted shop on the same float as Don and Claire's house and waited for the big move. The men had a daring and brash plan. If they waited a few days until the highest tide, they thought they could pull the float through the Bull Run instead of making the long trip all the way out of the Ahclakerho and around. The Bull Run is the local name for the narrow, shallow space between Greaves Island and the mainland at the Takush River estuary where GMG was situated. It is not on the charts because it is dry at about half tide and scattered with boulders; in the rising and falling tides, it becomes a rapids. Travel was timed for high tides whenever possible, saving the hours of time it took to go out the Ahclakerho at the eastern entrance into Smith Inlet, but no one had ever taken a wide float through the Bull Run.

On a calm, sunny September day at noon, Don and Claire Goertzen's float was uncabled from the camp and pulled out of place by the *Westpoint*. The float was lined with men wielding pike poles—Roy, Alvin, Louis, Don, Frank and, as helpers, Frank Junior and Lance. One of the men drove the *Westpoint*, and a friendly fish patrolman, Bob Allen, pushed from behind. The *Westpoint* chugged slowly through the narrow channel. At the narrowest point, cedar limbs scratched the windows of the house, and a corner of the float arrested on a boulder. The men hollered to stop towing and ran to pry it off with their pike poles. It was a very tense moment—if the float stuck at the highest tide, it could be stuck forever. But at last, it was pried loose and again moved forward. Finally, the float slipped out of the narrows into the open water, and everyone breathed a sigh of relief.

"Never again!" said the men.

Takush Harbour seemed to welcome the little float home newly birthed from the Bull Run. The sun sparkled on its calm waters, seagulls circled, mergansers, grebes, cormorants and loons ducked and unducked around them. The house inched past an old shipwreck rising from the water on the left and moved through scattered tiny islets, heading towards Kigeh (Indian Island). A row of diapers flapped white on the clothesline like banners declaring peace. Claire was still looking after Lily Johnny's sick baby, Judy, and Lily, tall and slender with long black braids and a beautiful smile, was the first to come meet them. She was eager to see her baby, and she came with a boatful of curious girls. The girls leapt to the float and surrounded Claire, and shyly met their new teacher, Mrs. Frank. After delivering the girls, the boat dropped behind, connecting its bow to the float and adding power to the tow.

Then, in one of those magical moments in time that is remembered forever, many boats appeared, unloading a crowd of happy people onto the float, each boat joining to push the float home in an act of welcome. Together, they propelled the new families into their village and their lives.

An opening in the wall of trees ahead revealed a sheltered bay. High on the rocky shoreline grew a cluster of eight or so houses of aged wood, shining silver in the evening light. Takush Village. There were also several floathouses in the bay, and the GMG men tied Don's float beside Joe Johnny's float.

In the morning, visitors began to arrive to meet the new family. Ada was doing wash when the girls—Margaret, Helen, Annie, Isabelle, Frances—arrived. Only Margaret could speak English. She held out a brown pail to Ada and said shyly, "Water for you."

Joe and Jane Johnny from the float next door brought gifts of pretty seashells, wood for the stove and a rowboat for them to use. Charlie G. Walkus came with his eldest daughter Janet, a sweet sixteen-year-old with pretty dimples. Robert and Bill, ages seventeen and eighteen, came to meet their teacher. Chief George and his wife Lucy came, the tinkling bells on their trolling poles announcing their arrival. The chief called Frank "Mr. Frank" and Ada "Mrs. Frank." He shook hands gravely with Ada and smiled at Frank Junior, Donnie and Ethel, calling them "ake kinanum" (good children). His wife, Lucy, nearly eighty, strong and plump with white hair, bare feet and a jolly laugh, spoke in Chinook with Frank and taught them all to say "halakas'la" (goodbye).

On Friday evening, Claire and Ada rowed over to the beach and climbed up to the village. Claire introduced Ada to Lily's husband, Alfred Johnny, and their four small children: Geraldine,

Alfred, Douglas and Judith. They went to the home of George Walkus, and Ada met George and Eliza and their family of six boys and one tiny girl: James, Alec, Robert, Archie, Andrew, Alvin and Clara. Then to Charlie G.'s house, the largest house in the village. Charlie G. and Jenny (Jean) were at home with their six girls: Janet, Margaret, Edith (Helen), Isabelle, Irene and Clara (Ruby). Several families were gone fishing. The family situation in the tribe was confusing. There was a Mrs. Chief Johnny, whose husband had died, and a Chief George Walkus, whose wife was Lucy. Edward and Sally's home had over twenty people in it—children, grandchildren and cousins living together. Who could keep track? But there was once a way—there was once a song.

Takush (Ta'kus) Village

Mrs. Chief Johnny drying herring roe on hemlock and cedar branches. Photo by Don Goertzen

CHAPTER 15

WAIL OF L!AL!EQWASILA, A GWA'SELA WOMAN

I t was a spring morning in Alert Bay in the year 1916. George Hunt was assisting Franz Boas in accumulating artifacts and knowledge of the Kwakwaka'wakw peoples, and on this morning in Alert Bay he heard a woman crying for the loss of her brother. And in her crying, she began to sing the history of her family. Hunt listened to her cry and sing from seven in the morning until three in the afternoon. When she was finished, he asked her if he could write the story of her cry song. She said she would be proud of it—none but she could sing her song, she said, because she was the eldest daughter of her family. George Hunt recorded her cry song, or wail song (lag"alem), in its entirety and called it "Wail of L!al!Eqwasila, a Gwa'sela Woman." He translated it into English to be recorded in *Ethnology of the Kwakiutl* by Franz Boas (1921, p 836-885). L!al!Eqwasila sang twenty-three generations of history! Using Wikipedia's definition of a generation as thirty years, her song traced her ancestry as far back as 1226.

She began:

> Haha hananē! Now I come to think of my forefathers and of my great grandfathers. Now I will tell the story of my house when we were chiefs in the beginning of this our world.

Haha hananē! YāqalE'nāla went about spouting. He was my chief in the beginning of the world. He travelled about in his canoe, a whale; for he was a whale, the ancestor of my people the Gwa'sela; and he went into NEgēL [Smith Inlet?]. He saw that there was a good beach, and he went ashore there; and YāqalE'nāla built a house and came out of his whale-body. Now, the whale-canoe of YāqalE'nāla lay crosswise on the beach. Then YāqalE'nāla gave a name to the village and called it GwēqElis. [Whale turned to stone, now commonly spelled Wyclese, or on the marine chart, Wyclees.]

Haha hananē! Then YāqalE'nlis said that he would go and see the country southward. [Into the lagoon.] He went aboard his travelling canoe, "Whale," and came to Padzō. There YāqalE'nlis saw a good beach, and the whale landed in the middle of the beach of Padzō. YāqalE'nlis went ashore out of his travelling canoe, "Whale," and went to look at it. He saw that it was a good place to build a house. And now Chief YāqalE'nlis, my ancestor, built a house ten steps deep. He closed the mouth of the river at EmxsdElis and therefore the river is called EmxsdElis (closed-bottom). Then YāqalE'nlis name was changed from YāqalE'nlis to TsExtsExŭlis (stranded whale); for that is what the whale did when it went ashore at Padzō. Now TsExtsExŭlis finished his house. It was ten steps deep.

Then a canoe came along, and TsExtsExŭlis went to meet (the travellers) and he invited them in. A man and his wife and a pretty young woman came ashore. They sat down. Then TsExtsExŭlis gave them to eat. And after they had eaten, TsExtsExŭlis questioned his guests, "O brother, who are you?"

Then the man said, "I am SēnLē'. My village is in the world above, and this is my princess, SēnL!ēgas; and this is my wife, O brother!" Then SēnLē' questioned him also, "And who are you, O brother!" Then TsExtsExŭlis replied and said, "I am TsExtsExŭlis. I come from North-End-of-our-World. I wish to marry your princess, O brother! So that our names may be really together." Then SēnLē' asked his princess to sit down by the side of TsExtsExŭlis, and they were married. Then SēnLē' gave as a marriage present the names Sēsazâlas (Sisax̱o'las, Cesaholis) and Sēwid to TsExtsExŭlis, and this was the first name obtained in marriage by my ancestor, the chief.

Haha hananē!

The woman sang on and on, naming the firstborns and the ones they married, like the litany of begets in the book of Genesis. Special care was taken in her song to describe the gifts and names given in marriages and at the births of the firstborn. The marriage of the son of TsExtsExŭlis and the daughter of SēnLē' was the first potlatch given by the Gwa'sala, and the gifts given out at the first potlatch are all listed: a speaking post, ten sea otter blankets, twenty-five marten blankets, twenty black bear blankets, two slaves, the seal house-dish, the wolf house-dish, the dzonoqua house-dish, and the beaver house-dish. The wedding feast of fifty seals was served in the house-dishes, and all the blankets were given away to the guests at the feast.

L!al!Eqwasila sang on through the generations and the gifts given and received. Families grew, and each family (numaym) had their own chief. They began to receive through marriage the rights to songs and dances with the accompanying tlug'we—masks, rattles, clothing and whistles intended to aid in connecting to the supernatural. Sometime between 1575 and 1600, according to the calculations of Franz Boas and George Hunt, the family of our singer, L!al!Eqwasila, received through marriage the right to the highest ranking and most supernaturally powerful dance, the Hamatsa, or Cannibal Dance, along with two slaves to be used for their first Hamatsa ceremony, which L!al!Eqwasila says was also the occasion of their first winter ceremonial.

Respect, power and elevation of status were dependent on the number of gifts given away. It was also insurance. For example, whatever a Gwa'sala chief gave another tribal chief in a potlatch was later returned with interest (usually double) in a future potlatch given by the receiving chief. In one of the last potlatches the Gwa'sala gave before "the white men had come to live at Fort Rupert," an impressive list of gifts was given: four slaves, four large canoes, fifty dressed elk-skin blankets, fifty lynx blankets, one hundred deerskin blankets, one hundred mountain goat blankets, a name, a house. And this seems to be the end of Gwa'sala wealth. (Fort Rupert, near Port Hardy on Vancouver Island, was built in 1849 by the Hudson's Bay Company for trading purposes.)

Sometime after 1849 and before 1916, when L!al!Eqwasila sang her song that morning in Alert Bay, her parents were married in Geg'aqe (Kigeh, charted as Indian Island on today's charts, on which island is the village of Takush). The gift list was ten woollen blankets and one hundred cedar bark blankets only. Because, L!al!Eqwasila sings, "The white men had come to live at Fort Rupert." Did they trade all their fur blankets to the Hudson's Bay Company in Fort Rupert? Or perhaps they lost their wealth to the Heiltsuk (Bella Bella) raid in the 1850s?

The singer's parents had "not been married long when my mother gave birth to twins." Twins were significant, associated with the return of salmon, and a greater effort was made for the twins' celebration held at Geg'aqe, "For now the Gwa'sela had left GweqElis" (Wyclese). The general consensus is that the Gwa'sala made this move closer to the mouth of the inlet about 1890 to be closer to trade routes and canneries. (The Royal BC Museum in Victoria, BC, has photos online of the abandoned village at Wyclese that are dated 1905.)

At the end of her cry song, L!al!Eqwasila says, "I did not mention that all of them had two or three wives, and some had four wives, and a great many children and the younger brothers and sisters of those whom I have named. Now, this great matter is at end."

She also does not mention the population decline in her song, but the Gwa'sala, like the other Kwakwaka'wakw tribes, had experienced a ninety percent population loss after European contact. Some of the decline was due to tribal warfare, and in particular a raid by the Heiltsuk tribe in the 1850s. The first superintendent of Indian Affairs, Israel Wood Powell, when he visited Wyclese in 1873, said, "Nearly the whole tribe numbering 250 souls" had been killed in the raid. But other population data indicates that this could be an exaggeration. The Gwa'sala population decline is considered to be similar to the rest of the Kwakwaka'wakw tribes, about thirty percent due to the smallpox epidemic of 1862, the rest due to raids from enemy tribes, measles, influenza, syphilis, TB and alcohol.[6]

The Gwa'sala told a second origin story, for a second family; this ancestor came to earth from above as a brilliant event wearing a sun mask and, taking it off, became a man, Tlagalixala. In 1873, Powell recorded the names of the two Gwa'sala chiefs as "Mantzie" and "Iolthkin," names not found elsewhere. But spelling has always been an issue in recording Kwak'wala words, so perhaps these could be "Pladzese'maxwa" and "Yax"Len" from the same time period in "Wail of L!a!Eqwasila." A photographer named Richard Maynard was travelling with Powell and took a handsome portrait of one of the two chiefs sitting on a bench in

---

[6]   Robert Galois, *Kwakwaka'wakw Settlements, 1775-1920:* A Geographical Analysis and Gazetteer, Vancouver: University of British Columbia Press, 2015

front of his house. He also took photos of the Gwa'sala, picturing about a dozen men, women and children on the beach. (These photos can be viewed in the British Columbia Archives online.)

In 1950, when the Goertzen and Johnson families joined the Gwa'sala tribe at Takush, the population was on an increase. The names of the two families in 1950 were Walkus (Wa'kas) and Johnny. Johnny, the second numaym in Takush, had fewer sons, thus there were fewer tribal members with their name.

George Walkus (born 1882) was the chief in 1950. He had a Chinook wife, Lucy. Chief Johnny had died, leaving Mrs. Chief Johnny (born 1874) and their children, including firstborn son Alfred. When the Willis Gildersleeve family arrived in Smith Inlet in 1937, their understanding was that there had always been some feuding between the two Gwa'sala numayms, the Walkus's and the Johnnys. But in 1950, the numayms were well-blended. Chief George's son Charlie George married Chief Johnny's daughter Jeannie Johnny, and they created a prominent family in the village with daughters Janet, Ivy, Helen, Isabelle, Ruby, Julie, Hazel and Irene, and two sons, Robert and Johnny. Then Chief Johnny's son Alfred married Chief George's daughter Lily and began creating another large family.

Though the genealogy was confusing, the newcomers soon discovered that, one way or another, every Walkus alive came from three brothers—Chief George Walkus (born 1882), William Walkus (born 1884) or Edward Walkus (born 1897).

Of course, everyone in the village had more than one name, both secular and spiritual. Historically, when the first child was born, he or she was given the name of the place of their birth. At ten months old, a son's family held a potlatch for him and gave him a child name. Later he was given a young man's name and a feast name, a warrior name (but only if he killed a man and kept the scalp), a sparrow (spirit) name, which was used during the winter ceremonial season, a hamatsa name (if he had this privilege), and a chief name if he became chief. Houses and dogs also had names.

Names were gifts to the Kwakwaka'wakw people because they meant something important like "One Who Gives Great Potlatches." (Even a tribe's name could change. A man once struck his chief with a pole, taking the position for himself, and the tribe's name was changed to "Struck With a Pole.") The names of the men in "The Wail of L!al!Eqwasila" changed so often in relation to their new circumstances or the gift of a new name, that Boas gave the individuals numbers in order not to lose track of who was who. (Later, Chief George would honour the GMG families by giving their children Gwa'sala names.)

When it became necessary for the Gwa'sala to choose an English name, it needed to be significant as well. In Takush there were many males named after the king of England. There was Chief George Walkus, Charlie George Walkus, George James Walkus, Harry George Walkus and Louis George Walkus. It seemed George was used as a last name as well, with Annie George and Charlie Walkus George. Their neighbours, the 'Nakwaxda'xw, often came to visit, and the confusion grew with their long list of males also named George. It would take several months before names and customs became familiar to the Goertzen and Johnson families.

The morning after Ada and Claire visited the village, everyone met at Charlie G.'s (Charlie George Walkus) house for church. When Don came in to give his talk, he said "Wik'shis" (How are you?). Everyone was silent because they were so surprised to hear Don speak their language. Finally, Charlie G. said, "Ake" (Good). A dog came in and followed Don around.

"Quate" (Go away), Don said to the dog.

Everyone laughed to hear Don speaking their language, and they encouraged him with new words.

"Say 'quate watts,'" they said. "'Watts' means dog."

It was a happy new beginning. The new schoolteacher was a notoriously poor singer, but she did record a list of birthdates—future ancestry to be sung by an eldest daughter to her tribe someday. Or more likely to be read by anyone who likes, in Google Books, along with the "Wail of L!al!Eqwasila, a Gwa'sela woman." Eventually Ada wrote an unpublished manuscript, which is invaluable to our understanding of the events that unfolded.

Group photo after church, Takush, 1950/51. Photo by Don Goertzen

CHAPTER 16

SCHOOL DESKS AND WA'DALLA DOLLAS

A tired old schoolhouse and teacherage, looking large next to the small houses, still stood in Takush. The United Church of Canada had operated the school from 1928 to 1939, but it was hard to find teachers willing to live so remotely. Since it closed, some of the children had been going to St. Michael's Residential School in Alert Bay, and some hadn't been going to school at all. The teacherage had been given to the chief, who now lived in it, and the school had also been used as a dwelling and needed a lot of work. The roof leaked, windows were broken, the walls blackened. Frank, Frank Junior, Don and whomever they could enlist worked on the school for a week, repairing and painting.

Sent Sept 6, 1950
To M.S. Todd, Indian Agent, Alert Bay, BC
Please advise what to do regarding broken windows, paper for walls, and heater for school. I have good oil heater will sell reasonable.
Don Goertzen, Margaret Bay, BC

Sept 7, 1950
Cheque Alert Bay
To Donald Goertzen. Re Tel, supply stove, make necessary repairs school, forward account in duplicate this office.
M.S. Todd

Sept 16, 1950
To M.S. Todd, Indian Agent Alert Bay, BC
Books arrived safely. School near completion. Understood desks were coming, have no lumber, please advise.
Don Goertzen, GMG, Bull Harbour

On Monday, September 25, the school bell rang for the first time in over a decade. In addition to the teacher's children Frank Junior, Donnie and Ethel, ten children came to school that first day. Six of them could understand English. Helen and Annie learned to write their names, Isabelle and Frances were encouraged to make a man out of clay and say their first English word, "man." Sisters Janet, Margaret and Helen were friendly and co-operative, listening closely. Janet and Margaret had learned to speak English from staying at Gloria's house, and Helen learned very quickly. James Walkus was in grade four and knew English from attending St. Michael's. The students called Ada "Teacher" or "Mrs. Frank." They sat on benches, orange crates and apple boxes. They were short on books, and there was no chalk, pencil sharpener or erasers.

On September 27, "Eighteen school desks arrived in good condition," and the boys carried them up to the schoolhouse. Attendance improved as the families who were fall fishing began to return and send their children to school. Alfred and Lily sent their oldest daughter, Geraldine. Then came Johnny, Robert, Bill and Edward Junior. The school improved as well when Don installed an oil stove, and he and Claire—the music teacher—brought in an old pedal organ. Joe Johnny made a bookcase.

Not long after school started, Clyde, Nancy and Heather arrived in the *Sea Gypsy*. As always, they were thronged by their many friends in the village who were happy to see them again. Clyde had gone to school as planned and then bought the *Sea Gypsy*. He and Nancy provided a kind of mission service up and down the coast, supported by some fishing and logging in season, and by selling Christian books.

Just as they arrived, a sad message was delivered to the village. A few days previous, Geraldine had become ill and stopped coming to school; she had a lump in her side. Then sister Judy became ill as well. No one knew what to do about this new illness, and by the time Alfred and Lily made the long, rough trip to Alert Bay Hospital, the doctor told them they were too late. Judy would not make it through the night, and Geraldine's condition was hopeless.

Don and Claire's house immediately became the location of a prayer meeting for the lives of the two little girls. They prayed for the girls for two days before they received happy news: Judy was out of danger, and Geraldine would get better, but she must spend a month or more in the hospital. Later, when Harold and Rosalie developed the same illness as Geraldine, they, too, spent over a month in the hospital. The children had acute glomerulonephritis caused by strep, which would prove to be an ominous enemy in the village.

One day after school, the chief visited Ada and said, "More children coming. Maybe eight or nine. Maybe next month." Ada had already gained the reputation of a good teacher, and now parents wanted to send their children to board with family in Takush and go to school. But this kind of announcement must strike a bit of terror into a teacher's heart. There were no desks or books for nine more students! Ada brought the tables and apple box chairs back out and ordered more books.

Nov 23
To R.F. Davey, Regional Inspector of Indian Schools
for BC
Office of Indian Commissioner, Vancouver, BC
Needed 8 each. Before We Read. Think and Do.
Workbooks for We Look & See, We Work and Play,
We Come and Go, Dick & Jane, Our New Friends.
8 Jolly Numbers Primers. 8 Jolly Numbers Book 1,
1 of all Grade IV books, any extra colour books.
Mrs. Ada F. Johnson

Of the nine new students, only fourteen-year-old Simon, who was in the fourth grade, and eight-year-old Gladys Hunt had been to school before. Gladys had a younger sister, Barbara, and they lived with their grandparents Edward and Sally Walkus, their four uncles and one aunt in a tiny two-room floathouse. Their uncles David and Moses and Aunt Marian were also new students.

From the Harry and Mary Walkus family came Albert, Mabel and Willie. Mabel loved school at once and learned easily. Claire used the hectograph ribbon on her typewriter to type out needed materials, and the hectograph was busy every night for weeks while waiting for the new books.

Ada taught the students English, and the students taught their teacher Kwak'wala. They wanted to know how to write the familiar Kwak'wala names of their family, so Ada spelled the words on the blackboard just as they sounded.

Up'bump: Mommy
Oom'pah: Daddy
Pa'quan'um: brothers
Wyulth: Chief George
Wee'yu'lee'nika: Jane
Kloo'kwee: Edward

Ah'pah: Grandma Johnny
Oh'lee: Alfred
Ait'sum'ka: Gladys
We'je'ta'kat'l: Annie
Kin'an'um'ka: Irene

Helen's name, K'aspa, began with an odd little click in the throat and ended with "aspa." Ada could find no combination of letters that would make that sound.

Halluchee: Harry
Patchy: Robert
Goojee: Old Willi Walkus

Then the children shared the words they were saying every day, and Ada spelled them as best she could.

Dolla: day
Wa'dalla dolla: cold day
Yak'sum yu'qua: bad rain
Suqua: mud
Wa'dalla, wa'dalla: cold, cold (it is cold)
Kan'i'ees: I am cold
Wa'dalla yak'sum: cold, bad night

And everyone was happy. The chief was happy to see the school full again, the parents were happy to send their children to school without sending them away, and the children were excited about going to school. Ada was happily learning as much as the children; she was learning a new culture and living in a new climate of wa'dalla dollas and yak'sum yu'qua.

Ada and students

Chapter 17

Bootleggers!

Roy and Margaret Graver (pronounced Grover) were a middle-aged couple from England who somehow ended up living in Takush Harbour. They moved into Charlie Sanden's little brown floathouse, and they turned a second one into a little store. They sold a few staples, particularly the ingredients needed to make a good batch of brew, such as raisins, sugar and potatoes. Roy also bootlegged liquor to the residents of Takush, so the Gravers defied the amendment to the Indian Act of 1884 and made a tidy living for themselves.

The Indian Act was formed by the Canadian Government in 1876 to regulate land use, resources, status, education and more. The amendment to the Indian Act of 1884 stated that it was a felony for Indigenous people to purchase or consume alcohol or enter a licensed establishment, and a felony to provide alcohol to them. This was not the first time such a ruling had been made against distribution of alcohol. The early fur traders supplied alcohol to the trappers prior to negotiating the price of furs which, of course, caused unfair prices. To protect the trappers, Canada (under British Rule 1763 to 1867) sent instructions in 1775 to superintendents, deputy superintendents, commissaries, interpreters and missionaries: "No trader shall sell or otherwise supply the Indians with rum or other spirituous liquors." In 1951, just about the time the Gravers left Takush Harbour, another amendment was made to allow drinking in permitted establishments only. (Not until 1985 were Indigenous people legally allowed to buy alcohol and take it home.)

Of course there were many opinions on these rulings; some viewed the laws as a protection for the Indigenous people, and others demanded equal rights for all. But in 1950, Don saw alcohol as the root of all his friends' problems and was vigilant in his persuasion against it. When a batch of brew was ready, the village became unsafe. There was the time Charlie G.'s daughter Margaret got shot; there was the head wound caused by the wielding of a broken cup; the girl with the knife wound; the fighting and abuse. All these troubles had the common denominator of alcohol, so the enemy in Don's war against alcohol was the Gravers. Had he actually reported the Gravers for bootlegging, their penalty could have been up to six months in prison and a $300 fine. But as it turned out, a far bigger penalty was paid.

Margaret Graver was not happy to be living with her husband on a float in Takush Harbour. She was a talkative lady and spoke her mind about it. It also seemed apparent to all, by the bruises on her body, that her husband beat her. But the GMG families remained friendly to them both, despite their disapproval, inviting them to church and dinner and outings. Maybe they hoped to convert them and solve the bootlegging and wife abuse problems that way.

On a late November day in 1950, Roy McGill rowed through the Bull Run to the Graver store. As he approached the front of the house, he saw a movement at the window, so he knew the Gravers would be home. While tying up his boat, he heard screams from behind the building and ran to the back of the Gravers' house. There he saw Margaret Graver hanging onto a rope, half in, half out of the water, on a boom-stick.

"Help me! Help! Help!" Margaret cried and screamed and carried on.

Roy noticed that though she was half in the water, her upper half was dry. Still, she seemed very distressed.

"Help me! Roy tried to kill me! He threw me in! I've been in the water for hours! He's trying to kill me! Help!"

Roy helped her out, though she was a nimble lady and could have hefted herself out easily. Don, Frank and Clyde arrived from the village about this time and found Roy Graver sitting in his chair, unconscious. A cup sat on the table beside him. Roy took a sniff and thought it smelled like rat poison.

Margaret said, "He wanted to kill us both. He tried to kill me by throwing me in the chuck, then he came in here and took poison."

Roy remembered the movement at the window, looked at Roy Graver's unconscious body and Margaret's dry upper half and didn't buy her story. Don jumped in the *Wakini* and sped through the Bull Run to GMG to call the police. His radio log entry was hastily written and incomplete:

> *Please come at once. Attempted murder and suicide.*
> *Immediate medical attention required.*
> Don Goertzen, Takush Harbour, Smiths Inlet, BC

Sgt. N. Beaumoff responded from Ocean Falls, and this time no one had to wait two days for the double-ender putt-putt police boat! The silence of Takush Harbour was split by the sound of a descending plane, and a police plane taxied up to the Graver floats. Airplanes were still a rare thing, and the children burst out of the school to watch Mrs. Graver and her unconscious husband load onto the plane and roar into the sky. But Mr. Graver did not live to reach the hospital.

An inquest date was set for January 16. Margaret used the GMG radiophone to call Sgt. McBaine, to request permission to dispose of the floats and balance of her stock without an administrator, and on approval, she did so. The little brown house and the store were sold to Frank Johnson, and because Edward had twenty-five people living in his house more or less, depending on the time of year, Frank sold the store to Edward. (Later, when the teacherage was built, Alfred and Lily bought the little brown house from Frank and raised their family in it.) Margaret packed up and disposed of the rest of her belongings and was anxious to leave.

> January 5, 1951
> To Sgt. McBaine RCMP Ocean Falls, BC
> *Everything sold. Am out of fuel and food. How soon can
> you come for me? Am at GMG Camp.*
> Margaret Grover

But the RCMP wanted to ensure Mrs. Graver made it to the inquest.

> To Margaret Grover, GMG Logging, Margaret Bay
> *Can you remain Margaret Bay until Jan 16? Will make
> arrangements for transportation for you.*
> Constable Davidson

Gloria took Margaret in, and she lived in the McGill home until the inquest date, though soon enough she was alone because the McGills went away for Christmas.

"She was in good spirits and glad to be leaving," remembers Lance. "One day we went for a walk on the tidal flats. Mrs. Graver grabbed a hatchet from the rowboat and began hacking clams out of the sand, eating them raw with great relish, juices dripping down her chin, and we watched in awe."

Margaret, Roy and Don were all required to attend the inquest. Margaret told her story, and Don had the opportunity to reveal Margaret's role in bootlegging if he had wanted to do so. Roy, as the first witness on the scene, told his story just as he saw it. When he was cross-examined, Roy felt they doubted his testimony, essentially calling him a liar, so he refused to answer any more questions.

"Well, believe what you want, that's just what I seen," he said, and he would say no more.

If either of the Roys had talked, the outcome may have been different, but the court ruled Margaret Graver not guilty. She moved to Ottawa, where she had a friend, Mary. But in Smith Inlet she was always afterwards referred to as "The woman who got away with murder."

CHAPTER 18

A BLENDED CHRISTMAS

By mid-December, everyone at GMG had gone to visit family for Christmas except Louis and Hazel; it was their winter to take care of camp. With Don and Claire also gone, Louis and Hazel took the *Westpoint* to Takush every Saturday morning to help Frank and Ada with church services. And they helped Ada create the first Christmas program.

It was a simple program of stories, poems and carols. No one seemed to know the carols, but Harry and Edward volunteered to sing a song in Kwak'wala, and the chief told a story of a time when he was a young man and an Indian Agent had visited Takush. The Christmas program must have been a very unusual experience for all, but the chief thanked the Johnsons for coming to the village.

"You make us happy," he said.

Then came the fun for the children. There was a Christmas tree with gifts! Frank was Santa Claus, and Janet and Margaret handed out gifts to the waiting children. Ada and Hazel were delighted to receive beautifully carved silver pins—an eagle with outspread wings—crafted by Charlie G.

The evening after Christmas, Robert invited the Johnson family to a party at his house, starting now! Donnie and Ethel weren't feeling well, but Frank, Ada and Frank Junior attended their first Takush Christmas party. Ada described the events of the evening in her unpublished manuscript "Green Point," and I have condensed them here:

> The big front room in Charlie G.'s house was full of tables, and a feast was in progress. Frank Junior was taken to Robert's table where the boys aged fourteen to eighteen sat. Frank and Ada were taken to the chief's table, and bowls of delicious potato soup were placed before them.
>
> "Two men walked up the mountain," Chief George told them. "Another man followed them, but they did not know it. They saw a porcupine up in a tree. The tree was on the edge of a ravine. They wanted the porcupine so they cut the tree down."
>
> At another table, Happy Boone turned to look at Chief George. Frank noticed that he was laughing.
>
> "The other man saw what they were doing," the chief continued. "He climbed down into the ravine. When they cut the tree, it fell into the ravine. The porcupine fell out and was killed. The other man talked like he was the porcupine. He said, 'Why do you do that to me?' The men were afraid. They thought the porcupine talked. They ran away down the mountain fast. The other man had the porcupine all himself."
>
> Frank looked at Happy. He was listening and laughing.
>
> "Was that man Happy?" Frank asked the chief.

The chief laughed too. "Yes, that was Happy," he said. He looked around the room. "Robert is giving this feast," he said. "It is for his baby sister. Her name is Julia. I will tell them."

The baby was to receive both an English and a Gwa'sala name, Chief George said to Frank and Ada. He rose and spoke in the Kwak'wala language for a time and then sat down. When the applause had died down, he rose again. This time he made no explanation. Frank and Ada listened closely for any word that they might know. They heard their own names and often the word "ake" (good). Then the chief mentioned Harry and sat down.

"He was talking about you," Harry said directly to Frank and Ada. "He said it was good that you have come here. Whatever happens in the village, you are a part of it. You are not different from us. We are glad you are here."

Frank stood up to answer. He thanked the chief.

"We are glad to be here. It is where we want to be. We want to be good friends to all of you. And I really am not much different; I was born and grew up on the coast of BC. You know where Bella Coola is? Bella Coola was my home."

Everyone clapped. Janet and Margaret moved among the tables with plates of cake topped with dainty pink, green and yellow icing. Chief George passed out coins—Robert's gifts to his guests.

At a table over in one corner, old Charlie George rose and made a speech in Kwak'wala. Then Happy did the same. Alfred passed around a box of apples.

Lily followed with a large kettle of oranges and some brown paper bags.

"You can take your apples and oranges home in the bags," she explained to Ada, who was happy to do so.

At other tables, apples, oranges, cake and even the bread that was left went into the paper sacks. It was the custom. Then the tables were put away, the floor was swept, and the fun began. Harry and Robert sat down on the floor, knees drawn up, arms clasped around them. A stick about two feet long was placed under the knees and in the bend of the elbows. Each man's wrists were tied together, and a short stick was placed in his hands. The game was to try to tip each other over. When a man was tipped over and could not get up, the game ended.

Back and forth they went, and round and round, bumping with their shoulders, pushing and prying with their sticks. Robert went down. He managed to roll onto his back and rocked himself into a sitting position once more. Harry went down but was soon up again. The game lasted for some time. Then Robert failed to get back into position to play. Their wrists were untied, and they rose to their feet. Harry raised his stick overhead.

"Champeen," he called.

Everyone laughed.

Benches had been arranged along the sides of the room so that the people were roughly divided into two groups. Another game began. The chief's youngest sons Harry and Louis were the leaders. First came a rhythmical chant that seemed to have no words. Harry's arms were swinging up and down, back and forth, round and round keeping time with the music. The chief was beating time on the floor with his cane. His wife, Lucy, was beating the bench beside her with a stick. Everyone around the room was keeping time, mostly with sticks. Even the tiny tots beat on the floor or a bench like the others.

Louis spoke, and all was still. Harry threw two sticks across the room; they were about three inches long and perhaps three quarters of an inch in diameter. One was plain; the other had a black band around it. The song and beating began again. Louis's arms began to swing until Harry called out to stop. A small pile of kindling sticks had been placed beside each leader.

The leader passed his short sticks out to someone on his side to hide them. The other leader would stop the singing and time beating while he tried to guess where the plain stick was. If he guessed wrong, he tossed a kindling stick to his rival. If he guessed right, it was his turn to hide the short sticks. Frank and Ada were on Louis's side. Frank played very well, but Ada got caught every time.

"Too bad," Harry said to her when the game was over. "No stick for you."

Joe and Jane put on their coats, lit their lantern and went out. The chief looked at Frank. "You can go home now, if you want to," he said.

So Frank, Ada and Frank Junior made their way down the hill by the light of a flashlight and rowed through the Wa'dalla yak'sum to their tiny house on the floats with the glow of Christmas in their hearts.

CHAPTER 19

LOUIS AND HAZEL GO TRAPPING

L ouis and Hazel's Christmas began quietly. They called their parents on Christmas Day, Hazel worked on her writing course and Louis on his ham radio course. Towards the end of the week, they went to the village to talk about church duties and found Ethel and Frank covered in measles. Ada said nearly everyone was down with German measles—a good thing for potentially pregnant women to stay away from! So Louis took Hazel on an adventure up GMG's newly purchased trap-line.

They bought the trap-line from the estate of the unfortunate Charles Sanden, who died of a broken heart. The arrangements were made over the radiophone:

> Sept 26, 1950
> To A. McGill
> *Your bid $200. Sanden trap-line accepted arrange transfer line to your name will be made on receipt of money referred in your wire 17 Sept. Please advise by wire when I may expect to receive the payment you mailed to cover.*
> Received from G.E. Forbes, Official Administrator
> Charles Sanden Estate, Prince Rupert, BC

"We didn't plan on trapping, but it was for sale," Louis says when he tells the story. "It was interesting country up at the head of Smith Inlet, way back in the Nekite River. It was really quite a wilderness because you would never see another human being there.

"It was an old trap-line, and there were cabins there, all up the river, that Charlie had built. They were very primitive, mind you, with mice running over your face at night, but it was all part of the adventure. There was one cabin pretty near, down at tide level, and it was kind of our main cabin because it was the more comfortable one.

"It rained a lot that winter, and there were a lot of slides. At night you could hear the rocks and trees crashing down the mountainside. But we were fairly snug. Hazel was taking a course in writing, and I was taking a course in ham radio operation, so we spent a little time there in this cabin.

"But one night it rained so much, and the tide was coming in, and the river kept coming up and up and up. We were hoping it would go down, but the tide had a few hours to go still before it was high and we knew it was going to come higher. So we thought maybe before the water gets too high, we should get out of there. So we put all our good things in True Milk cans. If you remember those cans, you can seal them. Then we put them up high on shelves—our blankets and sleeping bags and everything. By that time the firewood was floating around and the water was already in the stove.

"We jumped into the rowboat and went off for higher ground. That's where we spent the night, outside under a cedar tree. We did get a fire going. I slept not too badly, but I think Hazel was busy putting wood on the fire all night. She heard wolves howling and she didn't like that. She thought we were too much in the open for having wolves around, so she kept putting wood on the fire to deter the wolves a bit. I wasn't too concerned about the wolves."

Louis smiles.

"Next morning we went back to the cabin. The water had gone down, and we cleaned it up and made a fire. The water had just come up as far as the bunks where we would have been sleeping, so we actually could have slept there that night. But we didn't trust it.

"Another night, we were in the same cabin, and there was a bear in the area. There were a lot of bears in the area, of course, because the salmon go up the river and the whole place reeked of bear. But this bear, he was prowling around the cabin that night and we had our boat, a gill netter, a camp boat, that was up on kind of a dry dock so that when the tide was up, we could go out.

"But he was banging around where that boat was, and I didn't like it. And I really didn't want to meet up with him, so I just took, well, [chuckle] we had a big carbine, I think it was a 44-40, but it had a real big shell, anyway. So I went out the door and looked and I just took a shot with this big thing, and there was a flash. It made a big fire in the dark and a big crash and it rumbled through the hills with a big roar and we never heard any more sounds after that. I went to sleep and had a good sleep that night."

Hazel's version of the story spent more time on the mice running across her face, the huge bears at the doorstep, and the frightening howls of the hundreds of wolves that were surely lurking in the shadows just outside the light of the fire, while Louis slept right through it.

But cozied in the little cabin Charlie Sanden built in the Nekite wilderness, Hazel was inspired to write several magazine articles, as she attempted to describe something that many people will never see. She told Louis that she would like to share the wilderness with people for a living, instead of logging it.

"People would pay big money to see this," she said.

The trap-line did not make GMG wealthy. In fact, they seemed not to have the heart for it. But later, the line would provide employment for several of the Takush inhabitants, including Don.

Chapter 20

A Hymn for Simon

While Louie and Hazel were on their trap-line adventure, a life-changing event happened at the village. Edward's fourteen-year-old son Simon became very ill. Whatever it was, Simon was much more ill than the others had been with the measles, so Ada advised Edward to take him to the hospital right away.

Ada was a schoolteacher, not a nurse, but she had a first aid kit, and whenever there was an accident or somebody was sick, she was summoned. She got called for knife and gunshot wounds, burns, blood poisoning, problematic births and sick babies, pneumonia, measles and many things she didn't recognize; all she could do was urge them to go to the hospital.

"Gale warnings out! Fifty mile an hour!" Edward said.

He sent his son Jimmie and his friend Abel Dick to Boswell Camp to send a wire for an airplane to come. But no airplane could come in the gale, and Simon grew steadily worse. This was a real problem in Smith Inlet; if the weather was bad, boats couldn't make the trip to the hospital and planes couldn't fly in. Children died waiting for a storm to subside. Heartbreaking. Even building a new village could never change this.

At midnight, Abel and Jimmie knocked on Frank and Ada's door.

"We think there is no hope for Simon," they said. "We will fire a gun when he passes away. We just came to tell you."

"But there is hope!" said Ada. "There is hope as long as he is alive! Keep trying to get an airplane! Try that tug out in the harbour—it should have a radiophone to send a wire."

Morning came, and no plane. But Simon was still alive.

"Don't give up, Edward," Ada urged. "Keep praying. We are praying."

Edward desperately wanted the Christian God to be what Mr. Frank and Mr. Don said He was—powerful, loving and able to save—and he urgently prayed for the life of his boy. Edward promised to follow Him and give up anything in his life that would prevent it, if only God would save his son.

Another day and night passed, and Simon remained very ill. The storm died down, but the waves on the sound remained enormous. Edward prepared to make the journey anyway, hoping Simon could survive it. But first a boat was sent to Boswell to call one last time for an airplane. At that moment, a police plane flying overhead picked up the call. They dropped into the harbour, picked up Simon and had him in the Ocean Falls Hospital in less than an hour, saving Simon the eleven-hour trip in Edward's boat and probably his life. A message was sent to GMG:

> Jan 8, 1951
> From *Thomas Crosby IV* to Ed Walkus
> *Simon has pneumonia. Doing well.*
> James Walkus [Edward's son Jimmie]

That night, Janet came to the Johnsons' house to borrow all the hymn-books they could find. Boats began to dock at Edward's float. The Johnson family heard the melodies of familiar hymns floating across the water from Edward's house—the sounds of thanksgiving. From then on, prayer meetings in the Kwak'wala language became common at Edward's house. Edward began to translate hymns and compose his own hymns in Kwak'wala. Edward's hymns are now printed in a hymn-book and sung to this day.

CHAPTER 21

MOVE TO MOSES

Jan 15, 1951
To GMG from Langley Prairie
Advise mill coming on this boat. Going inquest first.
Don

When Don, Claire, Harold and Rosalie finally returned on the *Cardena* after attending the Graver inquest, everyone was delighted to have them back. Perhaps Frank and Ada most of all. Don brought a movie projector and screen with him and arranged to receive films from the National Film Board. Movie nights became a new and very popular social event. And Saturday night games at the schoolhouse were always more fun with Don and Claire. Once again, the older youth gathered at the Goertzen home in the evenings to play guitars and sing. But best of all, Don bought a mill, and it arrived just before he did. The mill signified the beginning of new homes and a new future for the village.

But they were interrupted by illness. The year began with German measles, then influenza and pneumonia hit. In February, Harold and little Rosalie became very ill, and Don and Claire took them to Bella Bella Hospital where they had to remain for over a month. Don and Claire returned to Takush without them.

"One of the nurses gave me a spanking because I kept getting out of bed to find Harold, who was in another room," Rosalie remembers. "They finally stuck Harold and I together—probably so they could have some peace."

Then Ada became ill. For almost three weeks she lay ill, and the children were without a teacher. Summer could not come soon enough.

At GMG, Petersen had secured timber sale X-51758 for them, and by the beginning of May they had ten sections ready for towing. Then Petersen sent them a very unexpected message.

> May 23
> To GMG Logging
> *Would like you to look at timber in Moses Inlet available for immediate operation. Contact for letter of explanation.*
> E. Petersen

Moses Inlet, off Rivers Inlet, was a significant location change for GMG, but they acted fast. On May 29, GMG told Petersen they had cruised the Moses Inlet timber. June 8, their logs and A-frame were ready for towing, camp floats ready June 10. And on June 10, Petersen sent a telegram asking, "Would it be possible to tow camp Millbrook Cove by own boat? *Otteren* will assist you from there. Please advise."

Millbrook is the last little cove before going around the corner to Rivers Inlet. What a ride they were about to have. For the first time, GMG Logging camp would be moving out into the open water of the Queen Charlotte Sound. Remember James Hanna, then Captain Vancouver's description of this water? Remember the lighthouse washing off the rocks and the floundering boats?

Everything was secured more tightly and more carefully than usual. The crosswalks were removed and the floats separated by several feet of cable to prevent damage in the swells. The ladies prepared for movement. Before the men unhooked the water pipes, they filled bathtubs and containers with water, but not full enough to slosh out. The little boats were pulled well up onto the floats and secured. Things were brought inside and put away, children were given safety lectures, and everyone hoped for calm. The men removed the last of the boom-sticks and cables from shore Sunday morning and attached the standing boom to the last float.

> June 10
> To E. Petersen, Logging Office, Ocean Falls, BC
> *Expect to be at Millbrook with floats sometime tonight.*
> *Will wait there for boat.*
> GMG Logging

When the kids woke up in the morning, their beds were rocking, and they did their correspondence lessons at the table while looking out the windows to Japan. They arrived safely. Their new home in Moses Inlet was on a mudflat, and the houses went dry at low tide—a whole new world to explore.

The men ordered a new McCullock power saw with oiler and a four-foot blade, and parts for their Burnett power saw model B6. And in July, more power saw parts were ordered—they were falling the new claim. The men didn't go to the Big Smoke that summer. In August, they ordered parts for the donkey, strawline, and blocks, all sent to Dawson's Landing in Rivers Inlet, where they picked up their supplies on boat day.

"Moses Inlet was a tough show," Lance remembers.

Apparently, it was tough enough to discourage the loggers. Logging was not turning out to be easy money at all, and the GMG families were each considering some big changes. Louis and Hazel were due to have a baby in December, and they talked about life in Kelowna near Hazel's family, living on the land and raising their family in the sunny Okanagan Valley. Hazel left for

Kelowna in the fall to wait for the baby, and Louis left just before Christmas to join her. They shipped some of their belongings to Kelowna and settled in on a little place with some fruit trees. Louis would need to come back to GMG to do some clean-up, but then he planned to work with his father-in-law at his mill.

Alvin and Gloria made plans to attach their float to Don and Claire's and join Don in rebuilding the village. Roy was still ordering building supplies for camp. Perhaps he thought he could stay and make a living by fishing the *Westpoint* and doing some hand-logging.

In December, E. Petersen asked for a production report, and GMG's reply was, "One million feet piled in creek-bed." There would be a month or so of work left to get it boomed, ready for towing and then cleaned up. After Christmas would be soon enough, but no one knew what was going to happen in a cold January.

CHAPTER 22

THE LAST T'SEKA

When Don and Claire went to Vancouver in the summer of 1951, they bought a projector and filmstrips. Now every Friday evening a new routine was added: visual Bible lessons. Don also bought a new guitar. He had lost part of a finger on his left hand when he was falling with Alvin; they were felling a tree with a crosscut saw and his finger got in the way as he was clearing brush away from the saw. The first thing he said when he saw his missing finger was "How am I going to play the guitar?" But he restrung the guitar so he could finger it with his right hand. Don taught the young men to play guitar, and they formed a group called the Takush Ramblers—sometimes Claire accompanied them on her accordion.

Several of the men had been cutting lumber on the mill in preparation for building, and Frank and Don started to build an addition onto the too-small schoolhouse. The government sent a barge load of building materials to rebuild the village. A ramp dropped from the barge to the beach in Ethel Cove, and all able bodies joined to unload and stack the pallets of shingles, siding, plywood and lumber. If the Gwa'sala and Don could obtain permission, they wanted to rebuild the village at Ethel Cove.

Then measles spread through Takush, and the work went slowly. There was a funeral that fall, for Lily and Alfred's new baby,

Arlene. Baby Judy was in Nanaimo hospital with TB, and now baby Arlene was gone. Don wept as he performed the funeral service, but it was just the beginning of a winter of many sorrows.

In late November, George Walkus's sister was lost at sea along with her husband and young son. A large search party of men and older boys spent two weeks searching the waters, but they only found fragments of the missing boat. Finally they returned, and the next morning, two men rowed over to the little camp of floats.

By this time, the Johnson and Goertzen floats were secured together in a small cove near the village. Frank had cut a trail to the school so Ada could walk to school every day instead of rowing the old cannery skiff the chief had given them. To get from the floats to shore, Frank built a "ferry" that moved from the rear of the Goertzen float to the beach. He split a three-foot-diameter, twelve-foot-long red cedar log in half lengthwise and laid the halves side by side, flat side up, then nailed a plank across each end.

This simple design, with the bulk of the rounded log in the water, was very stable and impossible to tip over. He fastened the end of a rope to one end of the raft and ran the rope through a clothesline pulley at the top of a pole on Don's float. He then pulled it back through a ring attached to the raft by a piece of rope about four feet long, on through another clothesline pulley fastened to a tree on the beach, and back to the other end of the raft. Now anybody on either side, or on the raft, could pull the ferry back and forth.

But the villagers still chose to row over, as they did on this morning. The delegates delivered a message from the chief: "Chief George sent us to ask you to be our guests of honour at the death dance on Thursday night. It will begin at seven o'clock. Bring your families."

The kids were very excited about this invitation, but the adults were not. They knew it was a great honour to be invited by the chief and elders to this spiritual occasion, but it was the spiritual nature of the event that concerned them. Refusing such an honour would be the deepest of insults, but attending an event designed to invoke unknown spirits might equate to condoning those spirits.

A year or two before, Alvin, Gloria, Don and Claire were in camp for the winter and had been invited to one of the ceremonial winter dances. (These are the t'seka, as opposed to the Tta'sala. The t'seka are intended for interaction with the supernatural spirit beings who live in the woods nearby during the winter, whereas the Tta'sala are often called chief's dance or peace dance. But they didn't know all this.) People tend not to believe things until they see them, and that's how it was with these invited guests. They had heard of the spirits of the Kwakwaka'wakw peoples and how they are evoked through dances with masks, costumes, rattles, whistles and other supernaturally significant items (Tlug'we). Boas recorded eyewitness accounts, too, at the beginning of the century. But that was then, and this was now. And maybe it was all just coincidence, or fabrication, or a product of imagination. So they went, and took Lance and Lloyd, Harold and little Rosalie with them.

They sat with several of the young men. The drummers beat a rhythm on drums and logs. There was singing—a kind of wailing chant—Granny Johnny, Jeannie Walkus, all the elders, Edward's voice rising above the others. They chanted and cried and shook rattles; they seemed to be pleading, their eyes closed, tears coming down their faces. They appeared to be in a trance.

The guests didn't know the dance they were observing, but they saw some of the men take Louis Walkus, the chief's son.

"They removed his clothing and put a kind of band on him—it was red, made of some kind of cloth, like a big rope," Lance remembers. "They crossed it over on his body in a sort of figure eight, and he danced wearing it."

Some witnesses say Louis walked on burning coals without burning his feet while in this trance, and other witnesses don't remember it. But if he did or if he didn't, the guests felt very uneasy with the spirit presence and the trance-like state of their hosts. They stayed the whole evening, not wanting to offend their friends, but vowed they would never go to another ceremonial dance.

But now they had been invited to another. Don and Frank stopped working and spent the remainder of the day and all of the next studying the Bible and praying for God's wisdom.

When Thursday arrived, Ada taught school as usual, though the preparations in the village were unsettling. As she completed her duties after school, she heard the drums beating, and a wailing, mournful song. The children raced up and down the village and in and out of the schoolhouse. The villagers and the guests from other villages had white down feathers in their hair and streaks of red paint on their faces. On the floats, the men were praying, but they still didn't know what to do.

They tried to eat a little supper, and then they got dressed to go. The families met outside, ready to take the raft to the beach, drums and mournful wailing in their ears, worry in their hearts. Frank and Don stepped inside Don's house for one last prayer. It's going to be all right, they told their families. God will work things out to His glory.

Frank Junior usually ferried the families across one family at a time, so he stepped onto the raft first and picked up the rope. Donnie stood beside him with the flashlight. Ethel and Ada stood on one side, then Frank hesitated. It was his rule that only one family should go across at a time, but tonight he felt certain they should all go at once.

"Are you sure?" questioned Don.

Frank Junior expected his dad to change his mind, as he was usually very strict about this rule, but Frank insisted.

"Yes. We're late, so why bother with two trips? It will be fine."

So Claire and Rosalie boarded the raft and stood next to Ada and Ethel. Don stepped on with Harold under his arm, and then Frank got on. Frank Junior noted that it didn't seem nearly as loaded as he anticipated, and he began to pull the families across. When the raft had moved only a few feet, strange things began to happen. Ada remembers water surging over her feet, and Frank Junior tried to return the raft to the floats but he fumbled the ropes. The raft listed sharply to the right. Frank jumped off, hoping somehow to save the others by lightening the load. Then the raft slowly rose up on its side, hesitated, and came down bottom side up. They said it felt like a hand under the big cedar log lifted the raft and gently dumped them into the water.

A lot of screaming and crying ensued. There had been ice on the water just that morning! Frank pulled himself out onto the float and began pulling the children out. The moms, heavy with soggy woollen coats, lifted their children up, calling, "Take Rosalie!" "Take Ethel!" Don pulled his family up onto the upside-down ferry, and soon everyone was out and dripping into their houses. The children were put to bed, and the adults thanked God for their cold, wet, unexpected miracle.

Then the delegates showed up.

"The chief has sent us. Why have you not come? We heard children crying. Is something wrong? The chief won't start until you come, and it is growing late."

Don took the delegates and showed them the upside-down ferry, the rounded logs encrusted with barnacles and mussels, and told them the entire story—the honour they felt at being included, the difference between God's spirit and the spirits invoked at the ceremonies, the prayers they had sent to their God and His answer.

The dance went on—drumming, stamping of feet, mournful wailing mingling with the howling of wolves—until morning. The next day, Chief George came to visit. His delegates had told him the story. The chief looked at the raft; he knew it could not turn upside down on its own.

"We believe what you told us," he said. "We believe your great Creator God kept you from coming to the dance. There will be no more dances to the spirits in this village ever again. This will be a Christian village. We are going to donate all our masks that we use for our dances to the museum in Victoria."

It was a Friday, and the men gathered all the ceremonial masks that very afternoon. The chief invited Don to take pictures of them before they were sent away. The men posed for Don's camera, wearing the masks, then packed them into crates to be sent to Victoria. That night was Friday night Bible study with filmstrips, as usual. But different.

Note: Though this story has been passed down through "oral history," for accuracy of detail, I have relied heavily, with permission, on the first-hand accounts of Ada Johnson and Frank Johnson Junior, from Ada's unpublished manuscript, "Green Point," and Frank Arthur Johnson's published book *Jesus Is There All The Time: A Canadian Story of Life and Ministry*. See the U'mista Cultural Society website for information on Kwakwaka'wakw spirits and dances and the significance of the masks.

Posing in masks for Don's camera

CHAPTER 23

THE HOLIDAY OF THE RED HAT

I n December, the students performed in their first Christmas program. It was a well-performed and well-attended event, with costumes, acting and singing. It had been a struggle to convince the children to sing, and Claire, Ada and the parents felt very proud of them. Louis Walkus played Santa Claus that year, passing out candies and toys. Then the *Westpoint* and the *Sea Gypsy* arrived, with Alvin, Gloria, Clyde, Nancy and their children, so the students repeated the entire program for them the following night.

The chief said, "Please, leave the school like this. We want to use it."

So the bedspread curtains remained hanging across the front of the school.

Later that week, everyone was invited to a Gwa'sala-sponsored event in the school, similar to the year before. It began with a small skit, described by Ada:

> "You showed us a doctor," Harry said. "Now we will show you a doctor."
>
> He drew back the curtains. Near the back of the stage crouched the chief. Flat on the floor before

him lay Abel Dick. At one side stood Edward with a drum, which he began to beat. The chief's voice rose in a chant. He swung his hands about, rhythmically keeping time. Then he began to feel his patient. He asked for water and was handed a wash pan. He placed his hand in the water and then put it into his own mouth. He felt over his patient for some time, then placed his mouth close to him and appeared to be trying to blow out the sickness. Again, he felt over the man. Then he raised his hands and held them together as if he had something in them and blew through them. This was supposed to drive the sickness away.

Then they played similar games as the year before, and did some wrestling, lying on their backs and wrestling with their legs in the air. This was followed by a tug of war. Ada described the activities:

In this game, two men sat facing each other, their feet braced against each other, and both men clasping a strong stick. Behind each man sat several others each holding tightly to the man before him. At a signal, all began to pull. When it looked like Louie's side would lose, Harry seized his brother's hair with one hand and his arm with the other and pulled too. The chief joined Robert's side. James leaped to his feet and rushed to Louie's assistance. Old, white-haired Lucy, the chief's wife, rose slowly, wrapped her arms around her husband and pulled. The two leaders parted and fell back. The stick was in Robert's hands. Old Lucy turned her wrinkled, smiling face to the clapping audience and waved her hand.

Dances followed. One showed a man hunting wild goats. Another was a wild man. The last one was a legendary bird that was supposed to have lived in the mountains long ago. One time, a man who was out hunting saw it. The bird was very angry because a man had seen it, and it chased him. The man ran away down the mountain very fast. The bird followed. It ran so fast that it ran into a large tree, and its long bill went right through the tree. Edward, wearing a large bird-like mask, did this bird dance. The bill, which was about three feet long, was made in two parts so it could open and close. At the end of the dance he chattered the beak at the audience.

Several of the children present remember being somewhat terrified of that chattering beak. Afterwards there was a feast, with many speeches, hosted by Joe and Jane Johnny. In the speeches they talked about their hopes for a new village.

And then there was a day of drunkenness. There had already been a "big drink" with its usual problems on the day of the second school program; the children had not wanted to go home after the program. Don felt discouraged but didn't say anything. But now when he went over to the village and found so many drunk again, he was heartsick. Ada recorded what Don told them:

"'It looks like you don't want me to help you after all,' he said sadly. 'If that's the way you feel, I will go away again.'

"Sadly, he turned homeward. Would they let him go? He feared that they would, and his heart was heavy. He loved the people and longed to lead them to a better way."

The next day everyone felt great remorse. They didn't want to hurt Don, and they didn't want him to leave. On New Year's Day, the men gathered in the chief's house and voted to banish liquor from their village. If anyone thought he had to drink he must go away to do it. They were happy with their decision and went to tell Don. They joined Bill, who was already at Don's house. Sometimes when Bill was drinking, he came to the Goertzen home and tried to quarrel with Don, but instead of quarrelling he always found kindness and patience. Now Bill took Don's hand and asked his forgiveness. Then he removed his new red hat, asking Don to hang it up in his house. Bill made a promise that as long as his hat hung there, he would never drink again. It was the happiest New Year Don could ever hope for.

CHAPTER 24

THE HARDEST HILL

Two days after the Happy New Year, Don fell sick. It seemed nothing to worry about at first, and Alvin and Gloria returned to Moses Inlet. Clyde remained to work on the *Sea Gypsy* and offered to take care of the Friday night filmstrips for Don.

Don had a terrible headache, and by Saturday afternoon he was unable to move his right arm and leg. When Frank woke on Saturday morning, he was sick with similar symptoms. On Sunday, Don seemed better but his mind was wandering. Frank's back and head ached terribly, and he had trouble with speech. Frank Junior became ill with the same symptoms. Fevers were high. By Monday morning, Claire was alarmed by Don's rapid decline and sent for an airplane.

"Why get it for me?" asked Don. "Frank is just as sick as I am. He should go to the hospital too."

Though Claire wanted to accompany her husband on the plane, it was not big enough for everyone. What should she do? When the plane came at noon, Frank's and Frank Junior's temperatures were going down, so Claire boarded the plane with Don, leaving Harold and Rosalie with Nancy.

Several men carried Don out. He had only been sick for three days but he looked so small and shrunken lying on the stretcher. The villagers reached into their pockets and gave Claire what they had. She might need it for the airplane or for herself, they said.

"When I get back," Don said, "I will put some logs in the water and pay you all back."

Every evening, Clyde, Nancy and Ada listened for a message on the radio. Monday evening, they learned that Don had meningitis. On Tuesday, the storm made it difficult to hear the radio, so they didn't hear the news that Don was doing poorly until Wednesday. Frank, lying in bed at home, was also worse. The storm continued.

On Thursday, Alvin, Gloria, Lance and Lloyd came from Rivers— they had heard Don was worse and were on their way to see him. Everyone wanted to go. The *Sea Gypsy* and every villager who had a boat that could make the trip, prepared to go. Friday was calmer, and George and Harry insisted they take Frank with them and make sure he was admitted to hospital.

Meanwhile in Alert Bay, the long hours would be short. Don's right side became paralyzed, and Claire never left his side. They talked and prayed together. When blood was needed to give Don a transfusion, the chief of the Alert Bay tribe and his wife came and gave their blood.

"Now you're a real Indian," said the chief.

When Don became incoherent, Claire praycd alone—surely it must be God's will for Don to live—his work had just begun. And she needed him; there was going to be another baby.

Life was beginning to fragment. Claire sent a message to the family.

It was January 10, and for a moment, Don's mind cleared. He smiled at Claire and squeezed her hand. That was all.

Claire, broken:

The doctor orders her to bed—she spends a day alone in a hospital bed, struggling, asking God the tough questions

Then people come—her Gwa'sala friends, her brother and sister, her children asking for their daddy, but she can't bear to tell them

Alvin prepares his best friend's body for the grave because everyone else is too afraid of the same death

Don's brothers, his mother and Elder George O'Brien come to offer comfort

Sabbath, and the *Sea Gypsy* is low in the water with mourners

On the Queen Charlotte Sound, a flotilla— *WestPoint, Sea Gypsy*, all the Gwa'sala boats—bear Don's body home

Everyone, broken:

Olive Point is covered in snow, cold wind and waves lashing the shores

Bent figures lead to a hole in the ground at the top of the hill

The chief, sad and alone on the snowy trail up from the beach

He holds out his hand, "Help me," he pleads

Ada, stronger than anyone knows, helps the chief up the hill

Frank Junior pulls up his sick dad, limping and ill with pain and sorrow and new responsibility

The truth is, it is the hardest hill any of us has ever climbed

It's a hill we all climb

And we still climb it

Asking "Why?"

CHAPTER 25

ETHEL

T akush felt very empty without Don. Harold and Rosalie played the resurrection game.

"Harold stood up on the old wooden desk and blew an imaginary trumpet," remembers Rosalie. "Then I would burst out from under the desk [grave] waving my arms [wings], and we both 'flew' out of the living room to the kitchen [heaven]."

But they didn't find their dad in the kitchen.

"My grandfather just sits home and cries," Gladys told Ethel.

Ethel tried to comfort her friend. "Tell him not to cry," she said, "we will get to see Mr. Don again someday."

A meeting was held at the village, and Alvin McGill was invited to take Don's place and live at Takush. Alvin accepted the invitation and the people felt hope.

Then on Friday night, Ethel became quickly and seriously ill. On Monday, Ada cancelled school to stay home and tend to her. Everyone knew if Ada cancelled school, it was serious. The elders called an airplane and brought money to pay for it. It didn't matter that they had so little money—they shared what they had. But the airplane couldn't come due to strong winds, and

Ethel grew weaker. Her neck and back were stiff, and she became unable to move her legs, then her arms. On Tuesday, the airplane finally arrived.

Ada dressed Ethel in warm clothes and the soft coat and hood she had made her for Christmas. She wrapped her in woollen blankets, laid her on the stretcher with pillows and kissed her cheek.

"Goodbye, girlie. We'll all be glad when you come back well and strong," she said.

Frank got on the plane with Ethel, and Ada made her way up the hill to open the school.

In the Alert Bay Hospital Ethel was put on oxygen—a blizzard prevented them from flying her to Vancouver to an iron lung. Frank stayed by her side while his own illness lingered. He recognised some of Ethel's symptoms as his own. Tired and heartsick, he limped in and out of the hospital, grateful for the friendship of Clyde and Nancy on the *Sea Gypsy*. But then Clyde got bilateral pneumonia caused by the same strep virus, and he too was hospitalized.

When Ethel's diagnosis of encephalomyelitis came to Ada, she looked it up in her medical book and was terrified. What terrified her the most were the words that told her this disease had the ability to alter character. She said she felt a heavy depression, a feeling that the powers of darkness were attacking the missionary families and trying to keep an ancient hold. Ada prayed into the night and went to school the next day feeling an assurance that they would be spared to carry on their work.

As she closed up the school for the day, Frank Junior came with a wire that had just arrived. "Ethel worse." Ada felt a clutch of dread and sorrow. She knew what the message meant. Everyone did.

Some friends on a clam buying boat called in a plane for Ada and paid for it; the plane would arrive in the morning. After the longest night, Ada and Donnie went to Claire's house to wait for the plane. Alvin and Gloria and their boys were already there. Soon the house was filled to overflowing with villagers singing hymns and praying that God would save the little girl they loved. Again, they dug into their pockets and gave Ada whatever money they had, insisting that Ada need not pay them back.

When the buzz of the plane was heard, everyone hovered around Ada. Gloria buttoned Ada's coat, tied her kerchief and then retied it. She and Claire would do their best to keep the school going while Ada was gone.

Ada arrived at her daughter's side only in time to hold her slender wrist and feel the pulse beats fade away. It was January 29, just thirteen days after Don had left. Elder A.W. Bauer and Ada's brother came to offer comfort.

A fierce storm followed, but it seemed fitting. They chartered the seine boat *Barclay Sound* and carried Ethel home through the storm. It was one of those storms that make you wonder how you can possibly survive. The green troughs opened and closed, the boat climbed the mountains and fell into the valleys. Water washed over it, unleashing the seine skiff and carrying it away; everything in the cabin came undone and crashed about them. Everyone was either throwing up or hanging onto their bunks except Frank, who drove through the storm, still ill, weak and unsteady on his feet.

When they carried Ethel up the hill, the storm had blown itself out. A sudden shower fell like tears, followed by a glimpse of sun, and then a rainbow—a perfect arch, one end resting on the raw graves. A quiet awe rested on the little group gathered by the graves. The words of a familiar hymn came to Claire: "Across the thickest darkness shines the rainbow of His love." She began to sing, her voice wavering:

After the storm the rainbow shineth
Promise writ in light above;
Even so across our sorrow
Shines the rainbow of His love.

Never was a hymn more meaningful or comforting to them; the rainbow and the hymn were a gift that gave them the courage to go back to Takush and carry on. But no one ever completely recovered from this terrible winter. It altered the future in more ways than can be told.

Then Alvin got sick.

Note: The accuracy of detail for the accounts of Don and Ethel is from the unpublished manuscript "Green Point" by Ada F. Johnson. We thank you, Ada.

CHAPTER 26

MOSES INLET TO FLY BASIN

After the saddest of Januarys, and after the Moses Inlet claim was cleaned up, Louis went back to Kelowna and Alvin went to Vancouver, sick, struggling with stomach cancer. Roy and Dorothy stayed to take care of camp.

Roy didn't like living in Moses Inlet, so he decided to take camp back where it came from. He hadn't been in camp for the tow to Moses Inlet the year before; in fact, Roy had never towed before, and all who knew him described him as "not a boat person." When GMG was towed to Rivers, the men had separated all the floats with yards of cable to prevent damage in the open swells, and the tug from Ocean Falls had pulled camp far out around the islands and rocks. But on a calm day in September 1952, Roy simply freed camp from the beach and hooked the entire string of five houses with boat sheds, A-frame float, fuel float, drag saw float, boom winch float and auger float together with the standing boom trailing behind to the *Westpoint* and towed. No small feat for either himself or for the thirty-four-foot *Westpoint*, with its 110 Chrysler gas engine. Dorothy and baby Murray were along for the ride, and Dorothy took photographs.

Remembering the story, Lance says, "When the locals travel in and out of the inlet, they keep inside all the rocks—close to the beach right on the breakers—the breakers nearly wash onto the deck."

And Roy did the same with camp following behind him in a long string, thirty-plus feet wide. He got a nice push from the tide going out of Rivers Inlet, but when he rounded the corner, he began having trouble going through the rocks. When he came to Tye Pass, a gap of a little over a hundred feet between Tye Island (spelled Tie on the new charts) and the mainland shore, he was nearly standing still.

But he was lucky that day because Jack Randle saw him leaving Rivers Inlet and heading for the rocks, so he came out and helped push camp through Tye Pass. Then Roy turned north to go through Shield Pass and headed straight across Smith Sound, up Browning Channel, into Ship Passage, Takush Harbour, and finally into Fly Basin.

In the spring, he wrote to Alvin in White Rock telling him to come back. Fishing was good, Roy said. Wood prices were up, and other loggers were starting to move into the area. If Alvin moved back, Roy promised to build a school. Gloria had just had baby Dennis, and Alvin was recovering from a surgery that removed most of his stomach and part of his intestine. When he could eat again, he started work for a construction company building the White Rock Customs and Immigrations building at the border crossing—but he always hated taking orders and working for another man's gain. He didn't feel strong enough to go logging yet but thought he could manage gill netting. He had a thirty-two-foot gill netter built, the *Tye Pass*, and the family arrived back in Smith Inlet in May of 1953 to prepare for the fishing season.

Just days after they returned, their house burnt down. The house had a history of doom. Alvin had bought it from Jack Randle nearly ten years earlier during the year between Gildersleeve Logging and GMG Logging, when Bill Jago operated the previous

Gildersleeve camp in Security Bay. Jack Randle had his house tied up to the camp and was working for Jago. One morning, the Union boat was delivering freight to the camp. It was preparing to cast off just as the men were loading into the *Jonah* to go to work. From the *Jonah*, Jack saw his wife Lois and son Emmett walk up the plank onto the Union steamship.

"Goodbye," Lois called. "I'm leaving!"

She'd had enough of "living in the sticks"!

"Goodbye," said Jack, waving from the crewboat.

He was so shocked he could think of nothing else to do. He worked all day and came home to an empty house. He decided he couldn't live without his wife, so he took a boom-chain, haywired it around his neck to prevent himself from changing his mind and walked off the back of his float. He landed on his feet on the bottom. He hadn't thought to check the tide—it was out—and he had only a few inches of water over his head. He took a couple of steps and his head was out of water, so he walked out.

The next morning, the men saw that Jack's face and neck were covered in black and blue bruises.

"What in the world happened to you?" they wanted to know.

"No woman's worth dying for," said Jack.

Soon after, he sold his house to Alvin and Gloria, who were only too glad to move out of their one-room home and into a bigger one, and Jack left camp—with the new nickname of "Jonah."

Now Alvin and Gloria and the boys were back in this house, in Fly Basin, gathered around the table for dinner. Alvin and Gloria sat at opposite ends of the table, Dennis was in his high chair, and Lance and Lloyd sat facing the window looking towards the water.

"Look at all that smoke," said Lance, looking out the window.

To his surprise, his dad didn't run outside to see the smoke, he ran to the stairs that went up to the attic. When the men turned the generator on earlier, there had been an annoying short, so they fixed the fuse by putting a penny in it. Now the whole ceiling was on fire.

"Out, out—everyone out!" Alvin yelled, chasing everyone outside.

Roy was "sick as a dog" with the mumps that Lance and Lloyd had brought him from White Rock, but he came out and called to Gloria to untie the boat and set it free. He tried to help Alvin cut the house loose, though he was very weak. Sparks landed and smouldered on Hazel and Louie's house, where the dynamite was being stored, and Roy and Gloria dipped bucket after bucket to douse the embers.

Gloria and the boys watched their house in flames floating in front of them. Alvin was trying to rescue a few things. I can imagine Gloria shrieking, "Oh Alvin! Save my piano, oh my beautiful piano," then shrieking for him not to. "Alvin, don't go in there!" Alvin did go in. He "rescued" his clothes, but not Gloria's, and not the photo albums. The canary did not survive either. The piano did survive and that made the disaster seem slightly less disastrous.

But now they had to live in a one-room shed. The boys slept in a closet with a curtain over the entrance. When they sat up on the bed, their knees hung outside the curtain. Every day somebody thought of something they needed or remembered something they would never have again from their house. Like those precious quarts of canned huckleberries.

Claire also returned to Smith Inlet in May. With a new husband, Arthur Crooks. She met him in Parksville while waiting at her parents' house for baby Donnie to be born. Arthur, recently from England, was attracted to the Gildersleeve home when he heard them singing. He introduced himself to Bill and Alice, and they invited him to sing and study the Bible with them. Then Claire came home, sad and pregnant, with Harold and Rosalie. Claire felt it was too soon, but Arthur told her he loved her and he would care for her children. After Donald was born, they married and moved back to Takush.

Arthur and Alfred Johnny built a boatshed together, and Arthur finished building the boat Don had started to build. Arthur fished and fell trees, and Claire kept very busy with Harold, Rosalie, Donnie and Aleta. Soon they moved their float to the GMG camp, and Arthur became a faller for GMG. When I ask Dad later why Arthur didn't stay at the village and take over for Uncle Don, he says vaguely, "We-e-ll, Arthur wasn't really suited for it."

Louis returned not long after, when his father-in-law's mill burned down. He bought a gill netter and let Hazel name it the *Rolamar*, after Roland and Marcia. Hazel followed in the spring, arriving on the Union steamship with Marcia on a harness and pregnant with Roland. In July, Hazel went to Bella Bella, which was the popular place to have babies at the time; Dr. Darby could do emergency C-sections if he had to, anesthesia and all. Roland was born in Bella Bella on July 31, 1954. He made an unforgettable entrance to camp—in a RC-3 Seabee, an all-metal amphibious sports aircraft.

"Hazel flew home in a Seabee," Lance remembers. "Everybody thought it was a pretty cool airplane. I remember Aunt Hazel handing a little bundle out the door to Uncle Louie—it was Roland."

Just after all the families had returned to Smith Inlet, an oil tanker beached itself on the north end of Calvert Island in a small bay, spilling oil everywhere. Alvin, Louis, Roy, Lance and Lloyd went up to see what they could salvage. The tanker was so high and dry the engines hadn't been flooded with seawater. Roy welded up an A-frame affair so they could drill right through the deck and pull out the engines; they salvaged one of them, a Cummins, in good condition. It was too big for their own use, but they would hold onto it and trade it later for a smaller Cummins diesel for a new camp boat, the *Surf Isle*.

For the next three, nearly four, years GMG stayed in the Fly Basin and Takush Harbour area and held a pattern of logging "'til the flies showed up," fishing when the fish showed up and salvaging when passing ships crashed into the rocks at the mouth of the inlet.

And what did they do about the flies in Fly Basin? Handwritten above the recipe for baked winter squash in the "For Additional Recipes" pages of Mom's *Five Roses Cook Book* published in 1915, is the recipe for fly spray!

Fly Spray

1 gallon kerosene
½ pound pyrethrin powder
½ oz. wintergreen
Shake well, let stand for several hours, bottle tightly.

Roy, Dorothy and Murray

CHAPTER 27

THE BIGGEST BROTHERS

L ance was three and Lloyd two when GMG formed in
1946—forever the older brothers to every GMG child.
Their childhood memories are of an earlier time when
the boats were smaller, the people fewer and younger, the work
harder. A seeming small difference in age between them and
the younger GMG children was actually a huge difference in
technology, comforts and lifestyle. Their lives were more closely
intertwined with the Gwa'sala as well because GMG was situated
closer to Takush. The boys share some of their unique memories
with us.

There were four children in camp that first year: Lance, Lloyd,
Heather, and Harold, who was born in August. Clyde and Nancy
left with Heather not long after, leaving just the boys. Louis and
Hazel had no children of their own, but the tiny community
shared children happily.

The boys spent nearly as much time at the "uncles' and aunties'"
homes as they did their own. Aunt Claire's home wasn't much
different than theirs—the sisters, Gloria and Claire, had many
similarities and they cooked the same food. But young Lance
noticed that Uncle Louie and Aunt Hazel's house was different.

"When Mom and Dad went away, I'd stay at Uncle Louie and Aunt Hazel's house," Lance recalls. "It seemed to me they lived on a diet of lentils and potatoes. If I got hungry and looked around for food, all I found was more lentils and potatoes. It was hard times for GMG in the early days, though nobody let on to us kids."

On Friday night, Aunt Hazel would put Lance in the tub. After he played in the tub for a while, she would ask, "Lancy, did you wash your whole body?"

"Yes."

"Well, did you wash up as far as possible and down as far as possible?"

"Yes."

"And did you wash Possible?"

"Yes."

His bed was made in the little office with the old army surplus radiophone in it, off Uncle Louie and Aunt Hazel's bedroom. After Lance got into bed, Aunt Hazel came and tucked him in, said goodnight and took the coal-oil lamp.

On Saturday afternoons, Uncle Louie and Aunt Hazel took him hiking—his parents preferred boating to hiking—and on Saturday nights, Uncle Louie always made popcorn, which gave Lance nightmares. It seemed to Aunt Hazel and Aunt Claire both that Lance and Lloyd were their sons, too, and sometimes they got into trouble with Gloria, who would remind them whose sons they really were!

Grandmas were shared too. Grandma Alice Gildersleeve visited more often than the other grandmas because it was like coming back home for her. She once came up on the Union steamship in rough weather, and the *Stewart K* met her behind Egg Island. The boys watched their grandma, hanging onto a pallet, lowered onto the heaving deck of the *Stewart K.*

Grandma Craig, Heather's grandma, wore martens around her neck; two or three martens stitched into a stole, a gold clip holding them together at the front. Lloyd could hear their claws clicking as she walked. Grandma Craig also made a memorable fall into the chuck. When a grandma falls in the chuck, you don't forget it! She was making her way over the crosswalk between the houses when she slipped and fell in. Uncle Roy got to her first and was trying to fish her out with a stick.

"Uncle Roy never swam on purpose," remembers Lloyd with a chuckle.

Grandma kept shrieking, "My pills! My pills!" as she watched her heart medication floating away.

When Uncle Roy saw she was losing her breath, he slid himself (though some say he fell) into the water with her to push her out and rescue the floating pill bottle.

Grandma Goertzen visited as well. Eva Goertzen was an old lady by now—*really withered*, young Lloyd thought. Lance and Lloyd loved when Grandma Goertzen visited.

"She was the neatest lady!" remembers Lloyd.

"A really upbeat lady," says Lance. "She was kind and didn't raise her voice, but she had a look. And you didn't want to get the look."

At the end of a Grandma Goertzen visit, the ladies and boys were delivered to Wadhams to catch the Union steamship *Camosun* to Vancouver. The *Camosun* did the winter runs and was famous for its roll. Passing by Smith Inlet on their way back south, the *Camosun* was rolling in the heavy swells of the Queen Charlotte

Sound. Gloria, Lance, Lloyd, Hazel and Grandma Goertzen shared a cabin. Aunt Hazel was laid out in her bunk fighting seasickness, as usual, when Grandma Goertzen got sick. Grandma opened the porthole to throw up out of it, but the boat was rolling to that side at that moment and water poured through the porthole and washed Grandma across the cabin.

"It caused quite a kerfuffle," says Lance.

As I imagine it would! Grandma, seawater and vomit washing back and forth across the floor with the swells, and little boys lifting their feet off the floor to stay out of it.

And in the village, there were more people to call grandma: Granny Johnny and Granny Lucy. There was something special about the smiling, friendly Gwa'sala grandmas.

In 1947, Aunt Claire and Aunt Hazel were pregnant at the same time, expecting within weeks of each other. Lance and Lloyd were delighted! Two more cousins to play with! Dale Malcolm Goertzen was born January 7, 1948, and Rosalie Ann Goertzen on January 26. But Dale was born with a cleft palate, and following a corrective surgery in March, he died. The event was so painful that Uncle Louie and Aunt Hazel never talked about it.

Soon after, two little girls came to camp, and the boys quickly became attached to them. Uncle Louie and Uncle Don's brother John was in a bad situation—his wife left him and their two little girls, and John needed caregivers for them so he could go to work. Marilyn became a well-loved little sister to Lance and Lloyd, and their mom had a daughter at last. Donalda joined Uncle Don and Aunt Claire's family.

The girls lived at camp long enough for everyone to assume they would be part of their families forever, but John remarried and came to get his girls. Everyone felt a terrible loss when the little girls were taken away. Gloria probably felt it the most; it happened near the time that she lost another little girl to a miscarriage.

"Mom cried for a week," says Lance.

And Lloyd says, "I remember Mom running down the floats, crying, and Dad chasing after her. She was just running."

The camp children now were Lance, Lloyd, Harold and Rosalie. The three GMG sons were immersed into the men's world at a young age; they had three or four dads including them in everything. Those first years, whenever the men took the boat anywhere, they took Lance. When he was tall enough to peer out the window, they showed him a point of land in the distance and told him to drive the boat to the point. They told him the name of the point and later asked, "What is the name of that point you're headed for?" They showed him how to find his location on a chart.

One day, the GMG men and Lance were travelling in front of Margaret Bay in the *Stewart K* when the southeast wind switched to southwest. Alvin was at the wheel, and Uncle Don, Uncle Louie and Lance were sitting on the bench at the little table.

"Oh-oh," Alvin said suddenly.

Lance knew when his dad said "Oh-oh" something was terribly wrong, so when Uncle Don and Uncle Louie got up to see, he stayed at the table and prepared for the worst. Suddenly, a huge gust hit the *Stewart K* and tipped it over on its side. The men were tossed against the wall, the table came unlatched and landed on top of Lance, the battery tipped over, and the engine stopped.

"We were on our side for what seemed like a long time," says Lance, "but was probably only a minute. Then the boat righted itself, and the men tipped the battery back up and restarted the engine. The southwest gusts can get up to a hundred miles per hour there and can cause water spouts—the water goes up from the surface in a sort of tornado. I've seen fish come up in them and land right on the floats!"

The boys' young memories include going to the Takush School every weekend for church, and picnics at an old mill site nearby. They remember their dad and Uncle Louie shooting the Bull Run rapids in a canoe, just for fun, and tipping over. The boys were with the men for the propeller incident—the propeller fell off the *Rolamar* at Iron Rocks, and Uncle Louie and their dad drew straws to see who had to row back to Fly Basin for help.

Lloyd remembers his mom and Auntie Hazel making lanterns out of peanut butter cans with candles stuck to the bottom so they could go find the men in the dark when they didn't come home one night.

With no school to go to, the first GMG children had different Christmas memories too. Lloyd remembers the year Uncle Don created an unforgettable Christmas for them. Alvin and Gloria's house had a ladder permanently nailed to the roof, and Santa Claus, in his big red suit, used it to create such a clatter, the children wondered what was the matter. To the window they flew like a flash! To see Santa Claus dropping from the roof onto the floats with a great "Ho, ho, ho!" Perhaps he thought the chimney on their house was too small that year—he had gotten too fat! He had a giant canvas mailbag of presents for all! Santa was real!

The early GMG community may have been short on kids, but there were lots of friends in the nearby village.

"The language barrier didn't stop us," says Lance. "We made up our own language—a combination of Kwak'wala and English. Neither the Gwa'sala adults nor the GMG adults could understand what we were saying, and it annoyed them to no end."

Lloyd was always trying to find a way to go visit his friend in the village. There were strict rules about not going alone through the Bull Run, which separated GMG from Takush Harbour, but he decided he would go anyway. He rowed through and over to the village at high tide and had a grand time with everyone, playing baseball with a ragball and a stick.

When he rowed back to the Bull Run, the tide was out and the Bull Run was dry. He knew he had to get home before his dad, so he tied the rowboat to a tree at the end of the Run, ran through, walked the boom-stick to camp and no one was the wiser. Early in the morning, he hiked back to get his boat before his dad discovered it missing. But a limb of the tree he tied to put a hole in the bottom when the tide came in, and his crime was found out.

The boys visited the village as often as they could, racing up and down the beach and trails with their friends, crouching inside the smokehouses in the thick smoke from the barrel fires, dog salmon hanging over their heads. Other times there were branches of herring roe on hemlock or cedar boughs hanging to snack on. On a lucky day, the irresistible smell of Eliza's homemade bread floated through the village, drawing the boys to their friends' house, where Eliza would slice off a crust for the boys. Eliza had a big family and baked twelve loaves of bread at a time, their crusts shiny and soft with Crisco, all lined up to cool. Not everyone had a real wood stove with an oven to bake bread. Eliza smoked salmon and jarred salmon berries, too, all without a kitchen counter or plumbing!

It was the Gwa'sala way to share food, and their neighbours at GMG did the same.

"Sometimes, in the winter, the Gwa'sala might have been hungry," Lloyd remembers. "They never asked for money, but sometimes right after dinner, we'd hear a putt-putt boat coming from the village. As soon as she saw the boat, Mom would start opening jars of salmon and making sandwiches. She'd fill the big enamel washbasin with sandwiches like Grandma used to do.

"One guy would come out of the tiny boat and tie up, then go back inside. Pretty soon there would be twelve people coming out of the boat, bending in half to get out the door. *Where did they all fit?* we wondered. They'd all come in and sit down, smelling of perfume. The ladies all wanted to go to the bathroom to see the flush toilet. Everyone would sit down and Mom put plates of sandwiches out. A few of them could speak some English and there would be a bit of conversation, but mostly a lot of smiling and nodding. They'd eat some of the sandwiches, then they'd wrap the rest up and take them back to the elders.

"And Dad and Uncle Louie really appreciated how honest the Gwa'sala were. GMG had a little gas-powered donkey engine at the A-frame. When the tanker came in, they'd fill the big fuel tank behind the donkey with gas. In the winter the tanker didn't come as often, and some of the guys from Takush would run out of gas. They'd come to buy gas from us. They would say, 'If we can buy some gas from you, we'll pay you back in two weeks.'

"Well, Dad and Uncle Louie, I could hear them talking, and they said, 'Where will they get any money in two weeks? In two weeks, things won't be any different for them and they won't be able to pay and then they will be ashamed and try to avoid us.' So the dads told them, 'No, you don't pay us now. When the fishing season starts and you start making money, then come pay us.' And they always did. Bill Walkus and all the rest—they came back after fishing started and paid for their gas."

And then there was old Tom George.

"He had one of those cannery skiffs, and he used to row up and down the inlet," Lance remembers. "He shot a seal, and we all wondered how he was going to get it in his boat. 'I'm a strong man,' he told us kids. He got the seal onto a ledge at high tide, and when the tide lowered—*whump!*—he pulled it down into his skiff. He went up the inlet, with this seal in his bow, taking chunks off it when he was hungry. After quite a while he came back, and he still had the seal in his bow."

Lance and Lloyd started school by correspondence.

"We went to school on a stump," says Lance.

Six or seven is old enough to hike the logging slash, follow orders and blow a whistle, in their dad's opinion, so they were set to work whistle-punking. They went with their mother at first, doing correspondence lessons literally on a stump. At eight or nine, they were considered sufficiently trained to whistle-punk by themselves.

"Whistle-punking was no picnic," says Lloyd. "When it rained and you pressed the button for the whistle, it shocked you. The juice for the whistle came from a battery on the donkey, and you had to move the wire all the time. When the loggers changed roads, you had to take the string all the way down to the donkey and back up another road. Nicks got in the wire, and sometimes it got broke and had to be spliced. So when it rained, the whistle punk got shocked. You had to be close enough to hear the guys holler at you and far enough away to be safe from flying logs. When they moved farther back, you had to keep moving the wire to keep up with them."

Lance and Lloyd saw the progression of equipment, watching the men take apart outboards, the 10-10 Lawrence, power plants, then power saws. At first, they listened to the shrieking of the files in the evenings as the men filed the old hand saws.

"And then they pounded the set in them," says Lance. "The teeth have to be separated a bit, you know, to cut into wet wood."

Then the first power saw arrived in camp, and its arrival was an event—the huge, bulky Burnett laid out on the floats in all its glory, everyone gathered around.

Occasionally, Alvin took his boys up the trapline. "We stayed in the same cabin that Uncle Louie and Aunt Hazel did, just up the river where the trapline starts," says Lloyd. "We followed Dad up the Nekite, up the Piper Valley, around Baldy Mountain. We would stop at Piper Lake to catch huge trout. But we called it Trout Lake. Dad showed us how to set traps and use the skinning boarder, and then we'd sell the furs to the "Gum Man." Ray Lamarche came down from Bella Bella to buy the furs, and he would give us sticks of gum, and point out as many imperfections as he could find, to reduce the price."

Lance, as the eldest, was quickly depended upon. When he was twelve, Alvin became so ill he asked Lance to take him to the hospital in the *Tye Pass*. The seriousness of his dad's illness was unnerving.

"It was night, and the weather was bad," remembers Lance. "I could hardly see a thing. Passing Rivers Inlet, we were bucking the waves, and on every buck, Dad flew off the bunk into the air and back down with a thump. And he was delirious—he was not my dad. Finally, at daylight, we arrived in Bella Bella. I tied up and started up the ramp to get help, but Dad called, 'Wait! I can walk myself.' So I tried to help him up the ramp, but Dad passed out and fell, and his head hit the ramp with a loud thunk."

The relief was real when Lance finally relinquished the responsibility of his dad's life to Dr. Darby.

The boys also began logging at a young age; Lance started running the donkey at thirteen, with Lloyd on the chokers. And at fourteen, Lance was given all the boat chores—commuting guests to and from Kelsey Bay on Vancouver Island (paved road went only as far as Kelsey Bay), towing anything that needed to be towed, picking up the freight and providing ambulance service to the hospital in Bella Bella.

Lance and Lloyd were raised by our younger parents. And like the firstborn children of any family, Lance and Lloyd took the brunt of the responsibility, paving the way for the rest of us.

CHAPTER 28

A TALE OF TWO SCHOOLS

In 1954, Miles Everett was logging with his dad in Fish Egg Inlet when he fell in love with Rose, a Vancouver girl. He knew he needed a nice house to make her happy, so he built a lovely home with a front entrance featuring a staircase going up to two large attic bedrooms. To the right of the entry was a parlour. Down a short hall beside the stairs was a bathroom, and to the right of that, behind the parlour, a large master bedroom. To the left of the entry was a great room—a large open kitchen with a breakfast booth, a back door and plenty of space for seating, a table or both.

Though the house was lovely, Rose hated living in Fish Egg Inlet, and she left. A sad Miles Everett sold his house to GMG for $3000 just in time for it to become the first GMG schoolhouse and dormitory.

Ocean Falls School District said they did not have the funds to build a school in Smith Inlet, but when Alvin told them he had a building, they agreed to open the school on one condition—there had to be eight or more students.

GMG was short three students. Clyde and Nancy returned so Nancy could be the schoolteacher, and Heather, Lance, Lloyd, Harold and Rosalie made five students. To make up the eight, Frank and Ada's sons Don and Frank Johnson would come from

Takush (the Takush school only went to grade seven) to make seven students. Hazel had a relative, Dennis Polkinhorn, living with foster parents in Qualicum who might do well in a smaller school, and he provided number eight. And from Rivers Inlet came Leonard Walkus, for a total of nine students.

Classes began in September of 1954. The parlour became a classroom, the upstairs bedrooms became a dormitory for boarders, and the master bedroom housed Mrs. Soper, the house mother. Nancy, "Mrs. Gildersleeve" to her students, had previously taught school at the Gildersleeve logging camp and gave the GMG school the same name, Avalon. The first Avalon, begun in 1920 in Nootum Bay, had been named by Alice Gildersleeve, after her rowboat, *Avalon*. According to the Arthurian legend, Avalon was an island paradise, or refuge, in a western sea, and the name seemed suitable to everyone.

Meanwhile, Roy was building a real schoolhouse. When school let out for summer in 1955, Alvin and Gloria moved their family into the old schoolhouse—finally Gloria had a home worthy of her endless hospitality! And when the students came back to school in the fall, they had a brand-new schoolhouse. When you entered the school, there was a boys' cloakroom and bathroom on the right and a girls' on the left. The remainder of the building was one big room with blackboards across the front and right-side wall, windows along the left wall, cabinets and oil stove at the back. Gloria and Hazel boarded the students from Rivers Inlet in their homes for the next two years until GMG bought a bunkhouse and cookhouse from Budd Mann in Wyclese Lagoon.

In Avalon's second year, Fred Anderson came from Rivers Inlet and James Walkus from Takush, so there were eleven students in the school. James was in grade eight; he rowed his boat the two miles to GMG, in Fly Basin, every day.

"If the tide was low, I'd stop and eat clams, and I'd get to school smelling like stink," remembers James. "Nancy Gildersleeve and

Ada really encouraged me to go to Auburn Academy and finish high school, so I did."

Fred started in grade one at ten years old and completed eight grades in six years.

"Camp life was good for us kids," Fred remembers. "They treated us like their own. Sabbath was always a special day. Sometimes we would go to the sand beach for picnics and fun. Sometimes they would let us go logging with them on Sundays, and they would pay us $5 for the day. I remember being so happy with that, so we would have a little spending money. Maybe we could order something from the Sears catalogue."

Towards the end of the year, twins Katie and Ed Crooks, Arthur's younger siblings, arrived straight from England and attended Avalon through the next year.

"One of the happiest school years of my life," Ed recalls.

Avalon 1955/56. Left to right back row: Donald and Frank Johnson, James Walkus, teacher Nancy Gildersleeve. Middle row: Lance McGill, Heather Gildersleeve, Dennis Polkinghorn, Lloyd McGill. Front row: Leonard Walkus, Fred Anderson, Rosalie Ann and Harold Goertzen

As news of a school in Smith Inlet spread, attendance increased, including students from families in Rivers Inlet and distant parts of Smith Inlet—the Hendersons, the Bachens, the Salos, the Andersons, the Baders, the Kaufmans, the Jeffries, and increasing numbers of students from the increasing population of GMG itself.

A large structure of six-inch timbers was built onto the school float with two swings and a monkey bar attached. The structure was as high as the schoolhouse roof, and the swing pumped up as high as the eaves. The seat was a wide plank, big enough for two smaller kids to sit side by side, or for two bigger kids to "double pump," standing up, facing each other.

The structure itself provided a challenging climb and a thrilling view from the top. Climbing onto the top was against the law, however, and if you got caught doing it, you'd get a lickin' from Uncle Alvin himself, or so he said! But when no one was around, or if it was dark, well, the risk of getting caught made the climb even more irresistibly challenging.

One day Marcia was on the swing and Eric Bachen wanted it. When Marcia refused to give it up, he brought a knife out of his pocket. *He would never stab me*, thought Marcia, and she swung happily higher. Shockingly, Eric stabbed her in the wrist and blood flowed freely over the floats under the swing, astonishing them both.

"I felt lightheaded and was scared to look at it," says Marcia. "I ran to show Mom, and she got Aunt Gloria. They rinsed it in Aunt Gloria's rain barrel so they could see what was under the blood. They were somewhat shocked to see a deep wound about one and a half inches long. They closed it with butterfly tape but still the scar is a quarter of an inch wide in some places!"

I'm sure Eric was aided into regretting it deeply.

When Nancy became pregnant with Darby (born September 1956), she resigned and there followed a succession of teachers—Ms. Baker, Mrs. Thorn, Mrs. Egolf, Miss Schneider, Mr. McCormick, and lastly, Katie (Crooks) Lambert, former student of Avalon. There were housemothers as well: Mrs. Soper, then Mrs. Gelbreth, who reportedly made a great meatloaf with real meat!

It was a time when physical punishment was meted out as deemed necessary to control the classroom, and it was expected and accepted as standard procedure. No student was exempt. Mrs. Gildersleeve thought a good whack with the pointer was occasionally needed. Mrs. Thorn was a knuckle rapper, and no one escaped her ruler. Mrs. Egolf somehow had the power to stop unapproved ideas with a special look and made disobedient students stay in at recess to do extra work. Mr. McCormick employed the yardstick. Of course, some teachers got more creative with their punishments, or "consequences" if you like, and used methods such as standing in the corner, extra chores or writing lines.

Of all the Avalon teachers, Molly Thorn taught the longest. Mrs. Thorn had seven sons and a daughter, most of them grown. She and her husband had arrived in Alberta from England in the spring of 1933. As a wedding gift, Mr. Thorn's parents bought them a section and a quarter in Athabasca. The family was meant to make a new life in Canada, but Mr. Thorn left his family and went back to England. The children were separated to live with relatives and friends while Mrs. Thorn, determined to keep her family together, went to school to become a teacher so she could support them.

At GMG, Mrs. Thorn had a teaching job, and her sons could work for GMG and support themselves through school. It was a good situation for everyone. Mrs. Thorn was an excellent teacher, and she and her family were beloved by all. Except for one thing: Mrs. Thorn was quick with the knuckle rapping, which wasn't popular. It was the British way.

Sometimes Mrs. Thorn and her students ran into trouble because of her English accent. She spelled "car" on the blackboard and touched it with the pointer.

"Helen, what is this word?"

Helen didn't know.

"It's 'caw,'" said Mrs. Thorn. "Say 'caw.'"

"Caw."

"No, not 'caw,' 'caw'!" said Mrs. Thorn.

"Caw," said Helen again.

And Dennis called out, "Caw—that's what a crow says!" And he got in trouble.

Avalon 1958/59. Left to right back row: Ken Saari, Fred Anderson, David Thorn, Lloyd McGill, Doug Henderson, Teacher Molly Thorn. Middle row: Don Anderson, John Salo, Marcia Goertzen, Rosemary Salo, John Henderson, Rosalie Ann Goertzen. Front row: Don Goertzen, Lorraine Saari, Dennis McGill

The same fall that Avalon struggled to obtain eight students, the little Takush schoolhouse was bursting at the seams with twenty-nine students! Everyone wanted to send their children to Mrs. Frank's school. The government had just built a new school and teacherage on a float, but the float was not big enough for the weight of the school, the teacherage and all the students. Recess was a disaster—there wasn't room enough to play, and the float sank at the edges.

Then one day the students heard axes and power saws on the hill behind them, followed by the crash of falling trees. For the next few weeks, recess time was exciting! The boys scurried across the boom-stick and up the rocks to throw brush on giant bonfires. The GMG men felled the trees, and everyone helped clear the land and feed the fires. Don's mill ran every day, slicing the felled trees into boards to build new houses for the Takush families. One day, the students saw a hundred-foot letter 'A' out their window as GMG's A-frame was pulled in front of the hill. The donkey roared, and they watched stumps rip out of the earth, bounce off the cliff and fly into the water with giant splashes.

Finally, the students were dismissed for an unscheduled school holiday to watch their schoolhouse crawl onto land. The men manoeuvred the float close to the piece of beach with the least slope and secured cables to the skids under the school. Slowly, with much creaking and groaning, they winched the schoolhouse off the float and up the steep bank, inch by inch. It took two and a half days to place the school so classes could resume. The students went back to school with a floor so slanted the fire wouldn't stay burning, the windows and doors no longer fit, and the bottom of the schoolhouse door was the height of the small children's heads. For weeks, Ada and the older children helped the little ones struggle over the rocks and through the mud and then lifted them up into the school.

After two more weeks of labour, rain pouring continually, the teacherage and outbuildings sat beside the school. Over the winter, the community levelled the buildings, built porches and steps and constructed boardwalks above the mud.

As students, we didn't appreciate the significance of attending school without being sent away like other kids. But the efforts our parents put into starting and building our schools, then choosing and supporting good teachers show that *they* certainly understood the value. We also didn't understand how difficult it must have been for our teachers to live in such unfamiliar isolation. Now, finally, after they're gone, I thank them.

Takush School before being winched onto land. Left to right: school, Johnson house, Claire house, sawmill in front

CHAPTER 29

1957: A SIGNIFICANT YEAR

T he year I was born was the beginning of the end for GMG Logging Company, but no one knew it. In fact, they thought the events of 1957 were the beginning of something big. On January 1, 1957, Louis opened up a nice new logbook—the kind with a little lock on it that I would call a five-year diary—and began recording the hours and job positions for all GMG's employees. He also recorded the weather, significant camp events, departures and arrivals of camp folk, every visitor, births, weddings, baptisms and funerals. But never deaths.

> January 1, 1957, Tuesday. Mild and sunshine. Arthur went to Bella Bella with Claire. Harold and Donnie, Rosalie and Aleta stayed in camp. John Setnes and wife over from Boswell. Vivian Paul over. Paid me $800 for Chrysler parts. Do some bookkeeping—1956 most prosperous year.

GMG had found a market for cedar by now and no longer relied exclusively on Pacific Mills in Ocean Falls. When they broke their ties with the mill in Ocean Falls, they began to make money (1956 most prosperous year).

"GMG was working out at the mouth, with camp right behind Hazel Island near Boswell Cannery, when lots of gyppo logging companies started moving in from Seymour," remembers Lance. "For a short while, there were about a dozen or so, including Nalos, Jeffries, Mann, Henderson, Ladret, Levesque, DeMars, Greening, Randall, Vandelle, Saari and Kaufman."

The moms, particularly Gloria, loved the influx of people. They piled their kids into the boats and boated to all the other camps to visit the ladies.

The largest of the new camps was Nalos Lumber Co. Ltd. at the head of Smiths. It was a Vancouver-based company whose presence in Smith Inlet was of enough significance to make it onto the marine charts as "Nalos Landing." There were two prominent men associated with Nalos Lumber Company: Joseph Haas, president and managing director, and George McBryer, director of logging operations. Nalos had a mill in Vancouver. They bought GMG's cedar, and GMG was glad to have a buyer for it. Nalos was savvy about what was going on in the logging industry; they knew all the details of the recently implemented quota system, calculated on the board feet logged in the previous three years. GMG had been so busy logging, they didn't look into what was coming down the pipe, and it would cost them.

The 1957 crew was Alvin, Louis, Clyde, Louis Walkus and Vivian Paul (Janet Walkus's husband), with Arthur Crooks and a guy named Rob falling. In January, the men were living away from camp, "roughing it" by living in their little boats and working on the boom. Every night the logbook says they "sharpened saws" and "worked on saws." The day after Louis fixed his saw by replacing the magneto, he "fell in chuck with chainsaw—saved saw." Twice in two weeks, Louis fell off those rolly logs into the January water.

Arthur and Rob were falling on the hillside nearby, and on the fifteenth, Arthur saw an explosion in the water below. The logbook says, "Arthur's boat burned up—go home for night." No one knew why the boat blew up—the boat that Arthur built from Don's plans—but the crew took Arthur home.

A couple of days later, Claire came home from Bella Bella with baby Alan—she'd been gone seventeen days. The ladies had a baby shower for Alan, and Louis recorded it: "Tow A-frame home 7.5 hours. Art falling by himself. Ladies have baby shower."

The upper-grade students went back to school after Christmas break: "James Walkus and George over, James going to Auburn Academy tomorrow." And the lower-grade students came back to GMG from their own camps: "Arthur came home from Rivers with Freddie, Donnie and Rosemary."

At this time, the students were boarded in homes, no matter how small the home. Louis and Hazel's house (the house Roy built for his wife, Dorothy) had two bedrooms, with Marcia and Roland in one, Louis and Hazel in the other. When Freddie and Donnie Anderson boarded, they shimmied up the corner of the bathroom wall into the attic where their beds were. On Sundays, if there was work for them and if they wanted to, the schoolboys—Lance, Lloyd, Freddie, Donnie and Leonard—went to work with the men for five dollars a day.

On January 22, the steamer brought Dad's new reel-to-reel tape recorder, which he would later use to record Chief George's message to his people, and a new film projector. Let movie nights begin! Visitors, which included Vivian and Janet Paul, the Moores, Harry Walkus and family, Willie Johnson, John Setnes and wife from Boswell, the Hendersons, the power saw salesman, were all invited to "pictures"—Bible study lessons one through eight! I don't know exactly what Bible lessons one through eight consisted of, but I'm sure a lot of polite people, unable to say no, were made to sit through them.

Most winters, everyone "got hit with the flu." In March, when Hazel was about three months pregnant, she got sick enough that she had to be flown out to Alert Bay. She was gone a week, and when she returned Claire went out, also sick with pneumonia. They shared the childcare.

In May, the men began wrapping up the logging so they could gear up to go fishing. The *Rolamar* and *Tye Pass* took turns on the ways in Boswell, about three days each of scraping and painting the hull, then off the ways to paint the entire boat and "monkey wrench" on the motor, which took most of May.

On Saturdays, everyone went to Takush for church, then the sand beach for the afternoons. On one rare occasion, Louis took the boys to Bader's camp just for fun.

> May 19, Sunday—Take boys to Randals for poker—
> go hiking up to lake—catch trout.
> May 20, Monday—Back from lake—pretty tired.

Then school was out for summer. Schoolteacher Ms. Baker left, and Alvin and Gloria took Freddie and Donnie Anderson and Rosemary Salo back home to Rivers. But the real sign of summer arrived June 28—Carl and Andy! Carl Janke and Andy Waterman showed up every June for decades to gillnet in Smiths and Rivers. When Carl and Andy arrived, it was time to go fishing. Except this year there was a strike, so Carl and Andy and everyone else, Louis says, "…loafed around waiting for the strike to blow over." On July 1, all the camps and the village met at the big sand beach for a Dominion Day picnic. Somebody caught 175 sockeye, and they canned them right there at the sand beach, over a fire, tending it carefully—four drums full!

The strike finally ended on July 11, and Carl and Andy left for Rivers. The *Rolamar* and *Tye Pass* headed out soon after; Louis was by himself on the *Rolamar*, and Lance and Lloyd were with their dad on the *Tye Pass*. They fished Smith Sound, Shield Island, Canoe Rocks. On August 1, Louis ran into trouble. His entry says: "Got shark in net. Go into Boswell."

"We were fishing right beside him," Lance remembers. "We were fishing between Table and Egg Island. There were a lot of basking sharks back then. There were so many they looked like a boom broke loose, like logs, all across Smith Sound. They sleep at the surface of the water and often got rolled up in the gillnets. The gill netters bought shark insurance, but in order to collect the insurance money, you had to give them the tail of the shark. So Uncle Louie started cutting off the tail.

"It was a huge shark! Uncle Louie had the tail up between the rollers, and the head was at the bow. We could see blood squirting as high as the overhead light. Blood everywhere, it looked like a slaughterhouse!"

Louie told Roland, never his girls, the gory details. He said when he began cutting into the spinal cord the shark began thrashing, and his head beat against the bow of the thirty-two-foot *Rolamar*, and he was afraid the boat would roll over or be damaged, so he stopped cutting the tail and cut the net. He lost his net, and that poor shark had it all around himself and only half a tail.

"The sharks were such a problem to the gillnet fishery that the Fisheries officers would put a big knife on their bow and run around and cut the big sharks in half. You don't see them anymore," remembers Lance.

The week after Louie's shark incident, *Tye Pass* and *Rolamar* fished "mostly around Humpback Bay" and averaged "better than one hundred fish per day." August 18, Louis took five-year-old Marcia out for a week of fishing. Marcia cooked eggs on the surface of the stove for breakfast, swept the floor and sang all the songs she heard at church.

"Dad said he was amazed I could remember the words to all the songs, and that I never sang the same song twice," Marcia recalls.

After a week of "fishing rather slow, fishing not so good," Louis decided to call it quits for the season: "September 8, Sunday—got rid of my fall net to Frank Johnson for $200. This means no more fishing this year." The very next day he heard reports that the fish had turned on: "Alvin fishing—fishing supposed to be good at Nekite." And the next day, "Should be fishing I guess." By the end of the week, he couldn't take it anymore and went fishing with Arthur's net. Naturally, as fishermen everywhere would know, the fish then turned off. So he went beachcombing instead and towed home a string of logs to make up for it.

The fall brought three things: great sadness, great joy (I like to imagine, anyway) and the beginning of the end. On September 18, Louis set his net for the last time (no fish) and Hazel left for Vancouver to have a baby. On September 24, the Crooks left for Vancouver on a plane to see Harold in the hospital. Harold was dying.

Harold started having headaches early in the year. He had periods of aloofness, staring off, eyes open, not responding. He got into serious trouble for it with his teacher and his stepdad. A daydreamer, they thought. One day Harold had a seizure at school, alarming everyone. Arthur and Claire took Harold to Vancouver, where he was diagnosed with glioblastoma—a brain tumour. For the remainder of the year, Arthur, Claire and Harold went back and forth to Children's Hospital in Vancouver. Harold had a surgery, but he died at Children's Hospital on September 28, 1957.

Three days later, in nearby Burnaby Hospital, I was born. The log says, "Wire from Vancouver. Baby girl born today, Gayle Maureen." As sisters-in-law and mothers, Claire and Hazel had experienced joy and pain before, when Rosalie and Dale were born only eighteen days apart and Dale died. Now Claire lost her firstborn son three days before I was born. Mom and I weren't home yet for the burial at Olive Point when Harold, just eleven years old, was laid to rest beside his dad.

The third significant event, though trivial compared to birth and death, began on October 7. "George McBryer in today—might go logging to Humpback Bay." Humpback Bay looks like a little divot on the marine chart, just before and on the same side of the inlet as Burnt Island Harbour. George came on a Monday, and by Friday the A-frame was on location in Humpback Bay and the camp was on the north side of Burnt Island with the water running in the taps.

The first week in our new home, the men measured out the claim, hand-logged a spruce tree for the standing boom and played ball on the flats with the Hendersons. Louis and Fred Henderson took the *Tahine* (the Henderson's camp tender) to Boswell for the freight, and Alvin and Louis bought a donkey from Percy Henderson for $6000. They would be going "three sticks" back into the woods, which meant three spar trees plus the A-frame— four thousand feet, the farthest back they'd ever been. If they were a bigger operation, they would have built a road and hauled with a truck, but instead they would swing every stick! On October 16, a week after their arrival, they began. "Al and I went to work— slashed out road—first day on Humpback claim."

What they didn't know but George McBryer did was that by logging for Nalos, GMG would be losing future quota and Nalos would be gaining it. GMG and their one little donkey had been logging about three or four million board feet a year—pretty good for a small operation that shut down to go fishing every summer. Their quota would have been three or four million board feet a year based on their three-year average, but now they were logging Nalos's claim instead of their own, increasing Nalos's board feet per year and decreasing their own.

"Other small logging companies in the inlet were caught in the same way," says Lance. "Everybody trusted everybody; nobody could imagine doing such a thing to a neighbour, and when Alvin and Louie learned the truth, they felt sick. Later, whenever anyone brought it up, they would hang their hard-hatted heads and mutter, 'Oh that was a dirty trick. Oh they pulled a dirty trick.' They got Joe DeMars to do their brokering after that and stopped selling their logs to Nalos."

I'm sure Alvin and Louie and many other gyppo loggers felt pretty foolish for losing track of the big picture in their industry, and getting caught off guard. But in the fall of 1957, they were innocent of all this and began logging the Nalos claim. When Mom brought me home, home was in a new location, and Harold was missing. Alvin and Louis bought more equipment, hired more loggers and grew their capability into a five million or more board-feet-per-year company. But they would end up with a quota of two million board feet per year. The beginning of the end.

CHAPTER 30

FOR THE LOGGERS

The Humpback Bay claim, claim x-67322, was challenging. Loggers old and new might appreciate a glimpse at Louie's logbook. They might remember the impenetrable brush of the deep, steep inlets, the reverence of standing at the foot of an enormous first-growth tree, the thrill of its thunderous crash and ultimate splash into the water. That splash into the boom had an incredible amount of work behind it. There was no guilt associated with these things at the time, only accomplishment.

Louie's logbook might also bring to mind the tedious days of rigging and de-rigging, the incessant rain and pesky flies, the pain of sore muscles and the frustration of broken equipment. Most of us will glaze over at this chapter and move to the next—I won't be offended. But loggers might appreciate the story of a historical and challenging claim that went three sticks into the cut. So here's for the loggers!

> 1957
> October 16, Wednesday—Al and I went to work—slashed out road—first day on Humpback Bay claim
> October 17, Thursday—Bought donkey from Percy Henderson, $6000. Worked on claim with power saw

October 18, Friday—Came home from work early

October 20, Sunday—Dig out trail

October 21, Monday—Al and I working on claim

October 22, Tuesday—Northwest wind—camp taking a beating—will move to more sheltered spot. Arthur and Claire home with new boat—*Sather Maid*. Mr. Soper came with them

October 23, Wednesday—Move camp—take all day

October 24, Thursday—Al and I moving donkey

October 25, Friday—Al and I work moving donkey—come home to tie up camp better

October 26, Sabbath—Quiet Sabbath

October 27, Sunday—Moved donkey—had boys come up and pull line to bring up skyline—start falling out spar tree

October 28, Monday—Al and I falling—Bill [Gildersleeve] gone on the 5:30 [floatplane]

October 29, Tuesday—Al went to meet *Cardena* [to get freight]—falling myself

October 30, Wednesday—Al and I falling—Art brought his equipment—started falling

October 31, Thursday—Art, Al and I falling

November 1, Friday—Art, Al and I falling

November 2, Sabbath—Stay in camp, weather fine

November 3, Sunday—Al tops tree—I move donkey with Lance and Leonard

November 4, Monday—Tie down donkey—run guy-lines out—Art falling

November 5, Tuesday—Hanging guy-line and falling—Arthur falling

November 6, Wednesday—Arthur has pain in chest—leaves job and goes to camp—Al and I start falling with 2 saws

November 7, Thursday—Al and I falling with 2 power saws

In the beginning, there were three men on a falling team. Louie says, "We carried two springboards, four of those big steel wedges, two big old double-headed axes, a sledgehammer, and we shared an eleven-foot falling saw and a nine-foot bucking saw. Two fallers and a bucker could lay down about the same amount of wood as one faller with a chainsaw today."

After the war when chainsaws became more common, they were awkward, huge and required two people to carry them. By 1957, GMG had progressed to the modern chainsaw, which is obviously worthy of noting. A power saw each!

> November 8, Friday—Al and I falling with power saw each—weather mild and nice—Henderson family over for pictures
> November 9, Sabbath—Raining—SS [Sabbath School] in schoolhouse—Claire and Arthur at Takush
> November 10 to November 21—Al and I falling
> November 22, Friday—Get guy-lines from Hendersons. *Lillian D* [forestry boat] in camp
> November 23, Sabbath—Stay home—Arthur goes to Takush with Clyde and Thorns [schoolteacher Molly Thorn and her two youngest boys]
> November 24, Sunday—Move donkey—Clyde, Al and I, Leonard, Donnie and Freddie—Art and Alex falling
> November 25, Monday—Move donkey, Clyde, Al and I—Art falling
> November 26, Tuesday—Al and Clyde move donkey, I top tree—Art falling by himself
> November 27, Wednesday—Alvin hangs guy-lines, Clyde and I helping—Art falling by himself
> November 28 and 29—Al, Clyde and I rigging—Art falling by himself

November 30, Sabbath—Stay home, Art and Claire go to Takush

December 1, Sunday—Falling around back spar— Al, Clyde and I—Art and Robert go falling about 11 a.m.

December 2, Monday—Clyde, Al and I hang guy-lines, Art and Rob falling

December 3, Tuesday—Clyde, Al and I working on back spar—Art and Rob falling

December 4, Wednesday—Robert and Art help on rigging—also Clyde, Al, Vivian, Donnie and I

December 5, Thursday—Clyde, Al, Vivian, Louis, Robert, Arthur and I work on rigging

December 6, Friday—Clyde, Al and I tighten skyline 'til three o'clock—Art and Rob home at noon

December 7, Sabbath—Raining quite hard— Hendersons over for dinner

December 8, Sunday—Raining harder than ever— logging—Al, Clyde, Lloyd, Leonard and myself [This is the first day of actual logging since starting the claim on October 16!]

December 9 to December 31—Logging—Al, Louis, Vivian and myself—Art and Rob falling. [The only variance in these dates is that Clyde joins them on Dec. 16, and John Thorn, the teacher's son, works through his Christmas break.]

1958
January 1, Wednesday—No work today

January 2 and 3—Logging—Al, John Thorn and myself

January 4, Sabbath—In camp—afternoon Lance, George Egolf come in on plane, John Thorn, Fred and Dick Henderson left for school

January 5, Sunday—No work—Al takes Egolf to Takush [his wife Joyce Egolf is presently teaching at Takush]—I pack coupling up to donkey. Arthur bringing school children from Rivers.

January 6, Monday—Put in coupling, Al and I—boat day—Clyde and family back

January 7, Tuesday—Log—finish tree. Clyde, Al and myself. Fill oil for light plant

January 8, Wednesday—Log—pull in spar tree. Take skyline down—Clyde, Al and myself

January 9 and 10—Work, Clyde, Al and myself

January 12, Sunday—Start moving donkey—Clyde, Al, myself. Oil in house barrel

January 13, Monday—Moved donkey to spruce spar—Clyde, Al, myself

January 14, Tuesday—Rig the spruce for logging—Clyde, Al, myself

January 15 to January 26—Log—Al, Clyde, Art and myself [Freddie Anderson and Eric Thorn on Sundays]

January 27, Monday—Log—Clyde, Art, Al and myself—breakdown—phone for clutch gear [I imagine this one deserved their worst swear, "Dirty rotten snake in the grass!" They wouldn't log again until February 4!]

January 28, Tuesday—Go to Henderson's to get donkey. Monkey wrenching, Al, Clyde and I. Maurice [Saari] and Percy [Henderson] helping

January 29, Wednesday—Move donkey onto A-frame, Al, Clyde and I. Arthur falling for Hendersons

January 30, Thursday—Working around A-frame, Al, Clyde and I

January 31, Friday—Working on A-frame—Al, Clyde and I—six hours. Oil in plant—Thomas Crosby here (United Church mission boat)—pictures

February 1, Sabbath—Mr. Soper had meeting—party—Egolfs here

February 2, Sunday—Log Percy's sleigh runners [logs shaped for the base of the donkey so it can pull itself up the hill.]—Clyde, Al Leonard, Percy and myself—grey whale here

February 3, Monday—Log other sleigh runner—Clyde, Al, Percy and myself. Start fixing gear for donkey

February 4, Tuesday—Finish putting in gear—log—Clyde, Al and I [the breakdown cost them seven logging days.]

February 5, Wednesday—Log, Al, Clyde and I—gasket out and put one in—oil in house barrel

February 6, Thursday—Hang skyline—Clyde, Clive Thorn and myself

February 7, Friday—Log six hours—Clyde, Al, C Thorn and myself

February 8, Sabbath—Quiet day at home

February 9, Sunday—Log, Clyde, Al, Clive and myself

February 10 and 11—Swinging pile—Clyde, Alvin, Clive and myself

February 12, Wednesday—Log, Clyde, Al, Clive and myself—Arthur falling at Percy's—supper at Henderson's

February 13 and 14—Log, Clyde, Al, Clive and myself

February 16, 17, 18—Log, Clyde, Al, Clive and myself, Leonard. Break brake band. Trouble with engine getting hot

February 19, Wednesday—No log—bring engine from P Henderson. Clive, Al and myself—Mervin Walker [Hazel's cousin] up on plane

February 20, Thursday—Log—Clyde, Al, Clive and myself—got engine cool running hose from creek

February 21, Friday—Log six hours, Clyde, Al, Clive and myself

February 22, Saturday—Home all day—Hendersons leave for Vancouver

February 23, Sunday—Log—Clyde, Al, Clive, Freddie and myself. 77 logs today!

February 24, Monday—Log, Clyde, Al, Clive and myself

February 25, Tuesday—Log, Clyde, Al, Clive and myself—949 logs in pile

February 26, Wednesday—Log, Clyde, Al, Clive and myself—1013 logs in pile (64 today)

February 27, Thursday—Log, Clyde, Al, Clive and myself—1062 logs in pile (49 today)

February 28, Friday—Log 6 hours, Clyde, Al, Clive and myself—1090 logs in pile (28 today)

March 2, Sunday—Crew plus several boys—1114 logs in pile (24 today)

March 3, Monday—Same crew—1182 logs (68 today) Art and Mervin falling [They fall steady 'til March 19.]

March 4, Tuesday—Same crew—1166 logs (16 today)

March 5, Wednesday—Alvin and Gloria to Vancouver. Log, Clyde, Clive and I—1232 logs on pile

March 6, Thursday—Log Clyde, Clive and I

March 7, Friday—Log six hours—Clyde, Clive and I

March 8, Sabbath—Quiet day—go for boat ride up Rivers

March 9, Sunday—Log 6 hours—Clyde, Clive, Eric, Leonard and I—Clive hurts his hand

March 10, Monday—Log, Clyde, Mervin, Art and I—brake chains—haulback brake—1278 logs

March 11, Tuesday—Art and Mervin falling 'til noon—on rigging with Clyde and I in afternoon—1290 logs on pile

March 12, Wednesday—Log, Mervin, Art, Clyde and I—1324 logs. FINISH PILE

March 13, Thursday—Art, Clyde, Rob and I—de-rigging, take skyline down—Alvin and Clive back—Mervin and Art falling

March 14, Friday—Work 'til noon, Clyde, Al and I de-rigging—go to Boswell in afternoon

March 15, Sabbath—At home—Art brings freight at night

March 16, Sunday—Hang shoe—start moving donkey—Al, Clyde, Clive and I—Art and Mervin falling

March 17, Monday—Move donkey

March 18, Tuesday—Working Clyde, Al, Clive and myself. Mervin and Art falling—Alvin tops tree

March 19, Wednesday—Put donkey in position—run guy-lines—Clyde, Clive, Al and myself. Mervin and Art finished falling

March 20, Thursday—Rigging—Clyde, Clive and myself—hang guy-lines and tighten

March 21, Friday—Hang skyline and tighten—Clyde, Al, Clive and myself 'til about 2:30 or 3:00. Do some welding, fix brake, etc.

March 22, Sabbath—At home

March 23, Sunday—No work—go to build [Nalos] landing—nobody there—weather fine

March 24, Monday—Work on rigging Clyde, Clive, Al and myself

March 25, Tuesday—Rigging, stringing out whistle wire etc. Clyde, Clive, Al and myself. Forestry boat in for night

March 26, Wednesday—Work on rigging, lace stiff leg, forestry boat in for night

March 27, Thursday—Tow boom-sticks—bring guy-lines and boom-chains—bag ready
March 28, Friday—Try a few logs into the water, Clyde, Al, Clive and myself
March 29, Sabbath—Hendersons here tonight, also George Egolf—gets our radio working
March 30, Sunday—Log a bit and rig up—Clyde, Clive, Al and myself, also some of the boys
March 31, Monday—Lace-up A-frame, pull cedar log under—Clyde, Al, Vivian, Clive and myself

April 1, Tuesday—Log—both machines—Clyde, Clive, Vivian, Al and I. George McBryer here—weather fine
April 2, Wednesday—Chrysler breakdown—work on putting in other engine
April 3, Thursday—Finish putting in engine—Oil in house stove
April 4, Friday—Log—swing both ends

The remainder of the work on this claim gets my *Reader's Digest* version to bring it to its end. April was a solid month of logging, interrupted only by three days of making boom-sticks and bagging logs, and two days of building Nalos Landing.

They logged until the twelfth of May, then spent the rest of May and most of June booming: "Making sticks, sorting logs, and bucking." They had a boom winch with a jeep engine on its own little float that was used to pull the boom together and a drag-saw for bucking on another little float. Bucking was very important for getting the best value from a log. Lloyd describes how it was done:

A tree had three grades, the butt part of the tree being number one because it had no limbs and thus no knots; the wood was clear and straight. A tall tree could have two or three number-one-grade logs. The middle section of the tree is graded number two, and the top, with the most limbs, number three. If you buck incorrectly and mix the grades of a log, the mills noted the lowest grade of the log, even if it was only a foot, and applied it to the entire log.

Sometimes the base of a tree is hollow, and it makes sense to cut above the rot. But if the faller cut higher, say five feet or so, forestry punished you with stumpage fees. If you sent the log to the mill with the rotted end on it, they culled it even though the log was almost entirely good. The mills would cull a lot of logs and you couldn't say a word. Then the mill would use the good part of the tree for number-one wood. So it was a lose-lose situation. Alvin and Louie tried to find all the imperfect logs and remove them from the boom.

If the hills weren't too steep, the falling team bucked the tree after falling it. The mill told you what they were looking for—the fallers carried the plastic paper with them that stated which logs they wanted in which lengths. Logs were generally bucked to thirty-four feet—four eight-foot lengths with a ten-inch trim. If it was a really big log, a giant spruce perhaps, they bucked it twenty-six feet; twenty-four feet plus trim. It was always divisions of eight for plywood and lumber. Sixteen feet was a popular size; two-by-fours were eight feet. Spruce went for plywood, the good logs referred to as "peeler logs." An old-growth Sitka spruce was clear and straight, and the "white spot," the clear centre, was sold to Yamaha for building pianos.

If the hills were too steep or access was otherwise difficult, bucking was done after the tree hit the water. The north side of the tree was always straighter, as the limbs preferred to grow on the sunny side. So when they were booming, they turned the limbs underwater, with the good side up. They used an old gear-driven Homelite chainsaw for cutting in saltchuck, and they had a drag-saw. The log was pulled over to the drag-saw, chained up tight, the broken ends cut off, the remainder cut into the correct lengths, and the leftover bits pushed out of the boom for Mom to hit with her boat.

"Don't tell Alvin," Mom would say.
"Alvin already knows, Mom."

By June 25, they had eight sections of pulp boom. Sadly, a lot of good trees in the early days were used for pulp. The boom was towed to Nalos to await departure to Vancouver (previously to Ocean Falls). Then they did one last week of logging before the fishing season; Heather Gildersleeve was the whistle punk.

In September and October, after fishing, the men spent a total of two weeks logging and the rest of the time bucking and sorting. On October 7, they "start booming lumber—hemlock" then they boomed the cedar. They towed their booms and Maurice Saari's booms, and they finally "clean up rigging on x-67322 claim" on November 2.

GMG finished Nalos's Humpback Bay claim just over a year after their first day on the claim. The next day they towed camp away to Dry Creek/McBride Bay to start the whole routine all over again! I had just turned one when we moved to McBride Bay.

Alvin and Louie

CHAPTER 31

IN SICKNESS AND IN HEALTH

In August of 1958, in the middle of fishing, Alvin and Louie took the *Rolamar* to Port Hardy, caught a plane to Vancouver and slept overnight at Dr. Ken McGill's house (Alvin's brother). The next day they rented a "U-driver" and drove to the Hope Camp Meeting to surprise their families. Camp meeting was a respite for everyone—their annual connection with friends and family, the larger church family and the world. But as it was in the middle of both summer logging and fishing seasons, the men didn't always make it; the wives and extended families were overjoyed to see their faces when they did.

This summer, though, Alvin wasn't feeling well, and he recognized the symptoms. He stopped on his way back through Vancouver for an X-ray. His cancer was back. Dr. Austin told Alvin he was riddled with it. He performed Alvin's second gastrointestinal surgery, removing more of his intestine, and told Alvin he might have only three months to live. Shortly before, his mother had died of the same cancer, so Alvin prepared for the worst. After a month in hospital, he went back to camp to help finish up the Humpback Bay claim and to generally get his life in order.

In Alvin's absence, Louie, with Lance and Lloyd, now age fifteen and fourteen respectively, had stopped fishing and were trying to finish up the Humpback Bay claim with anybody they could find who happened to be around at the time. Lance went falling with Louie, dragging Louie's big axe and the heavy bag of wedges.

"For each tree, Uncle Louie told me exactly where to stand," says Lance. "But sometimes it took a while to cut down the tree—those were big trees—and I got bored. I wandered uphill from Uncle Louie a bit, out of the way of his tree, and found a bouncy log lying across another log. It didn't seem the tree would fall in my direction, but when the tree began to fall, I could see it was falling my way. It hit the log under my bouncy log and I flew into the sky and came down in the brush. As soon as the tree started to go over, Uncle Louie was already racing up the hill, yelling, 'Lancy! Lancy!' When I popped up unharmed, I got a very stern lecture, the sternest I've ever seen Uncle Louie! 'Don't you EVER do that to me again!' he said."

For a short time, Lance, Lloyd and Louie logged, just the three of them. Lance was on the donkey at the A-frame, swinging into the chuck. Being short on crew, Lance had to jump off the donkey every turn and unhook the logs, jump back on and send the chokers back up. Louis hooked chokers with Lloyd.

Alvin started working soon after he came back. He was weak, so he took the job requiring the least amount of physical exertion—donkey puncher. He brought a big basket of zwieback and milk with him and ate and drank from it all day long.

"I have a gut like a seagull," he would say. "Everything goes straight through."

Every day, everyone in camp prayed for Alvin's GI system. And strangely, everyone carried on as usual. In fact, they expanded. Alvin and Louie went into Wyclese Lagoon to buy a Skagit (donkey) and a bunkhouse and cookhouse from Bud Mann. The Skagit's float wouldn't go through the narrows, so they tied it up until they could build a new float for it. Like the Bull Run, the lagoon narrows is a tricky passage, roaring with waterfalls and foam as the tide moves in and out, but quite passable at high slack. It took them a couple of tries to get the cookhouse and bunkhouse through.

The logbook says: "Unable to take float through, tie up and come home … Go to lagoon—too much water to take float." Finally, they brought the bunkhouse and cookhouse through on the afternoon of September 30, and the students moved in; Freddie and Donnie Anderson, John Henderson and Kenny Saari into the bunkhouse, and Rosemary Salo, Lorraine Saari and the housemother, Mrs. Soper, into the cookhouse.

Alvin's three months to live had come and gone, and he was still going to work every day and feeling pretty good! They built a float for a new light plant and an oil float for the oil tank. In June, Louis chose logs for a new float and house skids and ordered a house. It was a kit, and they started building it in July. Clearly, no one was planning to quit and die.

August came again, and everyone left for the annual trip to town. It had been a year since Alvin's diagnosis, and he almost didn't want to go hear what his doctor had to say. Dr. Austin told Alvin he was surprised to see him and ordered an X-ray. He examined the before and after imaging and said, "You are the luckiest man alive! Your body is totally clear of cancer. What have you done?"

Alvin said, "Well, there was a lot of praying going on!"

Alvin could see the doctor didn't know what to make of it.

"I don't believe in miracles," said Dr. Austin, "but I feel I have just witnessed one."

By now Alvin was racking up the miracles, and there would be more to come. In the bush, Louie and Alvin looked death in the eye several times and escaped it. I'm sure they thought *Why me?* just as they had asked *Why Don?* and *Why Ethel?* that dark

January of 1952. I don't know why either, but all of their lives, whether long or short, created a ripple on the inlet that reached far beyond it.

As logging partners, Alvin and Louie were a phenomenon. In their thirty years as associates, they never spoke a harsh word to or about each other. They shared the values of hard work and honesty, lending a hand when needed and treating everyone, even kids, with respect. They didn't even swear—which is considered to be very un-logger-like. Often at day's end, after hours of working together, they spent an hour, or several hours, in the office, talking and planning and figuring out life on this planet. There is a beauty in such a friendship, and an example.

CHAPTER 32

CHIEF GEORGE TELLS A STORY

O ld Chief George loved to tell stories. He could sit for hours and tell the children, or anyone, story after story. Often, they were stories of animals with spiritual and human characteristics. Children who listened remember the chief saying, "My animal is the blackfish [killer whale]. When I die, the blackfish will come into the harbour to get me. When you see them come in, that big one, spouting, will be me." And the children believed him because not long ago they had heard the wolves come for old Tom George on the night he died.

One evening, Chief George and Lucy came to visit Frank and Ada and, as he often did, the chief told a story. Ada recorded the chief's words.

"One time, my grandfather told me about a little boy. The little boy got dead. They put him in a box. He gets up. He takes off his meat and leaves it in the box. Then he starts to walk. Lots of people on the trail. When he sees people, he hides. He came to the end of the trail. He sees a big house. He hears his chum's voice. It says, 'Go into the house, but watch your blanket. If it gets on the floor and the woman step on it, they not let you go back where you come from. You are to go back where you come from.'

"The little boy goes into the house, but he not watch his blanket. One corner fell on the floor and the woman put her foot on it. Just then someone outside called and she went outdoors. The little boy heard his chum's voice again. It said, 'Run out quick while she not look. Go back where you come from.' The little boy ran out. He started back the trail. When he sees anybody, he hides. He came back to his box. His meat was still there. He puts it back on and was alive again. My grandfather told me."

The chief was quiet for a moment. Then he said, "I believe God. I don't believe that old story anymore. I believe God. My grandfather didn't have the Bible."

And Ada wrote those words down, too, because they were very important to her. For Ada, it must have seemed that the years of difficult work, sickness, isolation and the pain of losing her daughter were for this moment. Her reward was to witness Chief George change his allegiance—from the sometimes vicious spirits of his ancestors to the loving spirit of God.

Three baptism events occurred in the village, and Ada wrote a first-hand account of how they came to be. For five years, many of the Gwa'sala had been asking, "Why do you not baptise us?" And the answer was always, "We want you to understand what God asks of you before you make such a big commitment." For five years, Don, then Frank and Clyde, gave Bible studies so they would understand.

In the fall of 1955, seventy-five people crowded into the Takush schoolhouse for church. After lunch, Elder A.W. Bauer performed a baptism of five Gwa'sala individuals and one young person from GMG. He also officiated at a double wedding in the evening. Nancy wrote up the event for the *Canadian Union Messenger*, the church publication at the time, but unfortunately, she didn't include names.

On May 12, 1956, eighteen Gwa'sala were baptised. A crowd stood on the shore at high tide, hushed, waiting. Pastor R.A. Smithwick walked out into the water, the crushed white shells beneath his feet evidence of the lives of hundreds of years of Gwa'sala ancestors. The chief led by example and was first to follow the pastor into the water. At waist deep, they stopped, and Pastor Smithwick spoke a few words. Then, in a loud voice that everyone could hear, he said, "I baptise you in the name of the Father, the Son, and the Holy Ghost." He held Chief George and dipped him beneath the Smith Inlet waters—the waters that carried the Gwa'sala ancestor YāqalE'nāla in his whale canoe to Wyclese long ago, and the whale turned to stone. The people waiting on the beach sang as the chief rose from the water.

The chief's wife followed, and then I can only guess, because the photograph of the crowd that day, which was posted in the *Canadian Union Messenger*, is fuzzy. Some of the names are Edward and Sally, Vivian and Janet, Robert and Violet, David and Annie, and more. It was a day of happy tears. The people had been drawn by love, not fear. It was the love of their friends who were willing to die for them, and their friends' belief in one all-powerful Creator God who loved the world so much that he sent "His only begotten Son, that whosoever believeth in Him should not perish but have everlasting life." (John 3:16)

This can all sound like a bit of a stretch to some, but the supernatural was (and is) very real to the Gwa'sala.[7] None ever doubted a supernatural world—their winter ceremonies were designed to connect them to it, and did. But now they had new knowledge, and their new understanding changed their desire to be possessed by the powerful Baxwbakwalanuksiwe' of the Hamatsa ceremony (the cannibal who lives at the north end of

---

[7]   *Yax̱waȼłan's*, (we will dance) "The Supernatural" p. 9 (Book 12 of the "Learning Kwak'wala Series" presently (2021) used in public schools, from the U'mista Cultural Society, by Jay Powell, Vickie Jensen, Vera Cranmer, Agnes Cranmer.) Also, U'mista Cultural Centre Website.

the world) or the other spirits of their ancestors into a desire to connect to their friends' all-powerful Creator God who loved them.

Today, many people call this "stealing culture," but these "missionaries" thought it wrong not to share knowledge and hope ("The Good News," they called it) with their fellow humans, and it would be unthinkable to withhold this knowledge when they were asked for it.

On June 15, 1957, Elder Wells baptised another ten believers at Takush.[8] Now almost everyone in Takush was a baptised follower of Christ, and they formed a church of about forty or fifty believers.

But mixing beliefs and cultures is never easy. And what about the blackfish? Would they still come for the chief when he died now that he was a Christian?

---

[8] "Canadian Union Messenger" articles are dated December 14, 1955; June 13, 1956; and January 23, 1957. (These can be viewed at adventistarchives.org.)

Wyulth (Chief George Walkus)

CHAPTER 33

BUILDING ON WATER

O ur new house arrived on the freight boat on June 12, 1959, in the form of a kit.

"That kit had everything!" Dad told Roland. "Right down to the shims!"

The men unloaded the kit onto an empty float and towed it to camp.

It was the year for building things. The men had just finished a claim and took some time off. On May 19, the *Gulf Islander* towed away GMG's boom of four sections lumber, seven shingle, two pulp, and the following day people from the village and all the camps enjoyed a big picnic and a school sports day at the sand beach. After the picnic, the men towed the Hendersons to Rivers Inlet. The Hendersons were good friends, and everyone was sorry to see them leave. There would be many trips back and forth from Rivers from then on for visits.

Then Dad and John Thorn started building a float for our new house. The GMG men constructed floats using large cedar logs, holding them together with cross-logs on top at each end. They lashed the cross-logs to each individual float log with cables and staples. If they were building a structure on the float, they built it on skids laced onto the float logs, then planked the remainder to form a sort of yard. The men built five floats in the space of a year: one for the new Skagit, one for the new light plant that arrived on the freight boat on June 5, a new oil float on which they placed tanks and barrels for towing to the oil tanker to refill, a new A-frame float for the new A-frame, and the float that became my yard.

Our float was different from the others. Dad didn't want to use nice, long expensive logs, so he used shorter logs and put them crosswise instead of lengthwise. We ended up with a row of cross-logs in front of our house, which was planked over into a sort of raised landing dock and barrier to keep little kids from falling in. It took Dad and John four days to build our float, then they pulled the house skids into place.

On July 15, Alvin, Dad and John Thorn began building. They framed for eleven days, then Lance and Lloyd joined the crew to sheet and shingle the roof. They attended a very important event in Rivers on July 25—Dr. Darby's farewell—after which they spent a day canning fish. By July 31, the roof was finished and everyone went to Vancouver for a month. Our family took the *Rolamar*, and John and David Thorn hitched a ride.

While everyone was gone, Carl Janke did the wiring. Then John Moore, a Rivers Inlet local who fished the *Advise,* finished most of the remainder with Dad helping when he could. It took John forty-five working days. On Christmas Eve Day, we moved in. Mom insisted on a fireplace, so we had a lightweight metal, wood-burning fireplace, and Mom hung our stockings from the mantel. Dad put the Christmas tree in the corner by the front window, and Mom wrote "Merry Christmas" on the window with a can of spray snow. But I only remember this from photographs. Apparently, all I could say was a two-year-old version of "I want to go home."

Mom was happy with her new home. It was a simple rectangle, and the front door in the middle opened to the living room. The fireplace was at the end of the room, to the right, and there was a wide opening to the dining room. The dining room connected to the kitchen, which was behind the living room wall. The kitchen had an oil stove, a coal-oil fridge and wood cabinets with a sink in front of the window. A hall ran off the kitchen (which we kids polished by pulling each other up and down it on Dad's old long johns). There were two bedrooms on the left, and a bedroom, bathroom and back entry on the right. The back entry had a laundry sink, some cabinets and places for shoes and coats. After breakfast in the mornings, Dad sat on the back step to put on his caulk boots.

Dad built a wide porch with rose trellises for the front door and flower-boxes to line the entire front and right side of the house. Before they were filled with dirt, the flower-boxes made the most wonderful, cedar smelling train. "Chooooo, chooooo! All aboard!" But after many expeditions in the workboat to fill burlap sacks with soil to dump into the train (along with some dead fish and starfish), Mom planted it with red and yellow roses that she trellised up the porch, and dahlias, stinky feverfew, daffodils, rhubarb, even a Mac apple tree!

None of the ladies were home decorators by today's standards. A family living in a small house needs all the space for necessary things. But there were crocheted doilies under lamps, begonias on the end tables, a philodendron by the window, a couple of paintings on the walls, and one or two pretties. Our pretty things were on the mantel where we couldn't reach them: a multicoloured vase, two glass candlesticks that were a wedding present, and a wood carving from Ceylon—several elephants in a row, each elephant smaller and a paler colour of wood than the one before. Dad liked to show the elephants to people and tell them about his brother Clarence, who was working in Ceylon as a missionary.

In my first memory of our new house, old Chief George is sitting on a kitchen chair close to the cabinet by the front door where Dad keeps his reel-to-reel tape recorder. The chief is speaking in his language while Dad records his words, the reels turning slowly. Mom and Dad are sternly hushing us; it's possible that our protests about going to bed are on the recording. Chief George wants to leave a message for his people to hear later, when he's gone, and surely that must be soon because the chief looks very old and wrinkly. I fall asleep to the rhythmic clicking, shushing sounds of the chief's voice. Chief George died soon after, in May 1960. (Today, the tape is waiting to be professionally copied, then his recorded words will be heard for the first time since that night in our living room.)

In the new year of 1960, GMG continued to build. Lance was done with school now, and on March 4, Alvin, Louis and Lance began the process of building a new A-frame. They spent two days letting down the old A-frame and de-rigging it. Then they started building a float for the new A-frame. It took the three of them four days to build the one-hundred-foot float of cedar logs in the same manner as the float for our house. The last two and a half days were spent lashing it before they pulled the donkey onto one end.

On Monday the fourteenth, they began the A-frame. They found a beach with just the right elevation and cleared the trees to make a place to lay the selected spruce, long and straight, 100 to 110 feet each. With the help of the donkey, boom winch and cables, they laid the logs up the beach, with the butt ends near the middle of the float, against the cross-logs, which were on the outside edges of the float. Then they laced the logs together at the top and secured the crosspieces that formed the letter "A." All this required a lot of splicing of heavy cable, which is difficult and time-consuming.

On the twenty-fifth, Dad says in his logbook, "Al and I carry blocks to top." If you have ever seen these huge chunks of metal, you would know that was no small feat. They hung the blocks and rigged the A-frame. Then they trimmed and angled the base of the two spruce legs, secured them to the cross-logs and pulled the A-frame upright, off the beach, using the donkey. It took them six days to de-rig the old A-frame and build a new float, and eleven days to build, rig and raise the new A-frame, for a total of seventeen full working days. They immediately put it to use.

But they weren't done building things yet. Three more things would be built to complete the camp: a new house for Alvin and Gloria, a church, and a boat big enough to tow it all.

PART II
I Remember

CHAPTER 34

GLORIA

I'm only four, but I can remember now. Most things are shadowy, but Aunt Gloria keeps a diary in 1961. Thank you, Aunt Gloria! Uncle Alvin thinks her diary is inconsequential and a little foolish, but in the end, she leaves us a unique window into the past that he does not. Gloria was born in 1922 in Ocean Falls, grew up in her dad's float camp and moved to Smith Inlet in 1937—she's local history! A man once tried to write a book about her life, but it was disappointingly exaggerated and inaccurate. Her diary, however, is a true picture of daily camp life. She begins writing in March.

> March 6: Dear Diary, this was a lovely day and it looked like it would continue so, but after all my wash was out, it decided to be windy and rainy. I took the clothes all in again and hung them in the house. I also baked bread, white bread, because I am out of whole wheat flour.

Her entries always record the day's weather and how it affects her wash. She does a formidable amount of wash—sometimes she changes the beds twice a week! And nearly everything she washes needs to be ironed, which she likes to get done right away. One day she irons from 8:30 a.m. to 1:30 p.m.! She bakes bread twice a week, as well as two batches of cookies twice a week for the lunches. She cooks three meals a day for her family, the bunkhouse boys and whoever else might be nearby: visitors, pilots and any kids staying in her house at the time—like me. She likes to be the hostess of the camp, and her house has a large, combined kitchen and dining area that accommodates many guests at once.

Every day, Aunt Gloria lists any visitors who may have stopped by, any outings she may have made and (most days) what she cooked for dinner. "Made gluten today, and little Helen washed it for me." Yes, Aunt Gloria finally has the daughter she always wanted! Helen was born in Bella Bella on May 29, 1955.

Aunt Gloria does a lot of cleaning! She washes the walls, inside the cupboards, the floors, the curtains, everything. Her house is clean and tidy! It concerns her greatly to see some cases of poor sanitation at the village. (Though in my experience, it is a lot of work to be as clean as Aunt Gloria!) She banters and jokes with her friends in the village, pesters them into singing in choirs, talks the boys into having a "real" wedding and gives advice on cleaning. They've all been her friends since she was a teenager, so they don't seem to mind her advice. But washing anything is a problem at Takush; probably the biggest drawback to the Takush location is lack of water. There is not enough water for everyone to drink, cook, bathe and wash clothes.

James Walkus remembers being sent to fetch water. He took two pails to the shallow two-foot-deep well. He scooped up a pail of water and watched the wrigglers in it while he waited for the dirt to settle to the bottom of the well so he could scoop up the second pail. And, of course, there is no plumbing or washing machines or toilets. He remembers the chamber pots being dumped outside the door. When he picked salmonberries at the bottom of the hill, he could smell sewer but thought nothing of it. Aunt Gloria says these kinds of conditions, and close communal living, are the reasons for the high rates of TB, strep and staph-related illnesses, scabies and lice, and she wants to fix it.

So Aunt Gloria invites some of the girls to come live with her, and those poor unfortunate (or fortunate, if you like) girls get the works! She makes them a hot soapy bath and washes their hair with kerosene. She teaches the girls about self-grooming, even how to put pin curls in their hair! And she teaches them to sew and cook—Aunt Gloria style.

The girls' reward for all this torment, besides all Aunt Gloria's motherly love, is to learn English, sleep between nice clean sheets in soft, clean pajamas and eat their fill of Aunt Gloria's cooking. It's a gift from Alice Gildersleeve and Gloria to be regifted to the girls' future families—clean sheets, homemade bread, gluten, macaroni casserole. In 1961, some of these girls are already married, but Gloria is always on the lookout for another girl to adopt.

Of course, Aunt Gloria's diary is about more than just housekeeping. "I heard the first birdsong today, caught the first bee." And Aunt Gloria loves a warm wind, just like me! The kind that makes you run and run, up and down the floats, flying over the crosswalks like a soaring eagle, racing with the wind, the dogs, friends, nothing or anything! If it's a warm, windy day, Aunt Gloria always says so: "Today was a beautiful day—southeast wind is blowing ... the floats were bone dry when we got up this morning, I felt like running just like the kids ... we got up this morning with a warm wind blowing and the floats were powder dry—what a pleasure just to put your face to the wind and let the soft wind blow your hair."

But sometimes, when we're tied up in Security Bay, the warm wind turns into a katabatic. It begins with a warm chinook breathing on us, rising up the mountain, where it chills and morphs into a violent, roaring wind, forced back down the slopes, racing from high pressure to low (cold to warm). The katabatic has ripped our roofs off, blown our boats into the air, broken camp in half and, of course, wreaked havoc on the clothesline. But it doesn't stop Aunt Gloria from saving her sheets. "My sheets, my sheets, my beautiful sheets!" and she pushes off in her rowboat, hair flying. She scoops at the sinking white sails with her oar, pulls them sopping into the boat.

This spring of 1961, camp is in McBride Bay again, and, besides the Alvin and Louis families, there are Clyde, Nancy and Darby (Clyde is beachcombing, hand-logging and working for GMG on and off), Molly Thorn and David. Missing is Claire and Arthur and their family, who sold the *Sather Maid* the previous summer and bought a farm in the Fraser Valley. The older kids—Lloyd, the Thorn boys, Fred Anderson, Heather Gildersleeve and Dick Henderson (whom Heather will soon marry)—are boarding away at high schools and colleges. And boarding at GMG this school year are Donnie Anderson, Johnny Salo and Eric Bachen in the bunkhouse, and Rosemary Salo, who is living with us.

Eric Bachen is from Dawson's Landing in Rivers Inlet and has a dad named Lucky. Lucky survived two tours as a tail gunner in a bomber during the war, which apparently is very lucky. Johnny and Rosemary's parents are light keepers at Addenbrooke Lighthouse, and Freddy and Donny's dad works as a fish boundary patrol and fish guardian in Rivers Inlet.

Aunt Gloria is doing the cooking for the bunkhouse boys. She often notes what the boys in the bunkhouse are doing, and it sounds like the three of them have a lot of fun going to Gordon Lake nearly every day. They take a rowboat and an outboard, some fishing gear, sometimes their lunch or supper, sometimes their lunch and supper both. It's their hangout.

On Fridays, Gloria creates an enormous amount of food because you never know who will show up at church the next day and need an invite to dinner. "I did all my Friday cooking. I cooked a big rice pudding and set jelly. Baked beans, made potato salad, made pickled beets, made gluten." All the Fridays are similar. "Made apple pie, baked bread, made matrimonial cake and jelly. Made rice pudding, baked beans, made beet pickles and cooked potatoes and eggs for salad. Will have whip cream on the pie." (Probably whipped canned milk.)

Aunt Gloria is also the Sabbath School Superintendent for 1961 and is in charge of the Sabbath School portion of the church program. She stands up front as a sort of MC and facilitates the program. She takes it very seriously. Her programs look like this:

February 4 Sabbath

Poem: *To our Visitors*
Silent Prayer
Opening Song: #638 "I Have a Song I Love to Sing"
Scripture Reading: Luke 4: 14–20
And Prayer: Clyde
Remarks: Myself
Mission Report: Louis
Mission Exercise: Rosemary
Special Song: "In the Temple" — Dennis
Lesson Study
Memory Verses
Poem: *Jesus Loves Me*
Solo: "Love of God" — Gloria
Benediction: Alvin

She practices with all the kids, teaching us to sing solos, duets and trios, and makes us recite memory verses or read things up front. The camp ladies generally take turns with this responsibility of Sabbath School Superintendent and help each other out. They do this at the Takush community too. A few years ago Aunt Gloria and Aunt Claire created a girls' choir of about eight girls from Takush. They bought the girls matching skirts, blouses and scarves, and took them all to Hope Camp Meeting to sing for the crowds.

Aunt Gloria loves to have people over to her house, but she also loves to go visiting. She is the instigator of visiting adventures.

> March 21: Planned a trip to the Traylings camp. Asked Nancy and Hazel to go. We left at 1:30 p.m. Went through Bull Run. We visited until 3:45 then we came home. It was a very refreshing trip, everyone enjoyed it.

Uncle Alvin knows Gloria loves to speed about in her boat, and he knows how to make her happy. "We have traded Fred Henderson our speed boat for theirs. It doesn't seem possible. But Alvin bought it for me. He is very good to me." Though Uncle Alvin and Aunt Gloria argue sometimes (Alvin loves to tease her), they still adore each other. For Alvin's birthday, she buys him a trolling rod, and they go for a ride and troll a link for supper. And sometimes when she is feeling blue, Alvin takes her for a rowboat ride, which is the Smith Inlet equivalent of taking your wife out on a date!

The day after Aunt Gloria gets her new boat, she needs a reason to use it.

> Hazel and I went over to Boswell in the speed-boat today to get some groceries. The boat ran fine. Went to the A-frame first. Had quite a time with the shift, lots of fun though. We took our dinner [dinner is lunch] and ate it up on the trail leading to the oil dock.

But the next trip out, the Volvo breaks down and Lance has to tow her boat in. And this is the continuing saga of Gloria and her boats. She is elated when they are running well, and she speeds here and there. Then something happens to the boat—she hits something or it breaks down for one of a myriad of different reasons—and she is sad. Grumpy even. "And who knows when Alvin will get around to fixing it." Parts are ordered, Alvin finds time to fix it, and she is happy again.

When the weather turns in May, Aunt Gloria is going somewhere in her boat almost every day. She and Hazel (and us kids, of course) eat lunch on the beach then fill bags with dirt to take home for the flower-boxes. She and Hazel visit the Trayling camp in the Ahclakerho, then shoot the Bull Run to Takush to see Joyce Egolf, who is teaching there. They arrive home late for getting supper. Sometimes Aunt Gloria and Helen go to the tiny sand beach nearby to picnic by themselves, and sometimes she loads all of us kids in her boat and goes to get the mail—or the freight or anywhere just for the ride!

"A lovely day," says Aunt Gloria. "Decided to go to Randall Log. I took all the little kids—Marcia, Roland, Dennis, Helen and Gayle. We got up there about lunchtime. Just before lunch all the children went swimming. The water was real warm. It was a rough trip back. This boat isn't waterproof! We got wet."

And that's my memory of most of our rides! Beautiful going, pounding coming back! It could hurt—your innards leaping up inside you and pounding down hard. Pound, spray, pound, spray, pound, spray, on and on and on. But Aunt Gloria's boating enthusiasm is contagious, and we are all caught up in the ride.

Gloria and Alma Knopp boating to Margaret Bay

CHAPTER 35

GMG, RANDALL AND THE VISITING PREACHERS

Randall Logging is at the head of Boswell Inlet, and there are lots of kids we like to play with while our moms visit. Aunt Gloria's diary says:

> March 26, Sunday: This was a beautiful day. Hazel and I and all our little ones took flour and stuff for the makings of gluten, boarded the speed-boat and went up to Randall Log and taught the ladies how to make gluten. It was fun. We ate lunch with them all and had a lovely time together.

The owners of Randall Logging are brothers Cecil and Gordon Bader. Cecil and Harty have three kids: Gary, Norman and Cheryl, and Gordon and Joyce have Larry and Susan. Don Kaufman works for them, and Don and Marg have three children named Barbara, Brian and Brenda.

When the Baders started their company in 1956, they were in the Naysash Inlet, off Smiths. The GMG and Randall men really got to know each other while fighting fire in the forest fire of 1958; the source of the fire was Randall Logging's machine shop! The morning of the fire, the Randall Log ladies saw the shop on fire and tried to get the men's attention, but all they had was a heavy old rowboat with one oar! The frightened ladies managed somehow to make it to the boom and alert the men, but they were too late. The fire had made the leap to the trees, and the forest was ablaze. Every day the forestry airplane collected firefighters from the nearby logging camps and flew them to the forest fire near Randall's operation in the Naysash. For five days, June 18–22, Dad's logbook says, "Clive [Thorn] and Clyde on boom. Al and I fight fire."

Cecil and Gordon Bader had long before left behind their Seventh Day Adventist parents and their Seventh Day Adventist religion and were glad of it. They were far from home in remote inlets that were mostly empty but for loggers, and mostly those loggers were not the religious sort—all of which suited the brothers just fine. But in Smith Inlet, as far away from organized religion as you might imagine, here was a camp of church-going loggers. And Seventh Day Adventists, no less! It was a little disconcerting, and they may have even been annoyed by it, but they really liked Alvin and Louie. And the ladies and children got along so well too!

Then Cecil became ill and was flown out to Vancouver. The doctors could find nothing wrong with him and told him he should have a chat with his pastor. Cecil thought it was an unusual thing for the doctor to say—astonishing really—like God sending him a message. He found the phone number for the local pastor and was baptised the next Sabbath. He radioed home to tell his brother there would be no more working from Friday sundown to Saturday sundown.

When Cecil arrived back home, he was a well and happy man; he came to GMG for church on Sabbath and told his story. I can only imagine the joyous day that would have been for everyone at GMG, but Randall Log was less happy. In fact, no one at Randall Log was happy about it at all. The ladies realized they didn't know enough to make their case against Cecil, so they began collecting all the printed materials from all the mission boats to compare them with the Bible. They started a secret study group after the men went to work.

There were mission boats of several faiths that visited the inlets, so the ladies had choices. Father Fagan had a little plywood boat with a cabin and a 35hp Johnson on the back. He went up and down the coast, visiting all the camps in the name of his religion. Lance remembers Father Fagan fondly:

"We all liked him. He was very personable. He chatted with the ladies and jigged cod with us kids. One time he went to visit the Vandells in Wyclese Lagoon—they were Catholic. He arrived at the lagoon entrance when it was running out hard. There was a guy named Dick Ericson hanging out at the bottom, waiting for the tide, and Father Fagan hollered at him.

'Hey, do you think I could make it up?'

"Well, Dick Ericson saw the priest's collar and thought to make a bit of a joke. '*You* should be able to make it anywhere,' he called back.

"Father Fagan took Dick seriously and headed up. Dick watched him go in astonishment. Father Fagan made it nearly to the top, where he met a huge wave. He gunned his boat to get over the wave, and the next thing he knew, his boat was sitting on land, between two stumps, facing back down the narrows. When Father Fagan was rescued at slack tide, Dick figured God had been on Father Fagan's side despite his foolishness because both boat and driver were none the worse for wear.

"Once, Fred and I were going to Dawsons from Smiths. It was a nice day, and we spotted a little boat way out beyond canoe rocks. There was a guy in the back pulling on the outboard. We went over to see if he needed help. By the time we got there the guy was resting. It was Father Fagan.

'Father, do you need a tow? We'll tow you to Dawsons.'

'No, no, I'll be fine. It'll start on the fiftieth pull,' Father Fagan said.

'What number are you at?'

'I'm at forty-eight.'

"So we stood by watching, ready to give a tow. But sure enough, the motor started on the fiftieth pull!"

Sometimes, all the mission boats happened in to camp at the same time. If one boat arrived and saw the "enemy ship" docked, they didn't turn away, they stopped in for a visit with an old friend. One evening, Father Fagan with his little outboard boat, Reverend Bob Burrows from the *Thomas Crosby IV*, and Elder Ron Reimche from the *Northern Light* were all sitting on Alvin and Gloria's couch. It was a jovial evening, and the pastors were teasing each other. The United Church and the Catholic Church stood right next to each other in Ocean Falls, and recently Reverend Burrows had slipped on the icy steps of his church and cracked some ribs.

"I bet you poured water on my steps, didn't you?" Reverend Burrows said to Father Fagan.

Uproarious laughter.

"I've got to get a picture of this!" said Alvin. "Look at this! Three religions sitting beside each other right here on my couch."

And he took the photo: Father Fagan, Pastor Ron Reimche and Reverend Bob Burrows all lined up on the couch.

"The shantymen came in a few times in the early years too," Lance remembers. "They had loud music and beat drums and cymbals. But the most frequent was the *Thomas Crosby IV*. They brought the doctor from Bella Bella. The *Columbia*, the Anglican mission boat, never made it as far north as Smiths."

And now it's the spring of 1961, and it seems to be the spring for visiting preachers! The mission boat *Northern Light* arrives in April and uses Takush as home base. They bring boxes of clothes and food for the village, and they have meetings and show pictures and visit all the camps. On Sabbaths Pastor Ron Reimche preaches in the schoolhouse at the village in the morning and in the schoolhouse at GMG in the afternoon.

We all love it when the Reimches visit. Mrs. Reimche brings us strange foods to try, like avocados and green peppers. And Pastor Ron is a special kind of pastor. The first time the *Northern Light* went into Wyclese to see the Vandells (with Lance at the wheel), Pastor Ron could see that the Vandells were busy roofing a house.

"He got his tool belt on before we even landed," Lance remembers, "and went straight up onto the roof to help."

Extra efforts are made for church when the Reimches are here. And even more so when the group of visiting preachers arrive. Visitors, including the Hendersons from Moses Inlet, come to hear the preachers and then stay all day, sometimes overnight. The ladies are feeding a lot of people. Gloria draws a backdrop picture on the school blackboard on Friday nights, and she sings a solo, "Beyond the Sunset." There is special music at all the meetings. Gloria, Clyde and Lance sing "Shepherd Divine," and Gloria sings duets with Hazel and with Clyde. Clyde sings "His Eye Is on the Sparrow," a rendition which is remembered even today for its beauty and sincerity.

The first of the visiting preachers, Elder N. as Gloria calls him, arrives, and she makes him seasick trying to show him the sights in her speed-boat. Elder Kuester flies in next, and then somebody Aunt Gloria calls Elder H. (John Hnatyshyn) because, for obvious reasons, she can't remember how to spell his name.

The *Northern Light* and the *Silver Tide* (Clyde and Nancy's boat) ferry them around to speak at Takush, Margaret Bay, Boswell, GMG Logging, Stevens Logging, Saari Logging, Nalos Landing, Randall Logging, Ladret Logging, and Vandell Logging. They hold meetings in cookhouses and net-lofts and schools. The Vandell camp in Wyclese Lagoon is the trickiest to visit. The *Northern Light* is left at Stevens, and Lance takes the preachers into the lagoon in the speed-boat for an evening meeting.

Aunt Gloria says in her diary: "They had to come out in the dark, and the ministers were a little afraid, but Lance does know what he is doing."

Mrs. Reimche says in her book *Frontier Footprints*, "... as the channel narrowed, it became churning, fighting, swirling ... Lance poured on the power, and like a tiger, the engine sprang to the attack ... the speed boat reeled, twisted, and fought its way at planing speed against the torrent ... with the aid of a spotlight, we cleared the rocky shoals ...."

Lance, who has been through the narrows at least a hundred times, remembers, and, chuckling, says, "Mrs. Reimche prayed a prayer of thankfulness to God for getting us safely through the narrows."

The preachers only stay a few days, but their visit is life changing. On May 17, Gloria's diary says, "This was indeed a beautiful day. Also a day for rejoicing. Hazel and I went up to Randall Log, and on our way up we met the *Northern Light*, and they told us that Harty, Joyce and Gordon were ready for baptism. Hazel and I went up, and Harty could hardly wait to tell us. We all wept for joy. Thank God for His wonderful works."

Mrs. Gertrude Reimche Machan wrote the story in her book *Frontier Footsteps*. On the day Pastor Ron baptised Cecil's wife, brother and sister-in-law, she recorded Cecil's words: "Today we see a victory for God's kingdom because the Lord still has His fishers of men, searching even this remote inlet for His jewels."

Now the Randall Log ladies want the recipe for gluten, and everyone wants a floating church in Smith Inlet.

GMG Gluten Steaks
(Updated by Helen and Gayle)

To make the broth, add to the pot and bring to a boil:
3 qt. water
1 large onion, chopped
Garlic, fresh or powdered, if desired
1 bay leaf
½ – ⅔ cup soy sauce
2 Tbsp broth seasoning (these days use Better than Bovril veg paste)

To make the steaks, mix together:
2 cups gluten flour [In 1961, the ladies would have washed the starch out of plain flour to create the dough]
2 cups of water, or cooled, strained broth [Or, Helen says, 1½ cups water, ½ cup soy sauce and 4 Tbsp nutritional yeast flakes. Gloria and Hazel's washed-flour dough would have had no flavour, soaking up all the flavour from the broth.]
Pour liquid into the flour and mix quickly. Form into a two-inch log. Leave ten minutes. Slice ¼ inch slices off, flatten with hands and drop in boiling broth. Simmer thirty minutes with the lid on. Turn off heat and leave 'til cold.

Drain steaks, keeping the broth for gravy. The steaks can be fried as they are or ground for roast or burgers. To fry the steaks, dip them in a mix of ⅔ cup flour and ⅓ cup nutritional yeast flakes and fry in hot oil in a frying pan. These can be served plain or smothered in mushrooms, onions and gravy and baked in the oven. The steaks also make a favourite sandwich with mayonnaise and pickle.

Northern Light docked in front of schoolhouse

CHAPTER 36

BOATS!

A boat is so essential, and so much a part of daily life on the water that it becomes almost like a friend. For some unknown reason, boats are referred to as female. She takes you through a harrowing sea, and you praise her. After a long trip, she feels like home. When she doesn't start, you're angry with her. And she always holds a fond place in your heart, even when you have sold her and bought a new one. So the history of boats in the inlet is a history of the people who loved them, and the people who loved them feel like their boats are an important part of their history.

Originally, the boat of necessity was a dugout cedar tree; the Gwa'sala were renowned for creating and trading canoes, and there were still some canoes at the village in the 1960s. Then the canneries moved in with their little double-ended gillnet skiffs. There were still some of those around in the 1960s too. But soon, the boat of choice was one made of wood planks with a gas engine to power it.

GMG went through a few boats. The first was the *Stewart K*, which burned to the waterline. Then the *Rosebud*—one of those old double-ended, hand-haul gill netters with a two-cylinder "putt-putt" Easthope engine on it— got them by until they purchased the *Westpoint*. The thirty-four-foot *Westpoint* served as camp tender and gill netter until 1953, when Alvin and Louis returned after their year away and each bought a new gill netter.

Alvin fished the *Tye Pass* for the 1953 fishing season, and the *Rolamar* was ready for the 1954 season. Roy got too seasick to be a fisherman, but he kept the *Westpoint* until he left in 1955, when he sold it to Cecil Bader of Randall Logging. Later, Cecil would sell it to Robert Walkus in exchange for labour.

Arthur Crooks built a boat by following the plans Don had drawn up, but it blew up four years later, after which he commissioned the *Sather Maid*. Clyde bought the *Sea Gypsy* when he came back from seminary in 1950, and later the *Silver Tide*, which he eventually sold to Don Kaufman. George Egolf's boat, the *Joy Lynn*, also called GMG home for several years. Each boat, and today many of them are only boat names, brings enough memories of people and places and adventures to fill its own book.

Frank Johnson built a new boat he and Charlie G. designed. Old Chief George, who was a renowned carver, advised Frank on his use of wood. He told Frank to use yellow cedar for the keel, keelson, timbers, deck beams, etc., a natural crook yellow cedar for the bow stem, Pacific yew for the ribs, and western cedar for the planking. To curve the yew wood ribs, Frank placed a few of them at a time into a six-inch pipe full of fresh water that was placed on a slight slant. He then boiled the water (and the ribs) with several pressured naphtha-gas camp-stoves positioned under the pipe. When the ribs were ready, he rapidly fitted them into place. Frank named his new boat *Nuyims*, after his wife Ada. Nuyims is the name Edward Walkus gave their schoolteacher years before; it means "clever" or "smart."

Boat fondness extends to visiting boats as well. The *Tahine* loudly brought the Hendersons, the *Central Isle* brought the Baders, the *Advise* carried John Moore and Auntie Belle. Sometimes a boat brought apprehension or work. The sight of the *Lillian D* meant the forestry officer and all his regulations. The *Grisabel* came to tow away booms. Later, huge self-loading barges, looking enormous in our little bay arrived with boom-boats and with loaders to feed.

In the summer, fishing boats popped in, usually on Saturdays, so their skippers could attend church and get fed. They carried our favorite fishermen, like Gervis Betts, Andy Waterman, Carl Janke, Frank Johnson, Fred and Don Anderson, the Henderson boys, even Lance and Lloyd.

Fancy yachts from far away came to Smith Inlet too. When camp was in McBride Bay, Bob Hope and Bing Crosby came in looking for water. The GMG men gave them access to our water source, and they filled their tanks. The ladies were twitterpated, hoping to get a glimpse of Bing.

Some of those yachties didn't know what they were doing. One skipper hit a rock so hard it ripped a hole in the bow and threw one of the lifeboats onto shore. When the skipper went after it, he somehow also lost the boat he was using to get to shore and couldn't get back to the yacht. One of the loggers happened along and found the yachters fishing off their sinking yacht while their skipper shivered on the shore.

Maybe the most popular visiting boats of all were the mission boats. The *Thomas Crosby IV* visited most often in the early years, then the *Northern Light*. When the mission boats came in, there were movies and books and potlucks. The *Thomas Crosby IV* sometimes brought a doctor and a nurse, and then I tried my best to avoid it. But usually, I ended up sitting in the salon anyway, the nurse scratching me with smallpox or poking me with a needle. Before the famous Dr. Darby retired, the *Wm. H. Pierce* brought him with his wife, who was a nurse, and they offered check-ups and shots.

The really big boats—the steamships *Cardena* and *Camosun*, the oil tankers, and the freight boats—didn't come to us, we went to them. When the freight boat came into Boswell twice a month in summer and once a month in winter, we called it "boat day." Sometimes one of the men would pick up freight, but usually everybody went. We turned it into a mini holiday, visiting with people from the village and other camps, running around the net-lofts, racing up and down the trails and the huge water pipe, eating candy from the store, waiting for the freight boat.

The littlest boats were as important as the big ones. They served as lifeboats on the bigger boats, transported us from anchorage to beach and provided hours of exploration for us kids. In the early days, when the gas boat was away, a rowboat was the only boat left in camp. Don built the *Wakini*, Dad built the plywood rowboat *Tadpole*, and then someone built the *Banana Peel*. Fiberglass was a new concept. Lloyd remembers the first piece of fiberglass he ever saw. One day when the men returned from a business trip to Ocean Falls, Louie called everyone out to see this new, marvelous material.

"Look at this," said Louie, holding up his sample piece of fiberglass. "I can bang on it with a hammer, I can bend it, stomp on it and try to break it, and—nothing!"

He demonstrated as he spoke and sure enough, the fiberglass held firm. The next rowboat GMG bought was made of yellow fiberglass and, just as Dad said, it lasted forever—with a few patches.

They bought fiberglass workboats too. Workboats are generally unmemorable—just an open boat with an outboard motor and benches in it to transport loggers, and usually some teeth on the front for pushing things.

An exception was the *Jonah*, an old boom-boat GMG had inherited from Gildersleeve Logging. The *Jonah* was leaking, so Alvin and Louie tried to pull it up onto the A-frame float. It tipped to quite an angle when they were pulling it up, and it filled with water and sank. With two boats and a piece of haulback line, they lassoed it, shackled and choked it, and lifted it back out with the A-frame. And there it sat for a very long time, until Frank Johnson Junior got brave enough to go to the GMG office one evening and ask Alvin and Louie if he could have it. Frank Junior spent months in the boathouse at Takush bringing it back to life and turning it into a gill netter. The strange-looking boom-boat-turned-gill netter named *Jonah* brought a lot of chuckles out on the fishing grounds.

The young men in Takush loved to race their boats. They had a collection of gas boats, many of them "putt-putts"—one- or two-cylinder Easthopes and Vivians, most were unnamed. To start them you had to turn the flywheel and fiddle with the choke. Then they chugged to life with their signature popping sound.

"Generally, those boats go about six knots," Lloyd remembers. "But some of those guys could get a lot more out of them than that! They would take the boat to the beach and let it go dry, then they'd scrape it and hammer and file on their propeller and take absolutely everything off the boat—they'd even take all their finishings out! They went to great extremes. Johnny Walkus had the fastest boat. It had a Gray engine.

"So when we went to church at Takush in the brand-new *Tye Pass* from Sather Boatworks, with its 90hp Paragon Ford, here they were, all lined up, wanting to race. I was feeling so good because they had less horsepower, and I knew we would win. But we didn't! We were near the end of the pack! Same thing with the *Rolamar*, and she had a Chrysler Ace 90hp flathead."

James Walkus, who became a fishing tycoon, started fishing in 1954, the same year Louie started fishing the *Rolamar*. James was just fifteen. He found an abandoned double-ended rowing scow on the beach and asked the Boswell manager if he could have it. He patched it up with some boards and plywood that he found, and when fishing opened, he joined the other scows waiting to be towed out. BC Packers towed a string of these scows out from the Boswell dock with a gas boat.

"Where do you want to go?" they asked.

"To the lagoon," said James.

"Nope, sorry. Can't go there."

James wanted a boat with a motor so he could go where he knew the fish were. He made $250 his first week of fishing and went up to the Boswell manager's office to ask Doug Copley for a $200 loan so he could buy the *Little Billy*.

"I can't loan you money, you're too young," said Doug Copley. "Your dad would have to buy the boat for you."

His dad's floathouse was tied up at Boswell for the fishing season, way at the end of the docks. James found his dad at home, but he was drunk, so he dragged his dad out of the house, down the dock, up the ramp and to the office to sign the paperwork. Now James owned the *Little Billy*. It leaked and he had to pump it twice a day every day to keep it from sinking, but he didn't care. He could fish wherever he wanted. He out fished most everybody and upgraded boats nearly every year.

The many canneries in Smith Inlet and Rivers Inlet were all closed by the time James started fishing, but Boswell and Margaret Bay remained in Smith Inlet as fish camps for BC Packers and Canadian Fish. BC Packers packed all their fish to Namu Cannery, and Canadian Fish packed theirs to Goose Bay Cannery.

"There was no ice then," James remembers. "Sometimes the fishermen would have their fish on board for two or three days. Then the packer would take them to Namu, and it could be five or six days before it got canned."

James went away to boarding school in the winters and fished in the summers to pay for it. In the big sockeye year of 1958, he made $11,000 and saved $4,000 to buy the *Rolamar*. He was disappointed to find Louie had already sold it to Andy Waterman, but he found another boat instead. And another, and another, until in the 1980s and 90s his company, James Walkus Fishing, owned as many as nineteen seine boats at one time.

Lance and Lloyd were three and four years younger than James. They were fishing with their dad on the *Tye Pass* at the start of the 1957 season when an unusual opportunity arose. When they went to the packer to deliver their first fish of the season, the skipper told Alvin there had been a death in his family and he had to leave. He asked Alvin if he knew anybody who could run his packer for him.

"No, I can't think of anyone," said Alvin.

"What about that strapping young lad?" the skipper asked, pointing at Lance. "What's he doing?"

"Naw, he's working with me. He's only fifteen!"

But when the conversation was over, Lance stepped from the *Tye Pass* to the *Dorothy M* and spent the rest of the summer as a BC Packers skipper. He was based out of Wadhams in Rivers, and he packed fish to Namu.

The next summer he ran the sixty-five-foot *Klatawa*.

"It had a cabin in the stern, with a long bow, and a three-cylinder diesel you had to start with a blow-torch in the morning," Lance recalls. "In the fall, we ran springs to Vancouver. The springs were huge! We made ice for them, packed them in the ice and marketed them fresh. I'd load the fish and then run twenty-four to thirty hours to Vancouver. I had two deckhands, but I never left the wheel.

"Once though, I was so tired from loading the boat, I told my deckhand, 'I'm lying down, but if there's fog, get me up so I can get my bearings before it settles in.' We had no radar. The next thing I knew, the kid said, 'You better come up.' I got up and there was a whiteout! I made the kid go out on the bow to listen for the foghorn on Pine Island. Normally I went to the mainland and travelled up the mainland, but now I didn't know where to make the turn, so I had to go outside Pine.

"Well, the kid was in his Stanfields, and it was night, and there was a freezing fog. Finally, he heard the Pine Island horn. So I got my coat and went out and had the kid steer. I'd seen Dad and Louie do it this way many times. I listened to the horn. It got gradually louder. When it was at its loudest, I knew we were right across from the Pine Island lighthouse, about a mile or two out, so I listened 'til the horn started to fade, and then I knew I could make the turn. Then I'd watch for the Christie Pass Light. Goletas [Channel] was usually clear."

Later, when Alvin stopped fishing, he let Lance and Lloyd run the *Tye Pass* for a season before selling it to Carl Janke. The boys fished in Smith Inlet for a while, but James told Lance they should fish up by Namu because that was where all the girls were. He told them they could run to Ocean Falls from Namu, and there were lots of parties there.

"So we fished Namu," Lloyd says. "And James and Lance would be fooling around and they'd leave me at Namu."

Later, when Lloyd finally got his chance to go fishing on his own, he had a form of payback. Lance could never figure out how the two of them could be fishing side by side, whether it was jigging for a cod or fishing for salmon, and Lloyd would catch the fish.

But meanwhile, in Namu, Lance and his boat got into serious trouble.

"I took a couple kids out for a joyride in front of Namu in a speed-boat. It had two engines, but I only had a throttle on one engine. I opened the other right up. I hit a chunk of wood, and it hit the motor that had no throttle and we went end over end. My three passengers shot right out, but I was stuck inside, upside down. I got to the back door, but I couldn't get out—it was blocked with mattresses. I had to find the bow to breathe some air.

"I was sure I was sinking. The boat had no floatation, and the hull made cracking noises, like water pressure crushing it. It was dusk outside and dark inside the boat. I took a deep breath and went back down and kicked the windshield, but I couldn't kick it out. So I went back up to the bow for more air and went down again and managed to get the side window open. It was too small, but I had to give it a try. I went up for more air, and down again, and squeezed out. I gave a big push up so I could make it to the surface in a hurry. But I burst high out of the water—the boat was right on top! The boat wasn't sinking after all. My three passengers were on the hull of the boat, and that's what I thought was the sound of water pressure on a sinking boat."

I'm sure the story was modified for Aunt Gloria, who had a tendency to worry. As mothers do. But Lance knew where he was going in Smith Inlet even in the dark. He went everywhere in his little, open, twelve-foot boat with a 28hp outboard. He sometimes went to Vancouver in it, hugging the shoreline, "riding the breakers."

"The Gwa'sala taught me that," says Lance. "They would go out in some terrible weather, their boats loaded with people, keeping one foot on the beach."

Lance had no instruments or radio on these trips to Vancouver, and the weather report was whatever he could see for himself. If it was raining, he wore rain gear and rubber boots. If the weather became unmanageable, he was right by the beach and he could pull his boat above the high tideline, turn it over and sleep under it. It took him two days to get to Vancouver. Sometimes he stopped at the Reimche's home in Powell River for a shower, a meal, a good sleep. Sometimes he stopped at his grandparents in Parksville.

"Mom always worried about me," says Lance. "But Dad knew I'd be OK."

Eventually, all the GMG families got their own little fiberglass speed-boats with cabins, for exploring, trips to Boswell or the neighbours' or the beach. All the boys, with their need for speed, loved to borrow the family boat. Some of them found boats of their own and spent hours puttering on the motor and spinning doughnuts in front of camp. They sped ever farther away from camp, became stranded ever farther away and required rescuing ever farther away by their tired dads.

GMG's final boat, the *Surf Isle*, was launched in May of 1960. Sather Boatworks built exactly what GMG asked for: a sturdy boat for towing and transportation, forty feet long with an eleven-foot beam and five-foot draft. They traded the large Cummins they salvaged from the wrecked tanker on Calvert Island a few years earlier for a smaller, six-cylinder, 160hp Cummins diesel engine and put it in the *Surf Isle*.

The *Surf Isle* was named after the islet of the same name in Smith Sound. She was white with wood trim and an elegant shape. She could take some tough weather—green water over her cabin and the floor running like a river. She could haul freight and pull log booms. She took us on long trips to Vancouver, and she towed our homes to new places. We loved the sight of her as she came into view around the point. We dove off her roof and suntanned on her bow and painted her trim. Can you hear the love? Happily, the *Surf Isle* is still afloat in 2022. She is a gill netter, docked in Sointula, and beautifully refurbished by someone else who loves her.

Surf Isle

CHAPTER 37

SUMMER OF '61: A WINDOW INTO A TIME OF WONDER

On June 6, 1961, when I am nearing four years old, Aunt Gloria and Mom take Rolly and me to Boswell and leave us there with Ada Johnson. Aunt Gloria says, "Hazel left for town today. She is going to have an operation. I felt blue after she left." Rolly and I, standing on the dock at Boswell watching our mom speed away in Aunt Gloria's boat, feel a little blue as well. Mom tells us everything will be fine and she'll be back soon. But we don't know what an operation is, and we are nervous to stay with another family.

Frank and Ada are caretaking at Boswell, though Frank is gone fishing much of the time. Mr. and Mrs. Johnson are quiet and kind, and they always seem a bit sad. They have walls of books— Marcia loves to borrow them. She says when she grows up, she wants walls of books like Mrs. Johnson. Once when their float was tied near camp, Mom asked me to take Mrs. Johnson a bouquet of pansies; she said it would make her happy. So I rowed over to her house, timidly knocked on her door and gave her the pansies. But Mrs. Johnson didn't seem happy at all. She cried. Mom said that was because long ago she lost her own little girl who used to bring her flowers. I thought Mom was going to cry, too, telling me.

Mrs. Johnson is so nice to Rolly and me, and we always love Boswell. It has tall tarry black pilings with purple and orange starfish curved around them, and sea anemones and mussels and barnacles and other creatures clinging on below the waterline. We like to examine them from the dock when the tide is low. There are rows of docks for fishing boats and net mending, and up the ramp on top of the pilings is a big wide wharf where the freight boat comes on boat day. Around the corner are cavernous, musky net-lofts and huge rooms where the canning line used to be. There are empty houses, boardwalks and trails into the woods. There is a huge black pipe with ridges on it that brings the water; we use it like a trail and run along the top of it. Most importantly, though, there is a store—with candy in it!

The store is plugged full of one or two of every sort of thing, like rain gear, flashlights, net corks, shampoo, loaves of squishy bread, and tinned food. It is so full that things hang from the walls and the ceiling over our heads: fish gaffs and lamps and guns— even boots. Mom bought me some runners here once. It smells of cigarette smoke and something else—maybe tar from the black wooden floor, or maybe fisherman. Dennis says there's a cow hanging in the back, and the storekeeper whacks off chunks for people when they need it, but I've never seen it, and it sounds too horrible. Maybe he's teasing me. We gaze in awe at everything, but the candy counter draws us like a magnet. There are chocolate bars, and jars of suckers and gumballs and jawbreakers on the counter. If we can get a few pennies, we can buy something—five jawbreakers for a penny or ten suckers for a nickel—from the man behind the counter.

When Rolly and I stay at Boswell with Mrs. Johnson, I discover that mint grows. It is not a round white ball like Uncle Alvin keeps in his pockets, it's a leaf! I sit on the hill, fragrant with mint, and watch the busy docks below; the fishermen are getting their nets and boats ready for fishing. When Friday night comes, Mrs. Johnson puts us in a big copper tub for a bath.

Eventually, Dad comes to get us after the tug takes away his boom, and he and Marcia take care of us. When Dad's at work, we stay at Aunt Gloria's and she feeds us all lunch. We're all squished together, Marcy, Rolly and I, Dennis and Helen and the schoolboys and Rosemary on the benches around her table, eating sandwiches and soup. Mom is gone for what seems like forever.

After a month, Mom finally comes back on an airplane, and I feel safe again, hiding behind her skirt when strangers visit.

The rest of the summer is busy and fun, and Aunt Gloria tells all about it in her diary. Her sister Genevieve and other friends come to visit, and every weekend fishermen come to church and stay for dinner. Lorna Waterman, with daughters Diane and Nadine, stay for a few days while Andy is fishing his new boat, the *Rolamar*. One weekend, we have forty people at church!

Then it's time for our trip to town. Mom bakes bread and cookies, and packs all our summer clothes into a couple of suitcases. Rolly and I help Mom load things onto the *Surf Isle*—loaves of bread, cookies, peanut butter, jam, cans of soup and fruit cocktail and big rounds of hard tack. We tuck things into the tiny, narrow cupboards that appear when the table is put down from the wall, and into the cupboards under the sink. Beside the wheel is a can with a funnel shape on top. Rolly says it's the horn, and the liquid inside is apple juice. He squeezes the lever and the sound is so piercing I scream and cover my ears and Rolly gets in trouble.

Aunt Gloria is loading things onto the boat too. She brings potato salad and beans and raisin cake. Everyone is going, Mom says, so the kids will have to sleep in the hold. This sounds yucky to me because it always stinks down there. But our moms are fixing it up nice with mattresses and sleeping bags and pillows and throw up buckets. I don't get sick on the boat, but Helen does, and she's sure to get sick if she's down in the hold! When she throws up it makes me feel like throwing up too! Helen says the word "puke," but I don't like that word; it sounds too real. Mom always gets sick, so she stays flat on a bunk most of the time or sits outside on the hatch cover if the weather is nice.

Dad and Uncle Alvin fill the tanks with water and fuel. They wash the outside of the *Surf Isle*, make sure the bilge is pumped out and add oil and grease to unknown places.

In the night, we stumble to the *Surf Isle* in our pajamas and climb over the gunnel and down the ladder into the hold—boys on one side, girls on the other. The motor is running; it sounds like a big purring cat. I like it. When I wake up, we're in some big waves, and Helen is throwing up into her bucket. The hatch is cracked open for fresh air, and spray mists down onto our sleeping bags. Back and forth, back and forth we roll.

I have to go to the bathroom, so Marcy helps me crawl up the ladder and open the hatch. We creep carefully to the cabin and slide open the heavy door into the galley. The floor is rocking back and forth in here too. The table has been unhooked from the wall and let down, and Uncle Alvin and Aunt Gloria are sitting braced in behind it eating canned fruit and hard tack.

Marcy tells Aunt Gloria that Helen threw up in her bucket, and Aunt Gloria scurries out to take care of it. Dad is taking his turn at the wheel, standing, holding onto the big knobs sticking out of it, turning back and forth, back and forth. He's munching hard tack and looking cheery and asks how I am doing. I can see Mom down on her bunk, lying on her side, looking sick. The bathroom is down the steps from the wheel, on the right, just below Dad's feet. Mom murmurs, "You kids doing OK?" from her bunk.

After the rocking, we come into smoother water, and Aunt Gloria fixes some breakfast. We take turns crowding into the galley, then sit out on the hatch to eat our cereal. We cruise all day. We go past islands and inlets, inlets and islands forever. Trees and water as far as we can see. Aunt Gloria makes us lunch and dinner from all the things we brought, and Mom helps when it's really calm. In the evening, we can see patches of lights from the towns on the shore. When we're tired, we climb down into the hold and sleep. All night we travel, the motor purring. We wake up just before we get there, and we have some more waves. They're steeper, faster waves than before, and we let ourselves slide back and forth, bumping into each other, laughing.

Then suddenly it's silky smooth and we see huge buildings lit up and an enormous bridge looming in front of us. I go outside and stare straight up at the bottom of the Lion's Gate Bridge as we sail under. On land, lights are moving, red and white, like rivers. I ask Mom, "What are all those funny boats?" and everyone laughs. It feels different here; fast and bright and exciting. Everyone changes from bored to busy, and we start packing up our things and tidying up the boat to get off and go visit our grammas and grampas.

When we come back home again, my cousin Bruce Rafuse comes with us, and he and David Thorn paint everything that needs paint. Uncle Alvin and Dad do maintenance jobs, Uncle Clyde is away fishing, and Lance and Lloyd are gone packing for BC Packers in Rivers Inlet. We kids swim and play and laze about on the sun-warmed floats.

We go to Rivers Inlet, and Mom visits with a lady wearing red lipstick, who is cracking crab and smoking a cigarette. All of these things are intriguing to me—the lipstick, the crab cracking and especially the smoking. Lots of ladies in the other camps smoke. They have low, gravelly voices, and their laughter turns to coughing. Is it hot, all that smoke going inside you? Does it taste like campfire? Mom and Dad tell me never to smoke; it will kill me, they say. So I watch in fascination as the pretty lipsticked ladies smoke one cigarette after another, the red-stained cigarette angled elegantly between their fingers, little puffs coming out of their shiny lips. Are they dying? At Boswell, Helen and I buy cigarette candies and pretend smoke.

On a random Wednesday, we go to the beach. "We all got up and decided to go to the beach for the day," says Aunt Gloria's diary. "We had dinner [lunch], and after dinner Alvin, Louis and the kids went swimming. Hazel and I sat under a shady tree and talked. After the sun started to set, we went home."

The moms and dads are different when we go to the beach. In fact, it seems beaches are magical at changing adults—at making them more fun. They wear bathing suits and go swimming and sit around the fire chatting with us like they have all the time in the world. They show us animal tracks, hunt for moon snails and even bounce on the bouncy logs with us. The dads build a fire, the moms lay food out on a log—potato salad and baked beans and sandwiches to toast on the fire. Sometimes they put potatoes or corn on the cob in the fire to eat with butter, and they bring tubs of cookies, and marshmallows to roast. There is no better place to be in the whole world!

Then our taps run dry.

> August 9, Wednesday: The water is off this morning. There is no water in the creek. I don't like getting salt water to wash dishes with. We have to use water off the *Surf Isle* for drinking and cooking.

But Randall Log is connected to a good strong creek, so when our water goes dry, we go to Randall and swim with our friends, and the moms do their wash, and everyone has a bath.

The Randall Log folks invite us all over on the weekend.

> August 12, Sabbath: Foggy this morning but we went to Randall Log for church. We had to steer by compass. We had a big gathering at Randall. All

came out. Even Bob. We ate at Cecil's, the boys ate at Kaufman's, Hazel and Louis at Gordon's. After dinner we all went for a walk up their new logging road. What a pleasant day we all had together. God has blessed them. We came home about 7 p.m.

August 15, Tuesday: This morning was foggy again. It seems that we get it day after day, but no rain!!! ... Hazel and I went to Randall Log to go swimming. It was hot in there, and we really had a good swim after supper with Joyce. Came home before dark.

August 22 is Aunt Gloria's thirty-ninth birthday.

Got our work done early, and Hazel and I and kids got in the speed-boat with our dirty clothes and went up to Randall to wash them. It was a lovely day. It was my birthday, and the ladies sprung a party on me. Harty made the cake. I washed at Marg's. I like her. I also cut Joyce's and Marg's hair. We didn't get home 'til 5 p.m. Hazel asked us all to supper, and there we had a cake so I really was well treated. Hung out my clothes.

The lack of water stops nothing. The following weekend, GMG hosts the Henderson family, the two Bader families, the Egolfs, the Moores, Jessie and Maurie Saari, somebody named Ralph Amte, Freddie Anderson, and Lloyd and Lance, who are home for the weekend from Rivers. On Sunday, we have a picnic at the lake with all the same people. And then, finally, after eighteen days with no water in our taps, the rain comes. It pours and pours, and we have endless water and we wish it would stop.

And summer is over.

CHAPTER 38

BACK TO THE KLAK

D on Kaufman is trying to stay away from the whole church thing. In fact, he decides to move away from Randall Log altogether and go out on his own. Dad and Uncle Alvin tow him to the head of Smiths in September. It's a long tow from the head of Boswell to the head of Smiths—about as far away from Randall Log as they can get. It takes the *Surf Isle* almost two twenty-four-hour days to tow; first the buildings, then the A-frame.

Then we move. With the Kaufman move and ours, the *Surf Isle* tows for a week straight, night and day—excluding Sabbath. Aunt Gloria says she doesn't want to move. McBride Bay feels like the centre of things, and now we're moving back into the Ahclakerho—down its long hallway into one of the bedroom-like basins near the Bull Run. The A-frame goes first, then we go.

> Sept 17, Sunday: We are towing tonight. Got as far as Broad Reach. Had to stop and wait for tide.

> Sept 18, Monday: Still towing today. It is beautiful today and so still. We are tied in our new place in the Klakerho, and it is pretty here. Cleaned walls and cupboards. Scrubbed floor, cleaned out the speed-boat. We had sun on camp until 7:30 tonight.

The children all went swimming. I cut Joyce's hair. Also my own. Rosemary did Joyce's dishes.

Marcia is jumping-up-and-down happy that George and Joyce Egolf, with children Chris and Joy Lynn (and soon, baby Richard) are now living in camp. Joy Lynn is her bosom buddy. Joyce has resigned after teaching three years at the Takush School, and George will be falling for GMG when fishing is over.

So here we are, back in the Klak! I've never lived here before, but the older folks have. GMG is beside the Bull Run again, and Ada Johnson is teaching at the Takush School again. We visit all the old haunts: Mom's abandoned garden, the old mill site where they used to picnic, the secret caves holding bones and other things that Chief George says are not from his tribe. We wonder who the earlier tribe could have been. Old stories are remembered and retold; the early years after the war, and the epic year of 1950 when Frank and Ada, Don and Claire pulled their homes through the Bull Run at the request of Chief George, in this same month of September, eleven years ago.

It feels like the Ahclakerho is totally secluded from the rest of the world, but no one seems to have any trouble finding us. It's a busy little camp. Aunt Gloria's diary, straight up, lets us feel it:

> September 19, Tuesday: It was raining when we got up this morning, but it slowly cleared and became a beautiful day. The Finning tractor salesman came in, and he and the pilot had dinner with us. Also the BC Airways plane came in with Mrs. Thorn's suitcase. Which made Mrs. Thorn happy. Louis and Hazel, Gayle and Helen went to Ocean Falls to get teeth fixed.

> September 20, Wednesday: This was a beautiful day. But cool. Alvin got the boathouse through the Bull Run. I wrote six letters, and a plane was

in and brought in our plant parts. We can now have electricity. (Power plant quit last Friday.) Had potato soup for dinner. Marcia and Roland ate with us because their folks were at Ocean Falls. Made fruit salad for supper. Marcia and Roland ate with us for supper too.

September 21, Thursday: This was a beautiful day. Alvin got the plant running, and I did the wash late. I was glad to get it done. Salos also came in today. She is staying over the weekend. Roy [Salo] took Bruce [Salo] and went to Campbell River to get his eyes tested. Ruth and I both ironed, and we got it all done. I was sure tired tonight. I phoned Lance tonight, and he was at Parksville.

September 22, Friday: Got up and did my work up fast. Made pies, beet pickles, yellow salad, gluten, cleaned house, changed beds, made sandwiches. We, Ruth and I, took the speed-boat and went up to Randall Log to get Mrs. McGee [Joyce Egolf's mom, teaching at Randall] and George Duke [sleigh builder]. We met Clyde and George coming home … we went on up and visited for a while, brought George back the long way around, but I made it. Prepared my Sabbath program. Hazel and Louis home this morning. Helen had four teeth pulled.

September 23, Sabbath: Pleasant surprise to see so many out today. [GMG is farther away from the other camps now, with tidal runs to wait for.] The *Northern Light* also came in. We were all very happy. I sang for Elder Reimche's service. The Randall Log families went to the beach after church. I had Salos and Clyde and Nancy for our dinner guests. After

Salos left, I went over to Traylings camp and visited with the fellas. Just to say hello. They were very friendly.

September 24, Sunday: Alvin and Louis logged today [first logging on new show]. We woke up, and it was raining hard. I was very disappointed because I wanted to take Mrs. McGee home today. I left right after dinner. Mrs. Reimche went with me, also Hazel. We took Bonnie to Boswell for Bill Slader to keep. She didn't want to stay. [A sad day for me. Mom gave away our beloved dog, Bonnie, because she was getting nippy with the camp kids.] We were at Randall log for a few minutes, and then we started home. It was a bit rough, and the boat didn't run good. We shot the Bull Run. I was glad to get home. Reimche had a meeting tonight. The folks from over the way [Takush] came over.

September 25, Monday: Another lovely day. Alvin and Louis went to work. I visited with Reimches all morning. Lance came home before noon. He sure looked good to me. Nancy and Clyde are busy packing. Nancy looks tired tonight. The Reimches left for the head today. I made supper for Nancy and Clyde tonight. Made bread today. It smells good. Lance got a new needle for the record player.

September 26, Tuesday: This was a quiet, still day. A big ring around the sun. Clyde and Nancy finished packing today, will leave at high tide. I made a trip to Randall Log to get the tarps for Clyde. My boat didn't work good at first so Alvin fixed it. It ran good then—I got there in fifty-five minutes. Calm all the way. Met Clyde in the Bull Run. They have gone now. I sure will miss Clyde.

I love him so much. Lance ran donkey today. It is raining hard tonight.

October 24, Tuesday: Married nineteen years today. Doesn't seem possible. This was a horrible day, but I managed to get my washing done and dried. I did my ironing tonight and was just getting ready to go to bed when Hazel and Louis came in with a lovely chocolate cake. We had a very nice time together thinking back over the years. They will soon be married fifteen years.

I like to think of them, sitting around the table eating chocolate anniversary cake and "thinking back over the years." I wonder if they retell their romance stories—Alvin and Gloria's numerous attempts to be wed, Louis and Hazel's short courtship, mostly by mail. Perhaps they recall the first days of their GMG partnership, when Clyde and Don were with them.

"And then Louie shows up with this tall blonde," Alvin says, in his version of the story, begun on that November night long ago in 1945.

Mom's "Lovely Chocolate Cake" Recipe

When Mom makes cake, I scoot a chair from the table up to the counter, lean across it, under the cabinets, and watch. I love when Mom bakes. She dips flour out into a sifter. She gets out the little spoons with numbers on them, all different sizes, and spoons different powders into the sifter. Then swish, swish, swish, the white powder falls like a rain shower into her bowl. She cracks goopy eggs and puts them in a bowl and adds things and gets out the eggbeater and beats them. On and on, round and round 'til she's tired. There is a tiny bottle of the most lovely smelling stuff on the counter, and I beg and beg to taste it.

"PLEASE Mom, PLEASE."

"You won't like it."

"Oh please, it smells so good! Can't I just try?"

So she lets me taste it, and I choke and spit. How can something smelling so delicious taste so terrible?

"I told you you wouldn't like it," says Mom, grinning her mischievous grin!

The liquid from the bottle goes in the bowl too. Just a tiny bit. Good. Then the magic. She mixes all the things in all the bowls together with her eggbeater, and it turns out creamy brown and delicious looking. I really want a spoonful, but Mom says no, I won't like it. I try to believe her this time. But when I am old enough to make a cake of my own, I'm going to have a big spoonful.

Mom checks the dial on the stove and puts the cake in the oven. Now we have to wait. While the cake is in the oven, there is a most amazing smell, nothing like any of the things Mom put in the bowl. And somehow, magically, it has all turned into a chocolate cake, soft and fragrant, steaming on the cooling rack.

Mom's "Lovely Chocolate Cake"

3 oz. unsweetened cacao powder
½ cup sweet milk
½ cup granulated sugar
½ cup butter
1 tsp. vanilla extract
¾ cup granulated sugar
3 eggs
1¾ cups sifted Purity Flour
½ tsp. salt

2 tsp. baking powder
½ tsp. baking soda
¾ cup sweet milk

Combine first three ingredients and cook to a thick paste. Set aside to cool. Cream butter until it is soft and creamy, and add vanilla while creaming. Gradually add sugar and beat until mixture is light and fluffy. Beat eggs with rotary beater until foamy and add gradually to fat/sugar mixture, beating thoroughly. Add chocolate paste and blend well. Mix flour, salt, baking powder and baking soda and sift four or five times. Add dry ingredients alternately with milk, making three or four additions, beginning and ending with dry ingredients. Stir gently and quickly until batter is well-blended, but do not overmix. Spread carefully into well-greased eight-inch square cake pan and bake in moderate oven (350 – 375°F.) for 45 – 50 minutes. Allow baked cake to "set" for 15 – 20 minutes before removing from pan. Cool and spread with desired icing.

CHAPTER 39

IN WITH THE NEW

Mom is gone to the doctor in Vancouver, and I'm at Aunt Gloria's house when the plane arrives with my new friend on it. It's November 23, 1961, a Thursday. The men are at work, the floats are dusted white with our first snowfall. At the sound of the plane roaring up to the airplane float, school lets out so the students can welcome GMG's new family: Ernie and Alma Knopp and their children Ken, Doug and Laverne.

It is a rare thing for a new family to move to GMG, so it is a momentous occasion. Everyone has their own memory of the arrival. Aunt Gloria says, "The Knopp family came today. They seem to like it here. I will keep them fed until boat day, then they will have their own things."

Alma saw the vast emptiness of the inlets on her way in, and she sees camp and her new house, the one my parents first lived in, and is thinking, *Oh my, what have we done, what have we done?*

Ernie goes straight to work shovelling the snow off the floats, and Dennis thinks, *Why does that man wear the beak of his hat straight up? And why is he shovelling off the snow? I wanted to make a snowman with it.*

Helen notices Laverne's little red boots right away and wants some.

270

Marcia is excited to see that Mrs. Knopp has a guitar, and she wishes she could play it.

Dennis and Roland can't wait to show the new boys a thing or two, and Ken and Doug are eager to see anything they're willing to show.

We all gather in Aunt Gloria's kitchen. I can't stop staring at Laverne. She is about my age, with long brown hair. She is not afraid, or "bushed" like me. She walks right up to me.

"Do you know how to skip?"

Immediately I feel inadequate. I have tried and tried, but I cannot skip. Reluctantly, I say, "No, do you?"

"Yes, I do!" she says. "This is how you do it."

Laverne throws her skipping rope over her head, it lands on the big green and white tiles of Aunt Gloria's kitchen floor in a curve before her, and she steps over it. I feel so relieved. She can't skip either! I feel like we will be friends. And we are. Forever friends!

The Knopps are immediately thrown into the middle of things. The day after they arrive, Ernie goes to work with Alvin, Louie, Lance and Vivian Paul, with George Egolf and his brother Fred falling. Ken and Doug attend their first day of school. Saturday, we load into two boats and head to Randall Log for church. It's a big crowd—the Egolf family, Dad, Marcia, Rolly, me and Rosemary on the *Joy Lynn*, and on the *Surf Isle* the McGill family, the Knopp family, Gloria's parents Bill and Alice Gildersleeve, Molly Thorn and David.

Sunday is boat day, and the Knopp family's belongings and groceries arrive so they can set up house. On Monday, another family moves to camp: Vivian and Janet Paul with their girls Agnes, Rose and little Dorothy. Vivian has been working for

271

GMG for years now, since he married Janet, Charlie G.'s daughter. They're from Takush, but they have decided to live here with us for a while. I like Mrs. Paul. When she smiles at me her dimples show and you really think she means it. Agnes and Rose are older than me, both in school already, and Dorothy is little.

So when Mom comes home there are two new families at GMG, and she has a surprise for everyone! She announces that there will soon be a new baby in camp!

A few days after Ernie starts work, George Egolf breaks his leg while falling and they fly him out to Vancouver, so Ernie has to become a faller. But it turns cold, and the snow gets tall on the floats and deep in the woods, so the men can't go to work. They fix things around camp and go hunting, trying to shoot a goose for Christmas dinner. George can't go because he's on crutches, but it turns out he's the only one who gets a goose—he shoots it from his front porch!

On Christmas Day, Gloria cooks four ducks for Christmas dinner and has the Knopp family over. We have the Egolfs over; they bring their goose—watch out for the buckshot!—and the Pauls go to Takush to be with their family.

On New Year's Eve Day, Joyce Egolf takes all the kids for a walk in the Bull Run at low tide, and in the evening everybody who is old enough to stay awake—which doesn't include me; I'm sent to bed at the regular time—gathers at Alvin and Gloria's house to see in the new year. At midnight there are loud bangs and lots of hollering and running up and down the floats in front of my window. The new year of 1962 is heralded by five surprise, successive explosions of dynamite in five different parts of camp. It turns out the new guy, Uncle Ernie, is not only about work! He also has a mischievous streak!

CHAPTER 40

DRUMROCK

On the other side of the Bull Run is "the wreck," its jagged edges sticking out of the water where it broke its back on the rock upon which it still rests. We slow down to have a look. Dad says that the old, rusty metal above the water is just a small piece of what was once a great sailing ship.

"There used to be a lot more of it above the water," says Dad. "Every year it settles down a little lower."

I shiver and imagine a great sailing ship under the dark surface of the water, right here below us in Takush Harbour. Every ship has a story and people. What is the story of the jagged pieces of rusty steel submerging into a great sailing ship underneath our little speed-boat?

The *Drumrock* was a Cape Horn windjammer built in Leith, Scotland, in 1891 as a four-masted barque, 329 feet long and 3,182 gross tonnage. She started out as part of the "Drum Line," a fleet of British merchant ships owned by Gillison and Chadwick, who named each of their boats with the Celtic prefix "Drum." For several years she serviced the British colonies; there is a lovely photograph online of *Drumrock* in her prime.[9] In 1899, she was sold to a German company and renamed the *Persimmon*. As the *Persimmon*, she carried nitrate from Chile around Cape Horn. Just before the First World War, she was sold to another German company and renamed the *Helwig Vinnen*. The *Helwig Vinnen* left Germany in the spring of 1914 carrying a load of coke to a copper smelter in Santa Rosalia, Mexico, and on her arrival in August was interned there for the entire length of the war. After sitting idle in the burning sun for nine years, she would never jam the wind again.

In 1923, the now derelict sailing ship was finally bought, towed to San Francisco and sold again in 1925 to her final owner, Hecate Straits Towing Company, Vancouver, BC. The new owners valued her steel hull. There is a story in the October 1925 issue of the *BC Lumberman* explaining the details of the ship's transformation.[10] Her new owners removed the top-rigging and installed state-of-the art equipment at great expense to make her into a self-loading and unloading log barge capable of carrying a million board feet of logs. And they gave her back her original name, *Drumrock*.

On February 1, 1927, the steam tug *Pacific Monarch* was making its way across Queen Charlotte Sound towing the *Drumrock*, loaded with hemlock and spruce from the Queen Charlotte Islands. Captain Hugh Stanley McLellan didn't like the southeast gale with forty-knot winds, and he sought shelter in Takush Harbour. He entered the harbour mid-afternoon when the tide was going out. While he was anchoring his tow, the loaded *Drumrock*, drawing about twenty-two feet, arrested on a rock just in front of Drumrock Island. At low tide, 7 p.m., she broke in half. The

---

[9] The 'Drumrock' anchored in an unidentified harbour [PRG 1373/6/49]. Photograph, State Library of South Australia "collections.slsa.gov.au/resource/PRG", March 3, 2007 (Part of the A.D. Edwardes Collection)
[10] Rick James, *West Coast Wrecks: & Other Maritime Tales*. Madeira Park: Harbour Publishing Co. Ltd., 2011

bow and stern sank, resting on the bottom and leaving the jagged midship exposed above the rock.

"That would have been an amazing sight to see," Dad says. "There would have been a terrible racket, all that metal wrenching apart! And all those logs rolling off into the harbour! The village must have heard it!" Dad opens the throttle and we pick up speed. "But nobody died!" he assures us cheerily, his voice raised over the roar of the motor. "Everyone lived to tell the tale!"

The *Drumrock,* world traveller and bearer of stories, belongs to us now. She is part of our view, our history—a navigational point of reference. And she still has a bowsprit, an island named after her and a little teeny picture of herself on the chart!

CHAPTER 41

MOVING DAY

It's Monday, September 10, 1962, and Mom's too-cheery face pops through our bedroom door, lips smacking, teeth full of porridge.

"Good morning, Merry Sunshines! Time to rise and shine!" Marcia groans, and Mom says, "Come on now, today's a special day!"

I'm wide awake. *Why is today special?* I can smell the porridge cooking—oatmeal as usual. The radio is chanting the wind and the waves and the tides in weatherman voice, rhythmic and monotone, as it does every morning. The seagulls are fighting over something outside my window. I don't hear the light plant, that's unusual. And why is Mom running a bath?

I jump up to pee, and I see the tub full of golden, cedar-stained water, like apple juice. Or pee. The laundry sink is full, too, and several buckets and all the juice pitchers.

It's moving day!

Moving day changes everything! We need to get out there and see what's happening! But it's impossible to avoid the breakfast ritual. Everyone must be in their place at the table—hurry up Marcia! The daily devotional story must be read, the food blessed and the safety of our dad prayed for, also Marcia's and Rolly's brains so they will learn something in school today. Gratefulness for life must be expressed and problems addressed, Amen. The steam from the porridge pot fades to a few wisps, and the toast droops. Now we can eat. Baby Tammy is tied into her high chair while Mom tries to feed her pablum. I would rather eat pablum than porridge, but Mom says no.

Dad has eaten his porridge and gone already; I can see him and Uncle Ernie from my place at the table. They're behind camp wrestling a big cable off a tree into the workboat.

I pull my lifebelt over my head and push my feet into my shoes-with-no-laces Mom bought for me because shoelaces are impossible to tie, and I run outside to find Helen and Laverne. We race up and down the floats willy-nilly, no purpose at all, screaming, leaping long off the crosswalks. We watch our dads and brothers bring the cables and hoses to the floats and secure the boom-sticks and the family boats for towing. Uncle Alvin is hooking up the *Surf Isle* to the first float, giant cables again attached by boom-chains to the float logs, and the signal is given to tow. The workboats push the floats from behind and the sides, moving camp away from the beach, keeping the floats in line until a straight, steady pull tightens the whole string.

Moving day is a big day for everyone. For the dads, it's a chore they have to get right. The weather must be calm, and the boat can't breakdown. They drive in shifts, night and day. The selected site must be safe, not too much wind and no steep cliff that can slide down on us. There must be a water source—the dads explore a potential site at low tide so they can see the white water rushing over the rocks. They need to build a rustic dam or roll a big barrel up the creek for a holding tank, and they have to thread hoses down the hill and hook up to the camp water hoses, which can take a day or two. That's why our moms fill the bathtub and everything else before we go.

Our moms say, "No little kids allowed outside without an adult, and big kids stick together."

They don't want us to get sucked under the moving floats. They go on about it, trying to put the fear into us because we're certainly not afraid of being sucked under the floats. Last time, Aunt Gloria gave Helen the lickin' of her life for walking on a boom-stick while we were being towed!

Our moms like some locations better than others. Aunt Gloria likes being tied up beside Boswell for the good drinking water and the all-day sun. Mom likes the beautiful calm water and the gardening spot in the Ahclakerho, which we're just leaving. But they've been everywhere up and down the inlet over the years—Security Bay, Margaret Bay, the Ahclakerho, Fly Basin, Burnt Island, McBride Bay, numerous unnamed bays and nooks, anywhere with a creek that's near the logging show.

The beach grows smaller as the *Surf Isle* pulls us away. The big kids are in school by now, and the teacher has trouble making them behave. Laverne and I stay outside as long as we can, watching the flotsam inch by, listening to the crosswalks creaking, the water slurping against the logs. I imagine the water moving through the muscles and barnacles and weeds and unnamed things living on the floats under the water—what must they think of this? Are the little bugs and other squirmy creatures having trouble hanging on? And all the fishes under the floats—are they following us to get their morning scraps of porridge and peelings? I wonder if the little seahorse family is being swept away.

At lunchtime, the big kids are let out and we go in for lunch. It feels bright inside the house, floating out in the open with no beach out our back window, only water and distant trees. Mom cooks lunch on the oil stove as usual. The coal-oil fridge continues to purr, keeping our leftovers from rotting, as it always does. But when we go to the bathroom, Mom has to dip a bucket of water out of the chuck to flush the toilet.

No baths tonight. I fall asleep to the gentle hum of the *Surf Isle* tugging seven floats ahead of me, water slushing through the logs beneath my bed. There is no safer feeling than lying in bed, waiting for sleep, with Uncle Alvin and Dad pulling us all through the water.

We arrive at Boswell at ten o'clock in the morning. Our dads and the older boys push the floats and boom-sticks into place with the *Surf Isle*, the workboats and pike poles, and the tying up process begins. I can't wait to explore our new yard with Helen and Laverne!

CHAPTER 42

WATCHER ISLE

On Sunday, October 29, 1961, the *Surf Isle* tows Bud Mann's cookhouse out of Wyclese Lagoon. This 22- by 70-foot building on a forty-foot-wide float squeezing out of the lagoon is to be our new church!

The front door of the cookhouse opens to a large space that was once full of dining tables, the floor scarred by caulk boots, an oil heater in the corner, the far end partitioned off for a kitchen. The kitchen has counters and cupboards and a giant oil stove that reeks of recent and ancient bacon grease. The parents keep the cupboards and counters for storage, but the first modification made to our new church is the removal of the stove. It is pushed out the back door and into the chuck with an enormous splash. The kitchen is destined to become our Sabbath School room where we will sing songs about sailing to the mission land, drop our pennies into the little box for the missionaries and the poor ("Hear the pennies dropping, dropping one by one"), push little Bible people and animals around in a sandbox, listen to stories illustrated on a felt board, and recite our memory verses.

In November, Grandpa and Grandma Gildersleeve come to visit, and Grandpa begins remodelling. He tears down the existing entry wall and partitions a small classroom, a bathroom, and a foyer for the front door. Aunt Gloria helps him whenever she can, and Uncle Clyde comes to help too. Grandpa Gildersleeve builds twelve pews and a pulpit. (The pulpit that is now in use at the Gwa'sala Nakwaxda'xw SDA church in Port Hardy.) On the first of February, Elder Adams arrives and we all meet in the church for the first time.

The *Northern Light* comes to visit in the summer, and Pastor Ron Reimche builds a castle-like tower to increase the size of the foyer and to house a large bronze bell donated by the Canadian Pacific Railway. The front entrance is widened to accommodate double doors, which instigates a contest. The contest, with the Reimches as judges, is for the decorative hinges on the outside of the double doors. Everyone enters the contest, but no one comes close to the perfect anchor design submitted by Cousin Donalda. Donalda arrived in March to live with us and help Mom, who will be going away in May to have a baby. Everyone adores beautiful Cousin Donalda—she is like a joyful breath of fresh air. She loves to sing and laugh, and the boys, especially Lance, appreciate her beauty. We all know we don't have a chance against her in any kind of contest, and we don't even mind. The anchors look perfect on the big red doors that open into the wooden castle tower.

On Sundays, the GMG men help with the cookhouse-to-church transformation. They install a bathroom and lighting, build a platform for the speaker to stand on, and nail strips of wood to the front wall for decor. Pastor Reimche and some of the moms paint inside and out, and Ron lays a red carpet down the aisle between the rows of pews and on the platform. The outside of the church is painted white, with a red roof. The three front windows each have a red oar framing it on the left and are underscored by flower-boxes full of dahlias in summer. Beside the entry stairs is a carved ship's wheel with fancy letters curving around the white centre of the wheel:

Watcher Isle
Seventh Day Adventist
Float Church
Services Saturday
Sabbath School 10:30 A.M.
Church Service 11:00 A.M.
WELCOME

Entering the foyer, on the left, another carved ship's wheel
hangs on the wall that commemorates the labours of Uncle Don
Goertzen, who died while working for the Gwa'sala. Through
the second set of double doors is the sanctuary: rows of pews
against the walls, red carpet up the middle, a stage with piano
on the left and (later) organ on the right, a potted philodendron
in front of the pulpit. To the right of the stage a door leads to the
kitchen-become-classroom.

Everyone begins planning for the church dedication. Five
important pastoral couples—Adams, How, White, Baker, Kuester—
will be flying in from Vancouver to be part of the special service,
and there will be many local guests. Programs are designed,
special music rehearsed and extra groceries ordered. The *Northern
Light* comes early to help get ready.

Just five days before the dedication date, camp is towed out of
the Ahclakerho into Boswell Inlet, which takes all day Monday
through Tuesday 10 a.m. The men tie up camp and hook up
the water. The next day, the church is towed to camp from its
anchorage in McBride Bay, and Thursday, Ernie wires the church
to the light plant.

In the midst of the move, all are doing their part to prepare
for the biggest event in the history of GMG Logging. Everyone
is scurrying around, cleaning and tidying up every bit of
camp, sewing, cooking, filling oil barrels, finishing last-minute

carpentry in the church and practising special music! All through camp, the excitement hums like the buzz of an arriving airplane.

The ladies of Takush and Randall and GMG cook enormous amounts of food! Washtubs are repurposed as giant serving bowls for potato salad, and huge roasting pans are filled to the top with gluten steaks! The ladies make jellied salads of all colours, casseroles and huge pots of beans, platters of baked salmon and smoked salmon, and bowls of cabbage salad and pickled beets. The dessert table is heavy with pies and cakes and cookies and more jelly. Probably every single baking dish in camp is full of either a casserole or a cake. Admittedly, I remember the enormity of the potluck more than anything else about this significant event!

Friday, all the ministers and their wives arrive on two airplanes, and the hosting begins. There is a big dinner and a meeting, and some late-night practising. On the Sabbath morning of September 15, 1962, the boats begin to arrive. Boats from Takush and all over Smith Inlet and Rivers Inlet, and an airplane with the United Church of Canada minister Bob Burrows, who once skippered the *Thomas Crosby IV*. Somebody pulls on the rope in the foyer and the huge bell rings like a loud buoy calling everybody inside.

Pastor Reimche has a movie camera and takes movies of the event: the speeches, the prayer of dedication, the anointing of Dad as elder, the dedication of all the members, and the new trio—Gloria, Alma and Donalda—singing "His Harbour." It's a silent movie, everyone moving silently and too quickly and you can't hear the singing. He films loaded tables of food and everybody eating it, sitting on the church steps, the crosswalks, the gunnels of boats. I am in his film, sitting at a table on the school float eating a plate of food at high speed. He films adults visiting, kids running around in their lifejackets, and Mom walking at a very fast clip down the floats, carrying baby Tammy.

The church is named Watcher Isle after the islets of the same name at the south entrance to Smith Sound where the storms and swells are fearful. There is a blinker on the islet—a light, a waymark, guiding to safe harbour beyond. The nineteen new church members want their new church to be the light that guides people away from the storms of life and into safe harbour, the "harbour of His peace." The song "His Harbour," with words by Elsie Duncan Yale and music by Felix Mendelssohn, becomes the signature song for the Watcher Isle Church.

Potluck! Left to right: Laverne, Harty and Joyce Bader, Grandma Alice Gildersleeve, Gloria, Alma, Heather, Hazel

Watcher Isle Church

Chapter 43

Trucks and Teeter-Totters

Uncle Alvin and Dad want to try truck logging. They have a location in mind—a nice long valley full of big trees in Boswell Inlet—and they start planning. But they're still in the Ahclakerho. Though camp was moved to Boswell Inlet in September, just in time for the church dedication, the men weren't finished with the Ahclakerho claim yet, so they kept a house in the Klak and now they're weekend commuters. Vivian Paul and Louis Walkus usually go home to the village close by, but Alvin, Louis, Lance, Ernie, George Egolf and the new guy, Bob Betts, have to live together all week.

Nobody wants to do the cooking, so their story goes, but somebody always has something to say about it—particularly about the morning porridge pot. That morning bowl of mush is mighty important to them. At home, they get exactly what they want. Now it is either too mushy or too stiff, depending on who makes it. Some people are even ignorant enough to add the oats to cold water, if you can believe that! So they come upon a solution: whoever complains about the cooking is the new cook.

Dad certainly doesn't want to do the cooking, so he quietly eats everything that anybody is willing to make, perhaps even with a compliment or two, as is his way. But one morning everyone is gathered around the table for breakfast, and a plate of burnt toast is served up.

"This toast is burnt!" Dad says loudly.

He looks up, eyeing the cook and everyone around the table. Shocked, the loggers stop mid-bite and gaze back at him—Louis, the kind and gentle one, with never a bad word for anyone.

"But that's just the way I like it!" says Dad, breaking into a grin.

Relieved guffaws all around. And the chuckle stays with them. In fact, it becomes a camp legend. Ever after, if anybody has something bad to say about the food, we use Dad's method and have a good laugh.

By February 7, 1963, the loggers are back in Boswell logging a claim near the Cannery and timber cruising their future claim in the Coho Creek Valley. The valley cuts back into the hills for three or four miles, and they will build a road through the valley as they log it. Truck logging is a much bigger operation than A-framing, and requires a bulldozer, excavator, dump truck, logging truck, loader, a jeep to get around in, and more employees to run the equipment. There are long meetings in the office at night as Dad and Uncle Alvin plan their new venture.

Randall Log is still at the head of Boswell Inlet, and Don Kaufman is looking at a claim nearby. Don and Marg are glad to be back near friends, church and all, and end up joining the Watcher Isle Church.

"You can't run away from God," Marg tells her family.

Brian and Barbara Kaufman boat to Avalon School every day with Gary and Norman Bader.

A few days after the men return from the Ahclakerho, Dad goes timber cruising with Don Kaufman. They come back with a story, one of those stories that is told and retold into a fabulous and hilarious tale for sharing at a "remember the time?" session—a favourite pastime of loggers in which they reminisce about narrow escapes. Dad's own version of the story is fairly straightforward:

"We were walking through the woods, and I stopped in front of a big cedar tree, kind of looking it over, and Don says to me, 'Say Louie, do you see that bear?' And he said it so casually that I thought the bear was a way off. So I kept looking across the ravine and couldn't see a bear. Then I happened to glance down at my feet, and the bear was right there! Right at my feet! He was in the tree and he wanted to get away, but I was standing in front of him. It gave me quite a shock to see a bear right at my feet, so I just automatically took a big, long jump. I don't know how far I jumped, but Don thought the bear was charging me so he took a jump, too, and we both landed in the brush. And then we felt foolish because the bear was only too happy, of course, that we got out of the way, and he was gone."

The embellishing storytellers use pantomime and add great yells from the men, great roars from the bear, and two big logger bosses cowering in the brush, laughing foolishly.

"But it is a funny feeling to see a bear that close," says Dad.

At this time, Clyde and George Egolf have a hand-logging claim along the beach in Boswell Inlet. Clyde is becoming more permanently settled in the inlet; he builds a float, then builds a nice new house on it. Clyde has a bag of logs in Finis Nook. When he isn't hand-logging, he salvages, beachcombs, buys logs from the Gwa'sala, then booms them up and sells them.

One day when he comes back to Finis Nook after the weekend, his logs are gone. It looks like someone towed them away. He is so discouraged that he and Nancy decide they are meant to move to Port Hardy. They sell their brand-new floathouse to Alvin and Gloria, then build the exact same house on land, at Storey's Beach in Port Hardy. They start a church in Port Hardy and become the new operators of the *Northern Light*, which is exactly what their original dream had been when they were first married at the Nekite by Reverend Kelly of the *Thomas Crosby IV.*

When summer comes, Louis Walkus and Vivian Paul go fishing as they always do, and the student employees—three young relatives: Rolly Clark, Ron Goertzen and Bruce Rafuse, plus Lloyd—arrive at GMG for summer work. The bosses also decide it's time to put the younger kids to work. On the first day of summer vacation, Alvin takes a choker bell up to Dennis's bedroom. Dennis is still in bed, dreaming of a summer filled with swimming and camping and boating. Alvin hands him the choker bell.

"Can you lift this?" he asks.

Well, of course Dennis is only too eager to say, "Yes, of course I can!" so he sits on the edge of the bed and lifts it above his head several times.

"Good," says Alvin. "Breakfast is ready. I have some caulk boots for you. You're coming to work."

Dennis is thirteen; he's not expected to set chokers yet, but he is expected to work. Dennis, Roland and Marcia go to work, taking turns in pairs as whistle punks.

But this summer is different in another way too. Alvin and Louis go to Vancouver for ten days on business, and when they come back, they build a float for unloading all the equipment they just bought. In July, a road survey engineer comes to look at the valley. Truck logging is about to begin!

On August 20, 1963, a scow arrives loaded with a shovel and a bulldozer. An equipment operator, Roy Nimmo, arrives on the

289

same day. The equipment is unloaded onto the float and then onto the beach. The crew is set to work "making mats," and Alvin goes to Kelsey Bay in the *Surf Isle* to buy dynamite for blasting rock.

The estuary is soft, so the shovel sits on the "mat" of logs prepared for it, moves onto the mat in front of it, then picks up the mat from behind and puts it in front to travel. Every day, Alvin and Roy operate the new equipment, digging gravel out of the bay to make the landing—a large, flat area where a donkey will sit and pull the logs off the logging truck into the water. Next, the Cat is put on the beach and Ernie pushes the gravel around. Trees are felled and laid down in rows, rocks are blasted and the gravel pushed over the trees to make a road. In December, a dump truck arrives, and Lance drives it, transporting the gravel farther. The road begins to push up the hill.

When November's mail arrives, it brings bad news. The mailbags are sitting on Aunt Gloria's green-and-white tiled floor. They're stiff and grey with a rope threaded through the top, and they smell of damp canvas, must and stale cigarettes—sort of like if somebody was smoking inside our tent. Rain slides blurry down the windows. I'm playing with my friends at the far end of the room, and the adults are chatting, digging through the mailbags, sorting things into piles. Suddenly the room is different. The adults are hushed and solemn, saying things like, "Nooooo, it can't be true. Oh my, how terrible, this old world is surely nearing its end."

It's such a feeling of doom that we kids are drawn away from our play, begging to know what is so terrible. We are told that a very important man was shot and died. He was the president of the United States, the big country beside Canada, and his name was President Kennedy.

But, of course, we can do nothing about it, and life goes on. While the road creeps slowly up the first hill, Dad logs GMG's last

A-frame show. But they're short on crew, with two or three men always on road building. On March 13, 1964, Roy McGill flies in and works his first day at GMG since he left in 1955! The two Roys run the shovel and the Cat, building the road every day. Many days, Alvin and Ernie or Lance help them, and Dad logs with Louis Walkus and Vivian. On May 14, 1964, Dad writes in the logbook: "Last day on A-frame show." And truck logging begins.

Louis Goertzen admiring the log and truck

In the summer of 1964, Frank Johnson Junior, Bruce Rafuse and Simon Walkus come to work. Simon is Edward and Sally's son. Sadly, Simon's mother Sally dies on June 25, and after the funeral, Simon doesn't come back. Louis Walkus and Vivian go fishing in June as usual, and for the first time in a decade, they don't come back either. Changes are happening at Takush too.

Meanwhile, no one can decide where to put camp. For the first time, we need a more permanent spot. Three locations are under consideration. First, the men tow camp from its location near Boswell Cannery through Boswell Narrows and to the slide on the north side of Boswell Inlet. The slide is a bright, silvery gash in the green hill, young enough to have no growth, only boulders, tumbling pale in an ever-widening inverted V, like an opening zipper all the way down to the water. A crashing river runs down its middle, and there are infinite places to play. We kids love it! But it is rather exposed to the weather and a bit of a boat ride to work, so the men keep looking.

Across the inlet from work, at the narrows, there is a nice protected area with a natural rock barrier and a small island, but it has a puny creek. The ladies want to live across the bay from the new landing, which would be handy for going on walks up the new road. There is also a lovely waterfall, and eagles, like finials, mounted on cedar tops on either side of the bay. But the hillside is steep behind it, and the men worry about slides. Slides are a real concern in Smith Inlet, with its steep granite walls, and everywhere there are the inverted Vs of alder green, pale against the dark evergreens.

Not long ago, in the fall of 1961, Randall Log experienced a slide after a heavy rain—the loggers record two feet in ten days! On the morning of the tenth day, while it was still dark out, the Randall loggers were sitting around in the cookhouse, talking about not going to work. They were worried about pulling the tail-holds out while yarding. While discussing what they should do, they heard a loud, rumbling roar. The boom-man ran out and was immediately washed into the chuck by a jumble of hillside crashing right through the middle of camp. The cables split between Gordon's and Cecil's houses and the two halves of their camp swung out from the beach, with the boom-man awash in the mess. He managed to get out, but the speed-boats were swamped.

With no speed-boats, they were helpless. The summer before, Randall Log had sold the *Westpoint* to Robert Walkus in an exchange for wages, and the new *Central Isle* was still being built. So there was no way to pull their camp back into place or even go for help. They bailed out a speed-boat, took the motor apart, dried it out, put it back together, then ran to GMG for help.

With this illustration of their worst fears, Alvin and Louie don't want to put camp in front of a steep hill. But on Sunday, April 26, 1964, they tow camp to the waterfall across from the landing. They will just have to be on guard and move if there is excessive rain.

Three days later, a southwest storm blows up and nearly tears camp apart. I am trying to sleep, but the racket grows louder and louder, the logs squealing against each other, the crosswalks twisting, the wind howling. There's a loud crash, and another, and soon we are all up and peering out the window. When it's light enough to make out shapes, I can see our crosswalk rubbing on the log, making a wad of wood fiber, which I plan to collect as soon as I can and make paper. Also, the boathouses are broken up and the roofs caved in and the speed-boats are missing. In the morning, the dads make repairs, the boys chase after the speed-boats, and that very day, we move straight across the inlet into the protected nook with the rocks and the little island in front and the puny creek.

Tie-up takes the rest of the day, and Uncle Alvin, Dad and Lance roll a giant barrel up the creek to serve as a cistern. Here we are in our final truck-logging location. The puny creek will dry up most summers and freeze most winters for the remainder of our days in Smith Inlet, forcing us to boat across to the lovely waterfall to get water. Eventually, our dads will clear the brush behind camp for a wild playground of trails, thrilling and dangerous swings, teeter-totters with a view, musty hidey-holes under stumps, mossy thrones and challenging cliffs—even a garden. And in front of camp is the cutest little island, cedar boughs curtaining its mossy-floored room lit by Santa Claus-beard chandeliers. Sometimes I feel that this little bay is where my life begins—it's a child's paradise, forever the landscape of my dreams.

GMG camp on the left, Don Kaufman camp, right

CHAPTER 44

DEVIL'S DELIGHT

Soon after we are tied up in our cozy spot behind the rocks and the little island, we get some interesting visitors. My brother Roland writes the story.

At ten years old, I find myself sitting on the broad gunnel of the *Surf Isle*'s deck wearing one of Aunt Gloria's lifebelts and staring in utter fascination at the bubbles gurgling to the top of the calm waters of the bay. The bubbles move in an organized pattern, back and forth. I have never seen a person breathe underwater before. In an especially violent burst of bubbles, a strange looking head appears. Taking off his mask, the man yells across the water, "Only ten minutes of air left, any specific spot you want me to check?"

The disappointment is evident on my dad's face.

"No, just keep looking as long as you can."

Ten minutes later, the head bursts through the surface again.

"I found it!" the man yells excitedly. "I have enough emergency air to hook it to the cable."

This story spans three chapters, and maybe a fourth that hasn't been written yet, but it began for me several weeks earlier.

My dad had left several days before on an errand in the *Surf Isle*, a sturdy forty-footer powered with a Cummins diesel engine and built for versatility. She has a broad deck and roomy wheelhouse, the forecastle holds bunk beds and a head. The deck has a sturdy mast, boom and a powerful winch. She is equally at home as a tug-boat towing a log boom, a freighter hauling groceries and equipment, a yacht taking friends and family to various locations, and even as an RV for fun trips and events.

The *Surf Isle* was long overdue to be home, but that wasn't a cause for worry yet. The next afternoon, I finally heard the familiar muted roar of the boat's diesel engine, but it seemed to be going slower than usual. Eventually, it appeared around the headland, and soon after, the reason it was going so slowly became evident.

In tow behind the *Surf Isle* was possibly the strangest (and very likely the ugliest) looking craft I have ever seen. It was painted all black, it had a big flat deck with a squat wheelhouse in the middle, and a short mast and boom for lifting things. It didn't even have a bow, just a sort of barge-type front. Possibly the strangest thing of all was the name which I was unable to read until the vessel got close to the dock.

The *Devil's Delight* was manned by four young men who were trying to make a living performing salvage work along the coast. They had an interesting collection of things they had salvaged off shipwrecks and were hoping to sell, including some cannonballs. They were equipped with scuba gear and the equipment to service the gear, air compressors and such.

Dad had come across them drifting around the sound with a broken engine and had suggested he could tow them to camp where they were welcome to stay until they got the parts and repaired their boat.

We kids were impressed with these young men and their lifestyle. What could be better than boating around doing fun stuff and collecting things to sell from under the ocean? I don't think the young men felt quite that way; according to them, not much had gone right on the *Devil's Delight*. One even suggested maybe a name change would improve their luck.

As usual, the visitors in camp were given the A treatment—invited to dinner at various homes by the camp ladies, the men helped with the repairs, and we kids made friends with them. It took several weeks to get things seaworthy on the *Devil's Delight*, and the crew wanted to do something for the camp before leaving, so they asked Dad if there was any salvage they could do for free. After thinking about that awhile Dad said, "Well, we lost a big anchor in Security Bay. Maybe we could look for that."

WHAT! I had never heard of a big anchor. It turns out that chapter two of this story happened long before I was born, during the early days of GMG logging. In those days, Dad and Uncle Alvin logged in the winter and gillnetted salmon in the summer to better make ends meet. In between times they would putter around the coast in one of the little gill netters, exploring, salvaging old shipwrecks and the like.

The story Dad told me was that they were out on the west coast looking around one calm day when they noticed what they determined was a huge anchor deep underwater. Chapter one of this story will never be told, but it must have once been on a very large ship. One can only speculate how it ended up where Dad and Alvin found it, but they sure did want that anchor.

Putting their pioneering minds to work, they came up with a plan to get the anchor. It was far too large to put on one of the boats; it was too large even to tow underwater behind the boat. This is what they did: they went back up the inlet to GMG and found two nice buoyant cedar logs, fastened them firmly together in sort of a raft, got a piece of cable with a loop in one end and then towed the logs back down the inlet to where they had found the anchor. They waited for low tide when the anchor would be closest to the surface, and peering down through the water they were able to lasso one of the anchor flukes with the cable. After fastening the cable tightly to the logs, they waited for the tide to come in and lift the anchor off the bottom. They then towed the logs, with the anchor dangling forty feet beneath, to a gently sloping beach and waited for full high tide to ground the anchor on the sand.

From here it was a waiting game. Tides go in and out in twelve hours, about two full cycles a day, and six hours from low to high or vice versa. Tides in that neck of the woods average about fifteen feet with a big one about seventeen feet. Now you can see where this is going. At the next low tide, they tightened the cable back up and waited for high tide. Now the anchor was twenty-five feet below the logs, and they were towed closer to the beach where the anchor again grounded. Six hours later was low tide and time to tighten the cable. Now the anchor was only ten feet down. One more cycle had the anchor at surface level, and the logs with the anchor dangling from them were towed back to camp where it was a simple matter to lift the anchor from the water onto the A-frame float with the donkey engine.

Dad and Uncle Alvin were finally able to examine and touch this thing they had spent so much time and effort rescuing from the deep, but now they were left with a perplexing problem. What to do with it? GMG was tied up in Security Bay, which is known for occasional freak high winds, so they decided to use it to help anchor camp away from the beach. The cable was attached with a large tree shackle and again lowered to the bottom of the ocean. At some point the shackle must have lost its pin, or the cable rusted through or something, because the big anchor was lost.

There it remained for many years waiting for the intrepid young men of the *Devil's Delight* to help write the third chapter of the story.

With the cable hooked up and the diver back on board, the lifting process begins. The cable goes from the winch, through the fairlead rollers at the stern of the *Surf Isle*, and then straight down to the anchor. The winch labours, the cable snaps and crackles, and the stern of the *Surf Isle* dips dangerously low, but the anchor is wrenched from the grip of the bottom muck and slowly rises. My first view of it underwater reminds me of a monster. Far too big to be winched on deck, it begins its second journey while dangling underwater.

Once again, the donkey engine yanks the big anchor from the water and places it on the A-frame float. I eat my lunch, staring at this behemoth, now on dry land. Everyone else has left. The anchor is alive, covered with sea growth and nasty things. It doesn't even smell good, and I lose my appetite.

Once again, the question is "Now what?" About this time, GMG is transitioning from A-frame logging to truck logging. The trucks dump the logs into a small bay, the bay is closed off with boom-sticks, a long row of logs each chained to the next, so the logs can't escape. It is decided that the big anchor will be used to hold the boom-sticks away from shore so the circular shape of this big floating pen won't collapse. History often repeats itself, and sometime after the big anchor is deployed in this fashion it is again lost. There it remains to this day.

Will the fourth chapter ever be written? Not very many people know where this small bay is any more. Will a new intrepid salvage crew, like the men from the *Devil's Delight*, ever come along and find this extraordinary anchor?

I hope so.

CHAPTER 45

PLAYING AT LAVERNE'S HOUSE

In a childhood vague of schedules, there is time—endless, beautiful time. I love to lie on the sun-warmed planks at the edge of the float, soaking up their warmth, and watch things sink. It's fun to see how everything sinks differently. Flat things cut side to side through the water, back and forth all the slow way down. Tools drop so fast you can hardly see them go. Submerged cans and bottles sink steadily and straight. Cloth and paper can float around beneath the surface and travel great distances before reaching the bottom. Food scraps are attacked and torn to pieces a foot or so down.

With my head over the edge of the float, I can see all the life growing on the logs. There are a few sea anemones, which, of course, I touch to make their tentacles shrink, and a carpet of muscles sticking their tongues in and out. Lots of creatures live amongst the mussels: wispy seahorses, feathery worms and the tiniest of fish. Little black bugs dart in and out, and tiny eels worm around.

Laverne joins me there, our heads hanging over.

"Let's call those little black bugs Prince," she says, and we pick some out and put them in a bucket.

They are now officially called "Prince Bugs," and we create a world for them in the bucket.

When it starts raining, we go inside. I love going to Laverne's house; she has a big bedroom all to herself to play in. She has a bouncing horse on springs, and lots of dolls, named after her aunts, and even a walking doll nearly as big as us! She has a lot of horses too; about the size a Barbie doll can ride. When her brothers are being pests, torturing her dolls or pulling her hair, she uses their hard hooves to bash them on the head.

Auntie Alma brings snacks and treats upstairs to us, and sometimes we go down to the kitchen to drink hot chocolate. On bread day, Auntie Alma makes us dough codgers with butter and jam. Auntie Alma makes yummy white bread, not brown bread like my mom, and the best hot chocolate ever! She says she has a secret ingredient. She sits down with us in the cozy booth, three mugs of hot chocolate steaming in front of us, little marshmallow moustaches on our lips, and tells us stories of when she was a little girl growing up on the prairies. "The prairies" is a far-away place full of many creatures we've never seen.

Auntie Alma says when she was a little girl on the prairies, they had cows, ducks, geese, turkeys and chickens to look after every day. She had a favourite cow named Bess. Bess wore a bell, and all the other cows followed her to and from the pasture. When Auntie Alma was feeling sad, or if she had been punished, she would listen for the bell and find Bess and put her arms around her and bury her head in Bess's soft fur coat.

Auntie Alma went to school in the nearby town of Laird, three miles away. She had lots of brothers and sisters, and they all walked to school every day until the winter snow came. When it snowed, their dad took them in the sleigh. They had a cutter, and their mom heated a hot rock for them to put under their feet in the box of the wagon, and they snuggled under a bear robe.

"At Christmas time we sang Christmas carols as we rode along in the sleigh, with the bells jingling on the horses and the big snowflakes coming down. Oh, it was so beautiful," Auntie Alma says with a faraway look.

Laverne and I watch the rain sliding down the windows. We can see the rain circles all across the grey water outside. But we snuggle our warm mugs of hot chocolate, and for a moment we are sitting in a cutter beside Auntie Alma, who is a girl again, like us. Beautiful horses pull us through the snow, and we snuggle under a bear robe with our feet on a hot rock, and snowflakes land on our noses.

Laverne and Gayle

CHAPTER 46

FLOATING KIDS

According to my mother, I learn to row at the age of two and a half. At two and a half I am free and the world is mine! I can row wherever I want. As my arms grow, I row farther and farther. I row with my friends and I row by myself. Soon I row out of sight of camp, and there is no one but me, nothing but trees and water forever. I sit and float and fish seaweed out of the water and eat it and watch the ducks. I can only get as far as my two arms can take me, so I'm easy to find if anybody is worried. But no one seems to be worried. As long as I'm wearing my lifejacket.

The older boys, in their speed-boats, are harder to find. The dads spend a lot of time, after work when they are tired, retrieving boys when their boats breakdown and they haven't come home by dinner. But the boys are wearing lifejackets, too—if they haven't passed the test yet.

Everyone loves water—splashing in it, swimming in it, floating on it—and we live on it. Our parents do everything they can to keep us from drowning in it. In fact, all our freedoms to play in and on the water have been carefully considered from the beginning. In the beginning, when Lance and Lloyd were babies, Aunt Gloria saw that the commercial lifejackets tipped toddlers' faces into the water. So she designed and created her own lifejackets. They are simple—two canvas pockets stuffed with kapok on the front, another two on the back, with canvas straps holding everything together, and worn like a "jacket" over our clothes.

She makes one for every child—tiny ones when we're little and bigger ones as we grow. When we fall in, we float upright, our heads high and dry until someone rescues us. We fall in often enough that it is only mildly interesting news at dinner. As in, *Gayle fell in today. Oh? Who fished her out? Pass the potatoes please.* Forgettable news.

Occasionally a child falling-in-the chuck story is less forgettable. When Marcia was a toddler, she fell in when camp was tied in the Ahclakerho with its fast tidal runs. She was upright, proving the lifejacket's head-out-of-water feature with her screams, but floating away. Mom couldn't swim and, in fact, was terrified of the water. She leaned out, hollering for Marcia to kick. She grabbed a pole and still couldn't reach her.

"I can't reach her! I can't reach her!" Mom kept calling, and Marcia kept screaming.

Aunt Gloria saw what was going on and immediately kicked off her shoes, jumped in and swam Marcia into Mom's waiting reach. It's a breathtaking event to either fall or jump into that icy water! And if the float is new and floating high, getting out in a dress is quite a feat. None of the three ever forgot it!

There was another unforgettable time when Lloyd saw a rag in the water in a crack between two logs and discovered it was little Donnie, three or four years old, face down in the water. Lloyd yanked Donnie out by the hair and started pushing on him, and Donnie coughed to life with a growl.

All of us are encouraged to swim as soon as possible. Of course, no one wants to be the big kid who still wears a lifejacket, but before discarding our lifejacket there is a test we must pass. It is an old law handed down from the very first Gildersleeve camp, originating with the sad story of the little Gildersleeve girl who fell off a boom-stick and drowned.

Every camp kid has their own learning-to-swim story, and some would like to forget theirs! Because if a kid is taking too long to learn how to swim on their own, their dad ties a rope around them and throws them in. All for their own good, of course. The poor kid who has to learn this way screams bloody murder, and the dad calls out over their wails, "Don't worry, I gotcha, you're not gonna sink. See? I have this rope on you, and I can pull you right in, see? Now paddle."

When Rosemary Salo lived with McGills and learned to swim, she grew dependent on that rope. If the rope was on, she could swim, if it was off, she was certain she would sink, and she panicked. So the first time she took the test, she flunked it. I am fortunate to observe all the trials of the kids before me and learn from them. I have three strong motivators for learning to swim—I don't want to wear my lifejacket to school, I don't want to be thrown in, and I don't want to flunk the test.

The water temperature is part of the challenge—it literally takes your breath away! There are two ways to deal with the cold. Marcia likes to sit on a boom-stick and put graduating body parts in slowly, slowly, finally laying her belly on the log and lowering herself in, bit by painful bit. This is called "getting used." The other way is to jump in, come up screaming and get it over with. There are "get used-ers" and "jump in-ers." I'm a jump in-er.

I learn to swim thanks to a wide, peeled boom-stick that happens to be submerged under the end of the schoolhouse float. Standing on it, the water is up to my thighs at its deepest point. I jump in off the boom-stick at the back of the school float with my lifejacket on and swim to the submerged boom-stick. Then I take my lifejacket off and hold it in front of me, push off the log, kick around a little and come back to its welcoming, golden surface. The log makes the black depths, which I'm sure I will sink into without my lifejacket on, seem less terrifying.

Every day I have to convince my friends to swim behind the school float instead of elsewhere. Eventually, I make myself let go of my lifejacket to paddle in short bursts near the safety of the sunken boom-stick. Then I swim in front of camp with no security boom-stick.

Near the end of the summer, I feel ready to pass the test. I wait for Dad to come home from work and tell him I'm ready. Spectators gather to witness the event. I'm fully clothed, minus my lifejacket. I choose the float next to mine for the test because it's lower to the water. I hesitate a moment, then take a run and jump off, come up screaming, paddle back to the float and climb out on my own in front of the judge and witnesses.

Dad smiles and says, "Well, that's pretty good, pretty good."

Every kid is required to do the same before taking off their lifejacket; find a judge, Uncle Alvin or Dad, jump or dive in fully clothed and get out on their own. No ladder. But once we discard our lifejacket, we never wear it again. Not even on a boat ride! Somehow our parents miss that little safety issue.

Fascinating entertainment: baby seagulls trying to eat the lingcod. Left to right: Murray, (Dennis and Gary?) Roland squatting, Helen, Gayle, Donna

CHAPTER 47

GONE!

In the fall of 1964, the Gwa'sala have an enormous decision to make. The problem has been going on for many years, at least since 1950 when Don and Claire Goertzen and Frank and Ada Johnson arrived with their families in Takush as teachers and helpers at the request of Chief George. The conversation back then went something like this, and it started with Chief George, Don and Frank.

"This is no longer a suitable place to live. There is no good water source, no potential for modern plumbing, no electricity, not even a radiophone! And if the weather is bad, we are totally cut off from help in an emergency. People are dying because of it! What can we do?"

"Well, let's build some better houses at least, maybe get a generator—still not sure about water and plumbing."

"How about another location? Like Ethel Cove maybe."

"Yes! Ethel Cove! That's a great idea. It's flat and has a nice sand beach and a little creek."

"Yes," said everyone, "we agree, Ethel Cove."

"Now we just need to convince Indian Affairs."

Then Don died and the Gwa'sala lost their advocate. Frank was not a spokesperson like Don, but he did his best, and the chief asked him to write a letter. In January 1953, Frank sent a letter to W.J. McGregor, the regional supervisor of Indian Affairs, with a proposal for the Ethel Cove site. McGregor answered with a plea to consider a settled area such as Port Hardy or Alert Bay, saying Smith Inlet had "little to offer the coming generation." And Frank answered with the response of the Gwa'sala—a definite negative. Finally, the Indian Agent said he would arrive in spring to assess the situation.

The spring of 1954 was a difficult one. There was a drinking spree, Margaret got shot, Alvin Walkus was burned, got blood poisoning and nearly died, and then most of the families left to visit the Nakwaxda'xw at Ba'as (then called Blundeon), leaving the village and the school nearly empty. Students missed over a month of school and could not complete their grades. When two of the families came back, they brought a terrible, long-lasting flu, and anyone still in Takush became severely ill, including Frank and Ada and their children.

That's when the agent came. Only two families and Frank were in the village, and Frank did his best to speak for the rest of them. He gave the agent a tour of Ethel Cove. In the end, the agent's opinion went something like this: "We don't think Ethel Cove is suitable. There is still an insufficient water source, and it will be too difficult to obtain acquisition of the location. If you must stay in Smith Inlet, I will send in an engineer and we will build up the village on its present site."

Everyone was so disappointed. Lumber had already been dropped for them at Ethel Cove. But over time, the agent's proposal changed to something they liked even less. It became more like: "Smith Inlet is too isolated to reach in bad weather, and it is too difficult to reach, period. Teachers and any support persons don't want to be so isolated. It is too far from school, too far from the hospital, there are no entertainment facilities, and it's too hard to maintain adequate services in such isolation. If you want these services, you will need to move to Port Hardy."

"No, we don't want to leave our home."

The Wuikinuxv (Oweekeno) in Rivers Inlet above them could easily access Bella Bella and Ocean Falls, and the Nakwaxda'xw at Ba'as below them weren't far from Port Hardy and Alert Bay, but the Gwa'sala in Smith Inlet were in that in-between zone with the Queen Charlotte Sound between them and everything. The issue remained in limbo for years.

On December 3, 1963, Frank and Ada Johnson moved out of the inlet where they had lived since that momentous day in 1950 when their home was pulled through the Bull Run. They had remained close friends and advocates for the Gwa'sala, and now they were gone. Old Chief George was gone too—he died in May of 1962. The canneries, where they had found work for so many years, were gone, and now the gyppo loggers were leaving; soon there would be no employment other than fishing in the summer.

Now it's the fall of 1964, and time for school to start, but there is no teacher. The last teacher was Katie Crooks Lambert, and she is married and gone. Their acting chief, George Walkus (nephew of Chief George, and James Walkus's dad), already moved to Port Hardy two years ago and lives in a small house near the site chosen for the new village. The Indian Agent says he has some houses ready for them in Port Hardy. So they think about it.

"But not enough houses," says the agent. "Don't all come at once. Some of you can come now and some can come later, when we have more houses ready."

Finally, the Gwa'sala come to a decision. They will go. But how can they leave family members behind? They cannot, whether or not there are enough houses ready for them. So they all leave at once.

"We will come back to go fishing in the summer as we always do," they say.

I can only imagine the preparation for that journey. They put whatever they can into their boats and leave what doesn't fit. Then they motor right out of their homeland—the home they have lived in for as long as anyone can remember. Their home since the ice receded and revealed its shores, and Tlagalixala came down as a brilliant event wearing the sun mask and, taking it off, became a man. And since YaqalE'nala arrived at Wyclese in his whale canoe and the whale turned to stone. Now they are gone—boats pop-popping, wakes trailing back to the beach, boat decks loaded with people and dogs large and small, staring back at their shrinking homes, turning the corner out of the harbour and into Smith Sound, around Cape Caution, across Queen Charlotte Strait and into Hardy Bay. The village is empty, empty.

Weeks later, the village is burned to the ground and there is nothing to come back to, so they never come back. Not as a tribe. At least not yet. The inlet is not the same without its people, and the people are not the same without their inlet. The Gwa'sala begin a new story in Port Hardy.

Houses at Takush

Same Takush location in 2021

CHAPTER 48

A CANADIAN EDUCATION ON FLOATS

At nearly eight, I'm finally going to school. Marcia got to go when she was five! She wanted to go so badly that Mom and Dad relented. She was ridiculously smart; she took grades two and three in one year, did correspondence for grade eight and now she is gone at age twelve! Mom and Dad say they don't want that to happen ever again. At least Marcia doesn't have to go to boarding school like everyone else; she goes to live with Grandma Ritchey in Kelowna.

Marcia's best friend Joy Lynn Egolf is gone, too, along with her family, and we lost other students; the Baders towed their camp to Draney Inlet in Rivers to log the other side of their hill. Sometimes they walk over the hill to see us, just like Dad did when he first started logging for Doc Gildersleeve in Draney and wanted to visit the Willis Gildersleeve camp.

But the Kaufmans moved their camp next to ours, and now we have Brian, Barbara and Brenda. They row or canoe to school every day in the old leaky dugout canoe Brian found abandoned on the beach. And there is a new family in camp! When we came back home from Grandma's house this summer, Dorothy McGill, Murray, Gary and Donna were here. Murray and Gary are starting their first year at Avalon, the same as me, and Donna is a fun new friend!

On the first day of school, Mom gives me some coloured scribblers, a pack of crayons—a small pack, I save my big sixty-four pack for home—a packet of new Laurentian pencil crayons and a pencil case with pencils and an eraser inside. I like to put my initials on everything: G-M-G, just like our logging camp. I have new clothes too! Roland and I stand in front of Mom's flowers so she can take a picture of us on my first day of school. Roland is in grade five already. Donna and Laverne are still free—I can hear them running around outside having fun. Sometimes Brenda joins them. Sometimes they jump up and down in front of the school windows to look at us. Tammy isn't in school yet either, of course, because she is really little.

First thing at school, we say the Lord's Prayer. On the wall there is a picture of the queen wearing a crown and beautiful jewelry, and I can't stop staring at her. We get new books, and Miss Schneider teaches us how to open them properly and treat them with respect. There are a lot of rules and explanations about what will happen to us if we don't keep them. And talk of nuclear bombs and how to hide under the desk. How worrisome.

I like our desks. The desktop is a lid we can lift up to put our books inside. Helen shows me her stash of licorice fern roots, for sucking on, at the top of her desk. She also has a little cup of water with something in it. When the teacher isn't looking, she takes the little piece out and it starts burning.

"Phosphorous," she says. "From the science cupboard. Isn't it neat?"

My favourite thing about school is sitting at the round table for reading time. I love to read, and I can't wait until it's my turn so I can hurry things up and see what happens next in the story. But Helen hates reading. She can't understand why she has such a

315

hard time with it. Her teacher and her parents don't know either. They don't know about dyslexia. I can read fine, but I'm not brave like Helen.

"I dare ya," she says.

She ties a thread on a raisin and swallows it. Then she pulls it back up. She eats a muscle—picks it right off the logs and swallows it whole! She can do anything! If it is exciting, dangerous or forbidden, Helen wants to do it.

One day we find a fun catalogue of party supplies; you can order a box of supplies for all sorts and sizes of parties, and we want one.

"Let's order it!" she says.

"We can't do that! We don't have any money!"

"Let's do it anyway! We can always send it back."

We order a box of supplies for a party of twelve. It includes hats and streamers and little toys and bangers—exciting stuff! We fill out the order form in the back of the catalogue and check the box COD for "cash on delivery." We put it in an envelope, address it and borrow a stamp. It's easy to tuck our envelope into the mailbag without anybody noticing. Next boat day we look for our package, nervous and excited.

"What's this?" Aunt Gloria says. "A COD package for Helen and Gayle? Whatever could this be?"

I guess we're hoping, deep down, that one of our parents will see what a marvelous box of goodies it is and buy it for us. But they don't. They ask us what we were thinking. They seem flabbergasted, even. Helen begs a little, to keep it, but they send it back.

316

And that's how it goes. Helen proposes something preposterous, I say we shouldn't do it, and we do it anyway. Mostly we just do daring feats of bravery, like jumping off the *Surf Isle* roof, camping with bears or eating unknown flotsam plucked out of the water from the rowboat. If Helen wasn't my friend, I might still be curled up on the chesterfield reading my book.

When the Knopps move to camp, Auntie Alma wants Laverne to play with timid me more often than brave Helen, so Laverne misses out on a lot of adventures. Then Donna arrives, and Donna is game for any adventures proposed by anybody! Helen is about three years older and wiser than me, Laverne and Donna, so we listen to everything she says. She hates it when Mom takes her aside to say, "Helen, you're the oldest, you need to be a good example." Helen shares astonishing knowledge with us, such as the facts of life, and the time a man, a visitor, tried to put his hand in her underwear. Her dad made that man leave Smith Inlet and never come back!

We have a club, the Four Friendly Flickas, because Laverne loves horses so much. We gallop all over camp whinnying, and the boys laugh at us, but we don't care. After seeing the movie *Headless Horse* one Saturday night, we prance around in a string, hands on each other's shoulders, singing, "We love the headless horse, the headless horse, the headless horse. We love the headless horse, the horse without a head." We sing it every recess until the boys are annoyed.

We also have the Happy Club. Aunt Gloria started this club when Donna and Barbara and Brenda arrived because now we are a little crowd of girls. She says it will prevent quarrelling. We meet every couple of weeks or so and vote in the most thoughtful and kind of us to be "Happy Queen." Then Aunt Gloria brings out a nice cake and the Happy Queen gets to wear a crown while we all eat our cake. All our clubs are short-lived.

We go through phases of hula-hooping, skipping double Dutch, and then Chinese skipping with its never-ending stages of difficulty: ankles, knees, thighs and waist—even neck! After the hill behind camp is cleared, we spend hours exploring, swinging, running up and down the trails playing games of pretend. We explore and picnic in the rowboats. Sometimes on a rainy day, we hang out in an empty house and play Flinch all afternoon.

When it's suppertime, our moms start calling. They each have their own call; Aunt Gloria's is shrill, and it starts low and ends high: "Denn-US, Hell-UN," sort of like the varied thrush without the warble in it. Aunt Dorothy calls the opposite way, high going to low: "GA-ry, DON-na." Auntie Alma's is a straight call. If we're too far away to recognise the name, we all know the tone.

"That's you, Helen."

"I know, I know."

No one likes to be the first to go in because they might miss something. Mom blows a whistle, so there's no mistaking my call. At each call, another kid peels off.

"See ya later, alligator."

"After a while, crocodile."

The boys play with us at recess sometimes—Anti-I-Over, dare base, freeze tag, go-go-stop, capture the flag, even baseball with rowboats in the outfield. But any games we play with a ball just turn into a game of fetch-the-ball-out-of-the-water. We mostly save ball games, races and jumping for sports day when we go to the big sand beach.

It's hard for me to tell what the boys are doing. There are a lot of them now, always tearing around, playing tricks on each other and the teacher, laughing and hollering, and fighting on the school float. Brian and Doug seem to set each other off, and they start scrapping. Then Kenny steps in to help his little brother, and poor Brian doesn't have a chance. So Gary leaps on top of Ken and tries to pull him off, and a jumble of sweaty, grimacing, yelling boys end up rolling around on the school float getting slivers.

"Say uncle, say uncle!" Ken yells.

Sometimes Uncle Alvin, who is on the school board for Ocean Falls School District, has to go talk to parents.

It seems the boys are allowed to do anything. They run the speedboats, and they have axes and matches. They take their boats to the beach and chop down trees. They do a thing they call "double chopping." Roland tells us, "Each of us chop at a regular speed, but when the first chopper is rearing back for another strike, the second chopper is making his cut. You can chop down a tree really fast this way. But if your timing is off, you will whack the other axe, and that's not good."

Well, their timing must be off sometimes because once Dennis got axed in the head. That was a scary sight—blood everywhere and Aunt Gloria screaming. But no one took away their axes. They chop down big trees—big enough to sell to GMG. Dennis asks the forestry officer if it's OK.

They build fires on the beach too. When Roland was in grade one, he and Johnny Salo built a fire on the beach that got so big it almost caught the forest on fire! Another time, Roland put a can of beans on the fire to heat and it blew up and plastered everyone in hot beans. And then someone shot a seal, and the boys figured it would be the "real deal," Roland says, to melt the fat for boot grease. They put the chunks of fat in cans over a fire. When the fat tipped into the fire, it flamed up and singed their hair. In the end, the fat smelled so horrible they threw it away.

Doug is crazy brave along the lines of Helen. Once, Doug and Helen saw a bear swimming in front of camp so they jumped in the rowboat and rowed out to see him. Helen tells me:

"The bear just kept swimming along, so Doug says, 'Hey, let's tie a rope around him and tow him to camp.' So he ties a rope around the bear's head while the bear is swimming, and I row to camp, and the bear just swims along with us. Then when we get to the airplane float, the bear lunges out of the water onto the float in one big leap and takes off running towards the school with the rope dragging behind him.

"Well, everybody watching scatters like a shot! The bear runs around the right side of the school, the teacher following, and Ken and Lloyd run around the left side. At the back of the school, Lloyd, at a full-speed run, comes face to face with the bear, and in some kind of miraculous leap, flies right over top of him.

"Then the bear jumps into the water behind the school float, but he doesn't see the boom-stick there, because it's mostly submerged under the water, and he lands on it with a big thwump, the wind knocked out of him.

"Suddenly, my dad appears out of nowhere, still in his caulk boots, carrying a pike pole. He walks out onto the boom-stick in his caulk boots—crunch, crunch, crunch—and uses the pike pole to untie the rope from around the bear's neck. Then he takes me home and gives me a talk.

"Helen, you did a very foolish thing. You put your life in danger and endangered the lives of everyone in this camp. And not only did you endanger people, you also could have killed the bear. If that bear had got away with that rope around his neck, he would probably have died. The rope would have got tangled in the woods and strangled him or trapped him.'

"And to imbed his words in my mind forever, he gives me the lickin' of my life!"

Then there was the time Gary and Helen played with white gas. They discovered that if you dip your hand in gas and light it on fire, it will burn without burning your hand. But they got some gas on Donna, and the front of her dress caught on fire. Donna, in her little brown dress and blue sweater and her pageboy haircut, her front all aflame, screamed her head off. So they pushed her in the chuck. When the fire was doused, Helen pulled her out of the water by her hair, and Donna screamed her head off even more! Gary and Helen got in a lot of trouble.

The most serious thing that ever happened was when Doug and Ken were working on their outboard motor. Doug got some gas on his clothes and a spark ignited him. Kenny tried to push him in the chuck, but Doug ran for the house, adding oxygen to the flames, and was seriously burned. He frightened everyone badly and was gone for months, then back and forth to Vancouver for many years after that for grafting. Doug is really tough.

But mostly, school days are quiet. My bookworm is getting longer and longer above the blackboard, and now it's around the corner. In February, Valentine's Day month, we get a new flag. Miss Schneider makes a big deal of bringing down the old flag and folding it up, then sending up the new flag—red and white with a maple leaf, fluttering like a big Valentine at the top of the pole. We stand proud and straight and sing:

O Canada!
Our home and native land!
True patriot love in all thy sons command.

With glowing hearts we see thee rise,
The True North strong and free!

From far and wide,
O Canada, we stand on guard for thee.

God keep our land glorious and free!
O Canada, we stand on guard for thee.

O Canada, we stand on guard for thee.

Mr. McCormick's class. Left to right, back row: Sherman McCormick, Ken, Laverne, Roland, Brenda, (Gary out of picture). Front row: Donna, Helen, Barbara, Doug, Gayle

CHAPTER 49

AQUARIUMS, OTSCAR AND MR. BLUE

After boat day, there are always some big wooden shipping crates left lying about. As anyone can see, a shipping crate can be much more than a shipping crate. It can be a dollhouse, or a kitchen table in a playhouse, or a counter for a store. The boys see an aquarium, and thus begin a long string of natural events!

Roland and Ken nab a good big crate, sink it into the water and nail it to the logs on Ken's float. They put various rocks, seaweed and kelp in it, then they catch whatever fish they can and put them in the box. They want to put some bottom-dwellers in the box, too, so they design a trap.

"We created the traps with a wire hoop woven around part of a gunnysack with a rope harness that would lift it straight up," Roland says. "We tied a couple of dead puggles in the middle and lowered it onto the bottom. Next day, we pulled it up as fast as we could with the idea that the water pressure would keep whatever we had captured from climbing out."

Ken and Roland's traps catch some strange and ugly creatures; several of them are mean looking crabs. Just when the box starts getting too full, Roland spies a green crate and makes another aquarium on the end of our boathouse. When our brothers aren't around, Laverne and I spend a lot of time spying on all the weird creatures who live beneath us. It's a wonder we ever go swimming again after seeing all those things with teeth and claws who swim with us.

In school, the boys are learning about pirates in their socials studies class. Stories about pirates are popular, and Roland's and Ken's bookworms above the blackboard have a lot of pirate books in them. One of the pirate stories is about a pirate who successfully "singed the Spanish king's beard" by capturing Spanish treasure galleons, pretty maidens and the like. This pirate got the pirate's name "The Black Avenger of the Spanish Main."

One morning, Roland's box is ravaged, and the only creature left is a big, ugly, mean-looking crab. Ken helps Roland restock the aquarium, and they wait to see what will happen. Next morning, same thing: the box is ravaged, and the only creature left is the big, ugly, mean-looking crab, so they name it "The Black Avenger of the Spanish Main."

Then somebody buys a new piano. The piano is pretty enough, but oh, the beautiful wood crate that it comes in! It would make an extra huge dollhouse! But the boys claim it to make an extra huge aquarium.

Murray and Dennis co-partner on this one. Murray reads a lot of Sam Campbell books. Probably his whole bookworm above the blackboard is Sam Campbell books, and Sam Campbell writes about animals. When the piano arrives, Murray has just read a story about a wild fish that came when its name was called; the pike in the book jumped in excitement as it waited for a treat, so the story goes. And Murray gets thinking about fish and that piano crate.

Murray and Dennis repeat the aquarium idea and expand on it. They put rocks in the piano crate to make it sink and nail it securely to the side of the light plant float. They add more rocks, some seaweed and sand and start collecting creatures to put in it for observation and "to become friends with," Dennis says.

"First we caught puggles," he remembers. "These are shiny little fish that swim under the floats, and they are easy to catch. All we needed was a straight pin from Mom's sewing kit and some number 10 thread. Pick off some muscles from the logs under the floats and put some of the innards of those muscles onto the bent pin, formed into a fish-hook, and we can catch as many as we want. We transported them live and put them in the new aquarium."

Helen and I have been catching puggles for years. We help them deliver their babies by gently squeezing on the fat ones and watching their babies pop out, fall into the water and swim away.

"Well, we also caught some piling perch that are a little bit more tricky to catch," says Dennis. "They're a pretty wise fish. They aren't like the puggles. They don't just bite a hook. You have to chum them. Get a handful of mussels, smash them up and throw them in the water where there is a school of perch. They go into a feeding frenzy, feeding on the free food coming from above and, unbeknownst to them, we drop our hook with a piece of juicy muscle on it into the midst of the feeding frenzy and catch a perch. We caught several and placed them into the aquarium.

"We caught a tommy cod, too, and put him in the aquarium. Tommy cod is a small Pacific cod that swims in the shallows and hides close to or in amongst the kelp forests. They are a beautiful fish that can grow up to about twenty-four inches long and have bluish-green spots on them. We put a young lingcod in the aquarium too."

George, the tommy cod, is chosen for the experiment. Murray feeds him crushed mussels, and George nibbles his fingers. George always comes swimming to the top when Murray comes to the aquarium. So his story goes.

"Every day before school, we rushed out there to check on our fish in the aquarium," Dennis says. "We'd do a little bit of a headcount to make sure they're all still there and none are getting out. And one morning we noticed there were quite a few missing. We wondered if there was a hole in the aquarium that they had discovered. So at recess and at lunchtime and after school we replenished the aquarium.

"The next morning, however, there was a whole bunch missing again, and we could not understand for the life of us what was going on. We were very determined to discover what was going on, and so we kept a very close eye on it. Especially in the early hours of the morning. One morning, we caught the culprit in the act. It was an otter."

With poor George the tommy cod gone, Murray has a new plan. Instead of an aquarium, it will be an otter pond. But it's a lot of work to keep the otter pond stocked.

"One day," says Murray, "when I should have been doing my correspondence, I saw the otter checking the aquarium, which was empty. I had a fish saved, and I carefully splashed it back and forth in the water. The otter stretched its neck and coughed and snorted before slipping under the surface.

"I had no idea what it would do next, so I very gingerly held the fish half-in and half-out of the water. I did not see the otter but suddenly the fish was yanked from my hand. Then I flapped a fish up and down against the boards where I stood and offered it when the otter came closer. Soon it had no fear and was taking fish from my hand."[11]

Murray names the otter Otscar; an otterized version of Oscar the seal—another animal story. But we all just call him Oscar.

---

[11]   Later, Murray writes a book, *Dead Birds Don't Sing But Witching Rods Talk*, which includes many of his creature experiences recorded here.

Oscar loves anyone who will fish for him, but he loves Murray best. Murray spends hours fishing for Oscar, teasing him and playing games with him. He experiments with feeding Oscar large lingcod, longer than Oscar, and long eels, which Oscar eats from the tail to the head, poor eel. Oscar eats any kind of fish except dog sharks. Unfortunately, Oscar also eats loons.

The boys love to play tug of war with Oscar. They tie a fish on a string and throw it out into the water. Oscar dives from the wharf and tries to "catch" the fish before they retrieve it. If they win, Oscar waits for them to throw the fish again. In the winter, he likes to chase snowballs too.

But one day, Oscar comes swimming around with a lot of squeaky little pups trailing behind her, so we have to change her name to Oscarina! The pups get up on the logs under the floats, make a lot of racket and leave fish scraps on the logs that really stink. Sometimes our moms make the boys rip the planks up to clean the fish scraps off the logs and pour some bleach on them.

Before Oscar cleans out the aquarium, another visitor arrives. On an early morning aquarium check, Dennis sees him standing there. He is a tall, skinny blue fellow, and he stands incredibly still on the edge of the aquarium. Then ZAP, his head dives into the water and he comes up with a wiggling puggle in his mouth. With a jerk of his head, he flips the puggle so that it's going headfirst down his long neck. The blue heron stretches his neck and a bulge moves its way down, down that long neck until it disappears. He dabbles his beak in the water, gives his feathers a shake, then he goes for another.

When Dennis throws a puggle on the floats, the heron flies over and retrieves it, swallowing it in the same way as before—gulp, slide, gulp. Then he stands there waiting for more. Murray calls him Mr. Blue. Like Oscar, Mr. Blue becomes the best friend of anyone who is catching fish, and the most faithful to catch fish for Mr. Blue is Murray.

Eventually, Mr. Blue figures out what time of day we get out for recess. He gets impatient near recess time and struts around in front of the schoolhouse windows, even pecking on them. When we finally come out, he follows whoever has a fishing line. Usually Murray. He begins to follow Murray around everywhere, up and down the floats.

"If I stopped suddenly," Murray says, "he would bump into me. If I ran, he would run too. Once, I wanted to see how fast he could run, so I sprinted as fast as I could go. When I checked over my shoulder, panting and heaving, there was Mr. Blue flying effortlessly along beside me and looking at me curiously.

"I remember once while we were waiting for a fish to bite, Mr. Blue folded up and lay down at my feet. I didn't even know these birds *could* lie down. I thought they always rested, and even slept, while standing. I thought maybe he was sick, but when I caught a fish, he came to life.

"Mr. Blue could always tell when I had a fish. He would see the line jerking, and he would shift from foot to foot and peer into the water. He could see the fish long before I could and would often literally dive into the water to try and catch it. I was frightened that he would one day catch my fish, hook and all. He did once, but I was able to get the fish away from him before he swallowed it. I would sometimes push him so I could get the fish and hook first."

If Mr. Blue is out of sight, Murray, or anybody with a fishing line, can wave their hands in the air and call, "Mr. Blue! Mr. Blue!" and Mr. Blue will come in with a squawk and a crash landing. Mr. Blue is our friend for a long time, maybe two years, then trouble moves in. We would never have known this if Murray hadn't read it in one of his Sam Campbell books, but herons, capable of avoiding most predators, have no defense against the silence of an owl in the dark. Mr. Blue lets us know when the owl arrives.

He cries in unending and long, drawn-out shrieks while looking at the squawking gulls on the shore. Murray takes a rowboat and goes to investigate.

"I arrived at a crime scene," says Murray. "And no wonder the gulls were so upset! A large and beautiful great-horned owl had killed one of their own and would not retreat, even when I arrived on the scene."

One morning, Mr. Blue does not greet us on our way to school. He does not come no matter how much waving and calling we do, so we form a search party. The order is given, "All rowboats out." The boys find Mr. Blue's body floating behind camp, and the Great Horned Owl is nearby watching from a tree.

The boys must feel that it is too sensitive a scene for us because none of us girls ever see the poor, half-eaten body of Mr. Blue. They carefully put him in a box and take him up the hill behind camp. They dig a grave and bury Mr. Blue so deep that no animal will ever find him. I don't know if they cry, but I do. We all go through the five stages of grief, and when we get to the revenge stage, we consider the owl.

The owl has to die. A life for a life. Or at least it has to suffer for his evil ways. That's how we feel. The boys hatch a crazy plan to catch the owl that will probably never work. First, they need bait, and there happens to be a dead seagull floating behind camp. The bait is thrown in front of the owl's tree, and the boys wait in hiding, gunnysacks in hand. The owl drops on the seagull, just as they hoped he would. He digs his talons in. With his talons in, Murray tells us, it will be very difficult for the owl to let go. The boys creep up quietly and WHOMP! They have the owl. They stuff him in an apple box and take him to camp. Then there is a big discussion about what to do with him.

Ken says we should build a cage. His dad has some scrap wood and such around, and soon the boys have built a cage of wire mesh with a perch inside on the back of the Knopp float. They dump the owl inside and pronounce their accusations of murder upon him. I look at his staring eyes and his frightening beak, the huge talons clamped onto his prey; he doesn't look very sorry. He just plucks the feathers and tears the flesh off the dead seagull.

That night, the owl, just one float away from my bedroom window, hoots into the dark. I don't know if the boys named the owl but I name him Evil. Evil the Owl. I cannot feel sorry for him. This is justice.

How long should he be imprisoned to satisfy his sentence? That is our question. Meanwhile, he should be fed. Rations at least. So we catch him some fish and watch him tear them apart. What else would the owl eat? Dennis wonders what would happen if we put a live seagull inside the owl's cage. He regrets this later. So—the boys again—put breadcrumbs inside a circle of string, an old tried and true method, and catch a seagull. All of us kids cluster around the cage to see what will happen. We expect a big loud fight, but there is no fight. The seagull cowers in the corner and the owl lands on him and begins tearing him apart, live, as we watch in fascinated horror. I think we all feel that this has gone past the desire for justice.

And that is when Auntie Alma finds us and confirms our consciences in no uncertain terms. We disperse, abashed. That night, one of the dads, probably Uncle Ernie, pardons the owl, opens the cage and Evil flies away.

Now the aquariums and cage are empty. Roland's aquarium got washed away. We have no captives to observe or torment, no fish named George or crabs named The Black Avenger of the Spanish Main or owls named Evil. But we still have Oscarina and a little fawn named Specky, whose favourite food is Auntie Alma's roses.

Captured owl. Left to right (first visible face):
Helen, Ken, Gary, Doug, Laverne, Murray

Chapter 50

Loon Lake

May 26, 1965
To Kerr and Dumaresq Timber Co. Ltd, 8887 Osler
St, Van 4, BC
Phone 261-7242
*Great West Towing Barge #2 loaded with 1,560 logs
species approx. as follows: Hemlock 784, Balsam 431,
Spruce 185, Cedar 160, Log Mark 82305. Please notify
Supt of Scaling.*
GMG Log Ltd.

M om says to sing when we go around corners, so Mom, Tammy and I are singing as loud as we can as we puff our way up to the top of the second hill. We saw a grizzly here once, just after the second hill, and we don't want to see him again. We certainly don't want to surprise him. Mom picks Tammy up for the last part because her little legs get tired.

"This little light of mine (puff), I'm gonna let it shine (puff)."

I want to show Mom and Tammy a neat fort, a special secret room I found by Loon Lake, so I hurry ahead. At the lake, I stop short. What happened to the lake? It's ruined! Just ruined! Our beautiful lake with the loon's nest in it. The lake has broken logs sticking up everywhere, and the edges are a jumbled mess! I don't know where the poor loon is! I run to find my secret room in the curve where the creek meets the lake and the giant trees protect a circle of moss carpet and salmonberries bower it in a leafy screen. But there are only stumps and a tangle of bark, mud and fractured limbs as far as I can see. The beaver dam is gone. Did the beavers escape? Everything is gone and it's horrible and ugly. I can't help but cry.

"Why did Dad have to wreck our lake, Mom? Why? Couldn't he go around it? Why?"

But Mom is sad too. At suppertime we ask Dad why he wrecked our lake.

"Weelll," says Dad, under fire. "Well, we need to eat, you know."

"Well I don't want to eat then! It used to be so pretty and now it's so ugly!" Which isn't worth answering, I guess. "And what about the loon? And the beavers? What happened to them?"

"Don't worry about them," Dad says. "They'll be back. And it will be beautiful again, don't worry about that."

I can see Dad gathering his thoughts.

"There will be lots of berries for us to pick this summer with all that extra sun on them," he says. "Then the alders will grow really thick for forty or fifty years or so, feeding the soil, turning it into a perfect place to grow the big evergreens that come after the alders. When the alders start dying off, the evergreens grow—cedar, spruce, hemlock—all the trees we just logged off, and you won't even know we were here."

Dad points at the hill across from camp.

"See that hill?" he asks. "Right now, it's covered in alders. Gildersleeve logged that when I was a young man. By the time you're my age, or maybe a grandma, that hill will be all grown up with evergreens again."

"Humph."

Me a grandma is ridiculous, and I just want my lake back. And my secret fort.

Dad and Uncle Alvin see trees differently than I do. Uncle Alvin says, "Trees are beautiful standing and even more beautiful in the chuck!" But Dad and Uncle Alvin follow all the rules when they log. When GMG starts logging up the Coho Valley, they are required to leave firebreaks and burn slash. The road begins at the landing in the little cove and rises up two hills before it gets past the previous logging done by Grandpa Gildersleeve somewhere between 1937, when he arrived in Smith Inlet, and 1945, when he retired. This is the slash that includes the hill on the point I can see from my house—the one that Dad says will be full-grown trees when I am his age or maybe a grandma.

At the top of the second hill, which is quite steep and I have the scars to prove it, GMG begins their first show. According to forestry regulations, they can log for about a mile before they are required to leave a "firebreak" of untouched trees, which is also about a mile. And this has all been predetermined and marked with bright orange Xs on the trees and bright orange tape. The theory is that the firebreaks, which burn slower than logging slash in case of fire, will also reseed the logged areas by dropping and blowing seeds onto the nearby slash.

In addition, the loggers are required to burn their slash. Regulations to burn slash were made following a disastrous fire on Vancouver Island in 1938 which burnt seventy-five thousand acres. Its enormity was blamed on the quick-burning, dead and dry logging slash. In the fall, the dads take turns spending weary nights watching their slash fires, coming home at the end of the next workday exhausted and smoky. (Later, it is thought that burning could prevent reforestation, and methods move towards such solutions as pile burning or chipping.)

So by the time the road is completed, we will walk first through Grandpa Gildersleeve's old slash, which is becoming a baby forest, then through GMG's new slash, blackened by fire, then some tall trees, then even more recent slash, then more firebreak, 'til the road will eventually end at the last logging site, four miles into the valley, not far from Caroline Lake. By the time they have logged to the end, the theory is that enough time has passed to "green up" the old slash so they can log the firebreaks on their way back out of the valley. It will take GMG about five full time years and five extended summers to do this.

We can see all of this from the airplane when we fly into camp. I can see the pale patches where Grandpa Gildersleeve's logging slash is filling in. Randall Logging's slash, alder-pale, shows on the Boswell and the Draney side of the hill at the end of Boswell Inlet. From the south side of Boswell Inlet, after the narrows, there is a sharp rise over a hill which dips into our valley. Our lake is almost exactly a mile up the valley from the landing. We can see our road, bordered by trees and varying stages of slash, and the pale, thick alders lining the creeks, like ribbons rippling through the hills down to the inlet.

In mid-February 1965, GMG sends out its first bargeload of 1500 logs from the valley. No more log booms, no more weeks of booming before the tug arrives. They alert the receiver, Kerr and Dumaresq Timber Company in Vancouver, and the forest ranger in Ocean Falls via radiophone. On May 26, they send out 1560 logs, mid-August 1650. And so it goes. Dad says roughly thirds is a good approximation of the division of profits; a third for stumpage (the government), a third for towing or barging, a third for GMG, who pays wages and expenses from their third. Hard work for not enough, Dad says.

The barge comes approximately every three months. The loaders arrive first, by plane. Aunt Gloria and Mom feed them (they smell of boom-boat, sweat, trees and cigarette smoke, sitting at our table) until the tug and barge arrive, then they stay on the tug and are fed by the tug cook. I watch the squatty little boom-boats pushing the trees that came from my fort by the lake over to the barge. I watch the big crane pick them up, dripping, and stack them in rows across the barge. I watch the tug pull them away. Dad watches me watching.

"Somebody needs them to build their house," he says.

CHAPTER 51

SCHOOL OF HARD KNOCKS

The savage cables rattled through the mist.
The boxing chokers cursed the men they missed.

From *Like a War* by Peter Trower[12]

T he moms hate to see a workboat coming home in the middle of the day because it could mean trouble. In April 1966, Louie came home twice. The first time, he roared straight into the office, called an airplane and was off again without explanation. Soon the workboat came around the corner with the entire logging crew in it. Ernie was hurt.

"I was running donkey when Ernie got hurt," says Lloyd. "Ernie and Joe Deucy were on rigging. Ernie was standing on a long log and the turn caught the other end of the log and he fell, sort of dove, into a creek with a lot of rocks and he broke his leg and got pretty banged up. He got sent to Vancouver and was off work for the rest of the summer."

Ernie is tough. Once he cut his hand with the chainsaw while limbing a spar tree. He ripped off a piece of his shirt, tied it around his hand and kept on going. When he topped the tree, he

---

[12]   Peter Trower, "Like a War," *Raincoast Chronicles First Five*: Stories and History of the BC Coast, Edited by Howard White. Madeira Park: Harbour Publishing, 1976

hung on tight, whipping back and forth with the tree, chainsaw swinging, then rigged the tree with the blood dripping through his shirt bandage onto the brush a hundred feet below.

A week after Ernie broke his leg, the moms saw Louie coming across the water with Lance. He had caught his finger in the fan belt of the truck, and it was nearly cut through. He took a speed-boat to Port Hardy, then flew to Vancouver to save his finger. Now Lance was off work too.

On December 5, 1966, Gloria writes in her diary: "Louis got hurt today. The Angel of the Lord encampeth round about them that fear him. I'm so thankful his life was spared."

"We were at the second setting up the road, just at the top of the hill," remembers Lloyd. "I was running the donkey. We would hang two blocks at the back of the show—they get farther apart as you're changing roads, and the line has to stay straight between them. If the line gets strung around a tree or sapling, the tree or sapling acts like a brake, and when the log comes into the landing you can't get enough slack to unhook the log. So with the donkey, you have to lift the log right up, drop the end on the ground and then set it down.

"So on this day, we were having a horrible time because the rigging crew had strung the line around a sapling. Uncle Louie was on the landing doing everything—chasing, bucking, stacking logs with the loader and loading the truck. Uncle Louie's really good at everything.

"Well, the log came in, and I lifted it up, holding it in the air. I pulled forward to get slack, and it swung in and hit the spar. It turned out to be a hollow cedar log, and the bottom twenty feet or so just broke right off and started rolling towards Uncle Louie. I'll always have a picture in my mind of Uncle Louie running for his life, racing away from that log, rolling, running, trying to get out of its way. He almost made it, but it knocked him down, and

I ran over. Boy, was I glad to see him moving! But it got his knee really bad. His knee swelled up the size of a football and he was off work for quite a while."

The stress of a near miss is released in guffaws and knee slapping and teasing. But when somebody gets hurt, it is not a funny story!

"I guess we could belong to the Turtle Club," Louie says to Alvin.

Alvin nods his hard-hatted head. The hard hats do look rather like the shell of a turtle.

"I guess we could belong more than once," he answers.

The boys wait to hear the stories. As a warning or when they get a little cocky or, God forbid, careless, particularly while running the donkey, the "Remember the time?" stories get told. And all the turtled heads listen.

"Yaaa …" Louis says slowly. "I guess the closest call for you was that choker bell!"

"That *was* a close one!" agrees Alvin. "I blew the whistle to stop, we were just walking in to choke the log, and that's the last thing I knew!"

"I was on the donkey that day," says Lloyd. "The bell caught on a little sapling. Then it let go and whipped around in a 360 and got Dad on the back of the head. We were pretty worried. He came-to after a while. We got him out of the bush, and he flew out to Vancouver for X-rays."

"After the X-ray they told me I could leave the hospital, so I got a taxi and went back to my brother Ken's house," says Alvin. "Well, when I got there, Ken took me straight back to the hospital and told me not to move my head. They said my spine was just hanging on by a hair, right at the base of my neck; it was almost knocked off of the rest of my spine. They said one wrong move and I'd be paralyzed from the neck down."

"What happened?"

Everybody can see that Uncle Alvin is not paralyzed from the neck down.

"Well, they didn't really know what to do with me. I had to lay flat on my back. I could tell something wasn't right, that's for sure. There was a lot of pain. Then one morning it just felt right. It felt like my spine was back in place. So I got up, and they were all telling me to stay down. But they took another X-ray, and it was all back in place; the vertebrae were all lined up again. They didn't know what happened."

The faces are suitably impressed.

"What about you, Uncle Lou?"

"Well, not too long ago somebody fell a tree on my head."

Uncle Louie looks at the boys from under his dented hardhat with a small smile, and certain boys squirm uncomfortably. They truly had fallen a small tree on his head, then in nervous fear, they couldn't stop laughing when Uncle Louie was unable to remember anything.

"And Lance got me one time with a choker bell in the pelvis. I think I gave the boys a bit of a scare that day. I couldn't move. They took me out on a stretcher. That was in 1960 when Al was sick, so we had to stop working for a while.

"But one little experience was almost kind of funny. This was before we had our own operation and my brother Clarence and I were falling. In those days we didn't have power saws. We had misery saws, one of us on each end. You put the springboards in the tree, and sometimes the tree would be on the side of a cliff and one person would be a long ways off the ground. And so it happened that I was on the side that was off the ground, so I decided, well, I'm not going to get off. I'm going to let the tree go over and I'm going to stay up here.

"But as the tree was going over, it made a lot of noise and I guess I got cold feet so I grabbed the springboard with my hands and I hung down and I dropped to what looked like a log down there, farther down, or what looked like kind of a hump. And it so happened, as I landed on that log down there, the tree that we were falling hit that same tree, on the top, and it worked like a catapult. It was not too sudden, it was kind of a gentle start, but it catapulted me way up in the air. Clarence, he came around the back of the tree and he didn't see me anywhere. He wondered where I went.

"Well, I went up into a tree and I came down and I landed in some very deep moss. There was a little hemlock stump right beside it, but I landed not far away in this really deep moss and I really didn't hurt myself very much. I landed on my shoulders. There was a little tiny stick there and that was the only thing. I cut the skin on my back.

"So when Clarence came around the second time, he said, 'Where were you?' And I looked up and I said, 'See those hemlock branches way up there?' And he said 'Ya.' And I said, 'That's where I was!' And of course he didn't believe me because it was quite a ways up. But I said, 'Well that's where I was, because those are the only branches around and I felt those branches brush my face.' It was maybe thirty feet! I figure my guardian angel was with me that day!"

Chuckles and exclamations. Lance says he stabbed his foot with a spur once, when camp was in McBride Bay and they were logging Dry Creek.

"I was climbing a tree holding the rope. Dad was shouting at me to shorten the rope, and I was annoyed with him. I was about twelve feet up, and my spur got stuck in the tree. When I got it unstuck, I came down the tree fast, and one foot stabbed into the other—it went right into the other foot! I was groaning and moaning and about to take my boot off when Dad says to me, 'Don't you take that boot off! You have to walk out of here. I can't carry you.' So I walked out of the bush to the boat. They flew me out to Alert Bay. No bones broken—they taped it up. But it's still sore today!"

There are more stories. Gloria's brother was killed on a cold deck pile—the logs started rolling, and he couldn't outrun 'em. One of Gildersleeve's original partners drowned in the boom. Roy's falling partner was killed by a barber chair. But no one can remember all the stories at the same time. And anyway, no one wants to hear any more.

CHAPTER 52

GRANDPA AND THE SKYLINE

G randpa and Grandma Ritchey don't visit us for a long time, but when they do, Grandpa becomes a camp legend. Roland witnessed the event and writes the story of Grandpa and the skyline:

> Grandma Ritchey had high blood pressure, which she would use to her advantage, as in: "I couldn't possibly do that, I have high blood pressure." Mom would encourage them to come visit, and Grandma would say, "I'm not worried about the big jet, but that little floatplane could affect my high blood pressure." But after consulting with her physician, it was determined that her health would remain stable despite the rigours of floatplane travel. So Grandpa and Grandma flew into camp one day. Nobody imagined it would be Grandpa's health we should be concerned about.

> During the course of their stay, Grandpa, an energetic little man, asked Dad if he could come up to the logging site rather than stay at camp with the ladies. Maybe he could help out a little.

And so it was. Grandpa looked quite dapper with an old pair of boots someone had scrounged up, his town clothes, a brand-new pair of heavy cotton gloves, his Hitleresque moustache, and all topped off with a battered tin hard hat. He was actually quite useful, unhooking a few chokers, running a few errands, gassing up chainsaws and the like.

We were skyline logging, and everything was going fine until a turn of logs got hung up on a stump. The engineer poured on the full power of the donkey, and the unthinkable happened. The skyline broke. Well, lines break all the time, mostly chokers, which are considered a consumable item. Any line breaking under extreme tension is a very dangerous event; all the cables swing wildly, there is a lot of crashing and bashing going on, and if one of these cables hit you it could literally cut you in half.

All of us boys, now becoming young men, had been mentored about safety from an early age by the adult men in camp; when a cable broke you sought cover ASAP. A broken cable covered a lot of ground in a hurry, and you would have absolutely no chance to jump out of the way if you saw it coming towards you. So at the first sign of trouble, you hit the ground, in a hole or low spot, or behind a log or a stump.

This was the first and last time I have seen a skyline break. The skyline is the largest cable used in the logging operation for good reason—you don't want it to break. All of the other lines are smaller, in part so that if something has to break it will be a less important line like the choker—kind of like a shear pin. When a skyline breaks, several things happen. In this cable bigger than your wrist, there are dozens of strands, all breaking in a different spot, and as they pull apart, the heat from friction makes a huge sheet of flame in the sky. The ends, now free from tension, fly apart and make giant looping coils high above your head—I remember seeing these big snakelike coils, black against the sky. But then gravity takes over and you had best be in a safe spot. Getting hit with any part of this cable would probably end your life. The cable doesn't hit the uneven ground all at the same time so it sounds more like a roar than a bang, and the ground shakes from the weight of thousands of pounds of cable hitting it.

The crew took cover as if the Germans had opened fire; someone in a hole there, behind a stump or log over there, everyone except, yes, you guessed it, everyone except Grandpa. There he was, the only vertical thing on the landscape, standing with a bewildered look on his face, coils of deadly skyline all around. He knew something momentous had happened, but beyond that he had no clue. When he saw everyone in the duck-and-cover mode, he hit the ground too—right beside the coiled skyline that had almost killed him. What is the saying? "God watches over children and fools?" Grandpa was not a fool, but neither did he have the knowledge to be safe in that circumstance.

CHAPTER 53

SATURDAY NIGHTS

A s the sun sets on Saturday nights, the excitement rises. It's play night. Kids start tearing around the floats, chasing each other, teasing the dogs, checking to see who's doing what. On a warm summer night, we might play cops and robbers on the hill in the dark or go swimming to see the phosphorescence. The boys like to roar around in their boats in the dark too.

But it seems there are more winter nights than summer ones. In winter, we play Monopoly, Pit, Flinch and crokinole, and the adults play with us. Dad and Uncle Alvin play a mean crokinole game, and the boys like to challenge them. Sometimes we have a games night at the school, and sometimes we just invite friends over and eat popcorn and fruit salad. At our house, we eat cheese and onion sandwiches on Saturday nights.

We have "movie night" at least once a month now because all the new camps share movies before sending them back. Dad sits at the back and runs the projector, and Uncle Alvin sits across from him in the little nook beside the cabinet that's just big enough for one chair. The chairs have shiny wood seats and backs with metal legs and are usually stacked in that corner. Uncle Alvin eats peppermints—he has endless peppermints in his pockets—for his stomach. He even smells like a peppermint! When I am really small, I sit on his lap so I can see over all the heads, and Uncle Alvin passes me peppermints from his pocket one after another through the whole movie.

The adults often have their own movie night before we do to make sure the movie is suitable for us. At first, magic is frowned upon—if it was up to the moms, we never would have seen *Mary Poppins*! But the dads say, "Our kids know better than to believe that silly stuff. They'll be fine."

"What did you think when Mary Poppins brought all those things out of her bag?" asks Mom at bedtime. "You know that's not real, right? It's just for fun."

Lobo, *Big Yeller*, *Pollyanna*, *The Incredible Journey*, all make the good list. Silly movies, like *The Shaggy Dog*, *The Headless Horse*, and *The Absent-Minded Professor* with his "flubber" are noted afterward by the adults as being silly.

"Well THAT was a silly movie!" they say in disgust.

But between us, we girls remember all the words to the theme songs and sing them for weeks.

Whenever they can, our parents order films about Christian martyrs—examples for us. We'll watch anything, which is proven by the fact that we will sit through the whole volcano movie. Every time!

When Mom and Dad visited Hawaii, Dad was intrigued by the volcanoes and bought a movie about them. So in our little schoolhouse in Smith Inlet, we can see Kilauea, Hualalai, Haleakala and more, and one of them is erupting, the hot red lava bubbling and flowing. "Pahoehoe," and "'A'A," says the narrator about the flowing lava. Then the black crust with wrinkly red cracks moves slowly across the plantation, destroying the crop, and we watch the whole thing right to the last image of the hot lava flowing into the sea while the grand music fades. Ever after, whenever a movie is unsuitable for viewing or doesn't show up, the volcano movie is brought out so we won't be disappointed.

Dad also has home movies. He loves the newest technology and bought a 16mm movie camera in about 1960. He takes infinite boring pictures of trees and cables and donkeys and trees being felled, trees screaming down the hill at the end of their chokers, grappled, loaded on the truck, rolled off the truck, boomed and barged. Then, if we don't have a real movie on a Saturday night, and we're all desperate enough, he shows them. They're about ten minutes each, so a lot of time is spent spinning them back on their reels and threading the next one through the gadgets on the movie projector.

He also films birds and whales and fish jumping. We wait impatiently for the skiing and diving-off-the-*Surf-Isle* pictures. When at last we see Lloyd dive off the *Surf Isle*, the crowd goes wild. There are at least five minutes of people skiing and diving into the water, and we get a lot more footage out of it than is actually there.

"Backwards! Backwards!" we yell.

And Dad plays the film backwards. Dennis shoots backwards out of the water, feet first, the water zips closed behind him. He lands neatly on the *Surf Isle* roof. Then Murray, Roland, various others and, lastly, Lloyd. Hurrah! People diving and jumping out of the water backwards is hilarious! Our hilarity makes the adults laugh, too, and sometimes Dad even plays it backwards twice to extend the mood.

Then we beg for a sleepover with whomever we've been hanging out with—maybe just one friend or a big sleepover with everyone— Barbara and Brenda, too, in an empty house or a tent. The boys don't have sleepovers so much; I think they'd rather go camping.

One time, all the girls have a sleepover in Laverne's tent behind her house. Auntie Alma brings us snacks. Snacks, scary stories and secrets are the usual for a good sleepover. Laverne tells us a secret. She says her Grandpa Knopp had a big brown accordion that he used to play in the marching band when he was a major in the German Army. We are not allowed to tell anyone. It's a big secret because he escaped the German Army and they might come over here and get him and kill him. He was a sniper. We imagine him marching along with his big brown accordion, whipping out his sniper rifle now and then to shoot the enemy. Laverne says that her grandpa being in the German Army explains why her dad is so strict and talks like he is barking orders. In his house, you follow orders without question or else.

"Or else what? You get snipered?"

"Or else you get a lickin'!"

This we can all understand. Helen's dad gives her lickins'. Her worst lickin' was because of the time she and Doug captured the bear. Second worst was the time she walked out onto the boom-stick when camp was being towed. My mom gives ours. "Spare the rod and spoil the child," we hear the parents say to each other, often while observing some bratty behaviour, and it sounds like a hint that a lickin' is in order. Laverne got a lickin' for not eating her supper, so then she found that she couldn't eat supper.

"So what do you do if you can't eat supper and if you don't eat supper, you'll get a lickin'?"

"I just push my food around on my plate to look like I'm going to eat it. Then I push some food into my hand, then I yawn. When I yawn, I stretch my hand out to the side and drop the food behind the bench, right behind Dad's head. He never knows."

"So you go to bed without supper?"

"Ya, but I eat lots of food during the day."

"What happens to the food behind the bench?"

"I don't know."

We think maybe Rover eats it.

Donna's special torment is her brothers. They torment her in numerous ways and give her noogies, which wrecks her hair and hurts.

When Cousin Kathy McGill visits, we have a sleepover in an empty house. Kathy's dad is the Dr. Ken who birthed me.

"You should not wear your underwear to bed," says Kathy.

"Why not?"

"Because my dad says it causes infections. He says we need to air it out at night."

We sure don't want an infection down there, so we all take our underwear off.

"Dad invented a surgery for women who accidentally pee when they sneeze," Kathy says.

Kathy is already getting her period too.

"My dad says girls are getting their periods younger now because of eating meat. He says there are hormones in the meat."

So I think I will never get mine. I will be the last one. Or maybe never because I don't eat meat.

One Saturday night when the bunkhouse is empty, cavernous and dark, we have a sleepover in one of the big rooms. It's especially creaky and creepy, and we snuggle deep into our sleeping bags. We talk about what we want our husbands to be like and how many children we will have, and we make a game of telling each other what kind of husband they will have and how many babies. We choose favourite boy and girl names for them, even though Laverne only wants girl babies, the first of which will be named Proserpine. Helen wants both girls and boys, and she wants the boy to be named Ryan. And for some reason that I will never know, I get voted "first to marry and have babies."

"I will not be first!" I yell. "Why will I be first?"

"Oh yes you will," says Helen.

"Will not, will not, will not. YOU will!" I pummel her.

"No, YOU will." Shove.

The whole world is before us, and it feels like the possibilities are endless. We don't think, *What will happen to us?* We think, *What will we choose?* If we had known what the outside world was really like, we might have crawled back into our sleeping bags and stayed there.

CHAPTER 54

A SNOWY DAY ON WATER

The floats are low in the water, heavy with new snow. Chunks of it, broken off, are floating like icebergs submerged in the velvety grey. A row of seagulls, lined up quietly like teeth, float on a log. There's no sound yet. The snow has sent every noisemaker for cover and blanketed the crunchy, squeaky things, like the cables between the floats and the wood rubbing on wood.

A seagull's squawk breaks the silence and starts all the seagulls squawking, then the crows, ducks, loons, geese and herons, and morning begins. Voices, quieted by walls and sleeping children, begin to murmur, the porridge pot clangs on its way out of the cupboard. Probably the light plant will start now—the days are dark, and maybe somebody needs to do wash. There's a roar and the glare of light bulbs popping on.

Many porridge pots and many voices, sounds of scuffling, jockeying for the one bathroom. Breakfast noises—the news and weather droning, children chattering, dishes clanging and dads leaning into the radio calling, "Hush! I'm trying to hear the weather."

Doors squeal and bang, and the brothers feed the dogs the leftover porridge. Dad footsteps crunch on snow. Snow shovels scrape, and snow splashes into the water. Then the outboard motor revs up, and all the long-johned and work-clad dads pile into the workboat and take off across the inlet. Any more snow and the dads would have stayed home, tinkering in the toolshed or discussing important things in the office. Logging is hard enough without snow covering everything and making it slippery. In fact, they might come home early today if it's bad up there.

Kids in all sizes are out as soon as they can get bundled into snowsuits, mitts and toques. There is a noisy jumble to find something that fits this year, hand-me-downs are made, and puffy children with horizontal arms emerge from the houses. We make angels, throw snowballs, build snowmen and snow barricades, pull each other around on sleds or pieces of plywood with a rope, and suck on the big icicles that hang like fangs from the eaves.

By now the moms have cleaned up breakfast and are on to their next task. If it's laundry, it will be a steamy day in the house, with everything hanging on the drying rack over the stove. Mom pulls the rack down by a string on a pulley to hang the clothes, then pulls it back up out of the way of her cooking.

In the old days, Mom says, the winters were colder and it snowed more and there was thicker ice. They skated behind camp often and had skating parties with other camps. When camp was first in Security Bay, they got iced in, she says. When they started running out of food, Dad made skis by tying some shiplap onto his feet and slid his way, left, right, all the way to Boswell Cannery to buy some groceries. Everyone worried and kept peering at the corner towards Boswell. They were afraid Dad would fall through the ice and no one would be able to help. But he rounded the corner all right, loaded with groceries, and was the hero.

Another winter a nearby camp was iced in, so the men took them groceries. They went as far as they could in their boat, then they filled a rowboat with the groceries and slid it along the ice, running on both sides, ready to jump in if the ice broke under their feet.

Now our skating parties are mostly at Loon Lake, and they're one of my favourite things about winter! We walk up the road to the lake, crunching through the snow, packing our skates over our shoulder. The parents pack hot chocolate and goodies. There is already a fire on the edge of the lake when we get there, and the dads have shovelled off a space for skating. The parents skate with their arms around each other, swish, swish around the circle. The kids practise fancy things or just try to stay upright. We play a form of hockey, and a crazy, falling-down game of crack the whip.

The sky darkens, the wolves begin to howl, and we skate a little closer to the fire. On the edge of the dark, with the wolves howling, the stars over my head, the path of the moon at my feet, I feel shivers of fearful wonder. I wish I could save this forever.

At the fire everyone is cheery, chatting and singing and sipping hot chocolate and eating sandwiches. We talk about wolves. The adults all seem to have a wolf story.

"The wolves chased some deer into the boom the other day. The deer ran along the logs and jumped into the water and the wolves followed and chewed on the deer's ears."

"Remember the wolf sitting in the middle of the road and we chased it with the crummy?"

"Remember the time Roy came back to the road on a freezing night to put antifreeze in the Cat and the wolves surrounded him, eyes glowing in the dark. Well he couldn't stay on the Cat all night and all he had was a flashlight and a little short-handled shovel used for cleaning mud out of the tracks. So he waved them both around a lot and hollered his way back to the boat."

Wolves don't like fire, we are told, so we are safe. But what about when we walk down the road in the dark?

The distance to the boat is so much longer on the way back. We hurry into the path of our flashlights, nervously jabbing the beam into the forest edges to keep the wolves at bay. We jump over each other in our hurry to get back into the boat, and fly home with the keen breeze stinging our faces.

Clyde and Alvin with Christmas dinner!

CHAPTER 55

CHRISTMAS

My other favourite thing about winter is Christmas, of course! The season starts with the teacher assigning parts to play in the Christmas program. Practices are scheduled into every school day, a stage is built and sheets are strung on a wire across the front of the stage. At home, the moms spend hours sewing costumes and making props.

Ever since the school opened in 1954, the school Christmas program has been the biggest event of the year. There are great expectations, and every teacher makes great efforts, leaving behind a legacy of unforgettable moments. Marcia sings "I Saw Mommy Kissing Santa Claus," and Rosemary recites the entire *'Twas the Night Before Christmas*. Helen, dressed up to look like a stuffed doll, sings "Don't let me faint, someone get me a fan. And someone please run for the medicine man. Everyone hurry as fast as you can, cause I've got a pain in my sawdust!" My brother dresses up like an old woman who tries to sell everyone "stone soup." He's the star of the show, but kids still tease him.

My first-grade teacher, June Schneider, creates a special flower pageant for the girls. We dress like flowers and walk in special patterns on the stage to classical music played on the school's record player. Dennis is the curtain puller.

"You'll do great, girls," he says.

The curtain opens, and we see all the faces watching us—Mom and Dad, Aunt Gloria and Uncle Alvin, all the parents from camp and from elsewhere, some from the village, and the crew off a herring boat. They never all look at us like this. We can't disappoint.

The next year, Sherman McCormick is our teacher, and we put on a play about the origin of the song "Silent Night." Brian is the narrator, Dennis the priest, Ken plays the part of the frustrated organist who must tell the priest that the organ cannot be used. Donna, Laverne, Brenda and I, in little white capes with black bows, are the children's choir who sing "Silent Night" for the first time in the whole world. The parents clap as hard as they can as the curtain closes.

But the best part of the Christmas program is saved for last! We have been wondering and guessing and making silly bets about who Santa Claus will be this year. It is a well-kept secret. When Santa bursts in the door with a "Ho, ho, ho!" we shriek.

"It's Mr. Frank!"

"It's Uncle Alvin!"

"It's Dad!"

We all know immediately who it is. Santa Claus passes out brown paper bags filled with goodies—Japanese oranges, nuts and candy, a popcorn ball. The parents are a wild, chattering jumble, filling the school, and we crowd around the stage, waiting for our turn. "Well, hello little girl, have you been good this year?" Some Santas are better than others.

After school is out for the Christmas holiday, we have a huge dinner! The dads get sawhorses and boards and put a table down the entire length of the schoolhouse—you can hardly get around the end of it—and more tables along the windows for the kids. It's a sit-down dinner for everyone! There's turkey, vegetarian loaf, sometimes a goose. Mom makes a salmon roll with biscuit dough and canned salmon and slices it into pinwheels. All the Christmas favourites are on the table: gravy, stuffing, mashed potatoes, sweet potatoes with marshmallows on top, side dishes unmemorable, cranberry sauce, the infamous and gagful jellied salads full of shredded vegetables that only adults like, various pickled things, and fresh white buns with butter. The back counter is covered in pies, cakes, cookies and fudge.

At home, our Christmas tree seems to be left to the very last, until it becomes a great urgency. Dad piles us into the workboat, and we roar off to scan the shoreline for the perfect tree, lifting our feet every time the boat slows down so the water rushing forward doesn't give us a soaker. Dad goes to a logging slash with trees the right size. I don't even get out of the boat. He cuts it down in about one second, and we're sharing space with limbs and pokey needles, speeding home to the smell of tree.

Mom has been baking while we're gone, and the house smells like molasses and spice. She makes us hot chocolate, and we huddle in front of the fireplace. Dad drops the tree into the corner, pushing the chair aside, and twirls it around until Mom is satisfied that the fullest side is forward. Then somehow it gets decorated, and I lay under it and smell the lights warming up the needles.

On Christmas Day, every family in camp has their own Christmas, their own favourite foods and traditions. Ours are the traditions Mom learned when she was a girl. On Christmas Eve, Mom hands us a present from under the tree to unwrap—always pajamas— and Dad reads the real Christmas story from the Bible. Christmas morning, we can get up as early as we like to open our stockings, which are Dad's baggiest work socks hooked into the fireplace vent with diaper pins! Inside are nuts and Japanese oranges and candy to keep us happy until we gather around the tree, and Dad, in his Santa Claus voice with many a "Ho, ho, ho!" passes out our presents.

Aside, Dad says to Mom, "So much! The children won't learn to appreciate things."

This is Dad's most annoying quality. We shouldn't have too much stuff because we won't appreciate it unless we work for it, he says. Mom buys us things anyway, but I'm sure she would buy us more if it weren't for that consistent, disapproving comment.

"What was *your* Christmas like, Dad? When you were a little boy? What did *you* get for presents?"

"Weeell …"

He pauses. He always thinks a moment before he begins a story. But his stories are good and his voice soothing, so we snuggle in.

"Christmas in those early homestead days was different than we have it now," he says. "During the hungry thirties there wasn't, well, most people didn't have much money to spend. But it was always a pretty big day because Dad would bring home a big bag of peanuts, and we could eat as many peanuts as we wanted."

Yay. Peanuts. But we don't say this out loud.

"We didn't hang up stockings in our home. What we did was, we set the table on Christmas Eve, the same as we would ordinarily for our meal, then after we were in bed, we could hear our parents filling all the plates. There were peanuts, of course, and maybe some other nuts and some candy and maybe an orange or something, which we didn't ordinarily have. We had happy times around our table. And Father always prayed the blessing in the old language: 'Komm, Herr Jesu, sei du unser Gast, und segne was du uns aus Gnaden bescheret hast. Amen.'"

"What does that mean?" It's strange to hear Dad talking in his old language.

"It means: 'Come Lord Jesus, and be our Guest, and let these Thy gifts to us be blest.'"

"And if there had been a good crop," Dad says, "or if there was any money, then there might even be a little present beside the plate."

"What kind of little present?"

"Well, I can remember Christmas 1925 because I got a little bronze elephant, which was like a bank with a slot in the top to put coins in. I must have thought it was kind of special because I still remember that. That was when we still lived in the Carson area, Saskatchewan, before we moved in the covered wagon to the homestead in Flat Valley.

"In the Carson years, I remember huddling under the fur blankets with Frank and John on the sleigh, and we rode to our grandparents' house in Waldheim on Christmas Day. The horses had bells, and Mother and Mary would sing Christmas carols all the way. My grandmother always had a big tree blazing with real candles all over it. I'm still amazed the house didn't burn down.

"So toys, if we had any toys, it was usually something we made ourselves. But Christmas was still pretty special. We had goodies, and dinner; it was usually a roast goose, a farm goose, because farmers in those days had everything. They had geese, they had turkeys, they had ducks, they had chickens, they had guinea hens, and you name it. It seemed to be the thing to do.

"And New Year's Day was special, too, because Mother would bake these New Year's kuchen, and they were quite tasty. They're like a doughnut; they're deep-fried, but they have raisins in them. And we thought they were pretty good."

We're feeling a bit of awe and wonder at Dad's strange and toyless childhood. Poor Dad. But the cookies that are really a doughnut—that's pretty lucky. And the sleigh ride under the furs, over the snow, to grandmother's house—just like the song—we want to do that!

"I have another little story if you want to hear it," Dad says.

And of course we do.

"It was the first Christmas I was away from home. It was the winter of 1933. I was about sixteen, and I went fishing with a guy named Howard up in Cold Lake and Pierce Lake and Lac-des-Îles and, in this story, Island Lake, which is too small to be on the map. We lived on a quarter section between the towns of Goodsoil and Peerless, not too far from these lakes.

"Well, some of the best fishing was done in winter. Howard had a caboose, which is just a small hut with a stove in it, on a sled pulled by horse, and he would stay at the lake for the duration of the fishing opening—several weeks. In winter, trucks could easily drive across the lakes, so it was easy to ship the fish out.

"When the gun went off, Howard, myself and another guy—I can't remember his name—were at the ready. Howard was a huge, strong man and he used a large, pointed pick, and he hammered that thing into the three-foot-thick ice like Paul Bunyan, ice flying everywhere. When the water started to flow, I started to trim the edges of the hole with a sharp tool. The other guy shovelled the ice away. Speed was important because we had to get our nets in the water before the other guys! Lots of guys were out there with their cabooses all over the lake.

"When there was a nice rectangular hole with a slanted edge for the net to slide down, we shot the jigger [a board with a slit in it, a shackle and a rope] over and over 'til we figured it was about a hundred feet away. Then, if Howard had figured right, we would dig the next hole right on top of the jigger and pull the net through. Nets were a hundred feet long. Howard let me have three nets, and I also got five percent of the profits—that's how I got paid. And Howard paid all the expenses."

"How many nets did Howard have?"

"Howard had way too many nets; he was cheating the government."

Dad makes a frowny face at us to make sure we know that he doesn't approve of Howard cheating the government.

"Once a day we pulled the nets, picking the fish [white fish] into boxes. We delivered the fish to two Scotsmen every night, who packed the fish in boxes with ice then put them in a caboose to keep the fish from freezing. The truckers came every few days and took the fresh fish to market to fancy restaurants in places like Chicago and New York.

"Well, the opening lasts through Christmas, and the market is good at Christmas, so I spent my first Christmas away from home fishing for Howard. Unfortunately, on this trip Howard gave the job of buying grub to the other guy. The other guy was cheap, and he didn't buy enough grub. When we ran out of grub, we ate two white fish a day, between the three of us, for many days. We were pretty tired of it.

"So when Christmas day arrived, there was a Metis who lived nearby, and he saw our situation, and he invited us for Christmas dinner. We were pretty happy. The man had a wife and two kids. They lived in a small cabin—there was a picture of the Mother Mary on the wall. The man told us stories about how he used to scout for Louis Riel during that war. He said sometimes he walked eighty miles a day delivering messages and scouting. Louis Riel kept the seventh day sabbath, he said, and told his scouts that was the day to keep. So I found that very interesting, of course.

"Well, we had dinner, and it was dried blueberries in hot fat for the main course! It was a special meal for them. But I just about couldn't eat that."

"Ewe!"

We have a discussion about how disgusting it would be to eat a bowl of hot animal fat with dried blueberries in it. Especially on Christmas.

"Well, Howard seemed to like it all right, he downed a great heaping bowl full!"

"Ewe, yuck!"

Dad chuckles at our response.

"He was a Dane," says Dad, and I wonder why this matters for eating hot bowls of fat. "But we had biscuits with tea for dessert, and that was quite nice. But I sure was homesick for Mother's Christmas baking. And peanuts.

"When we got out of there and got to town, we ate at a restaurant—a huge meal of meat and potatoes and all the fixings, even dessert, for a dollar. While we were eating, we could see that the restaurant across the street was having a dinner special for a dollar that looked pretty good. So when we were done, we walked across the street and had a second meal. We were that hungry!"

We think about Dad's stories all day while we play with our toys that Dad never had. In the late afternoon, we have Christmas dinner and are grateful that it is not hot animal fat with dried blueberries. Mom invites people over for Christmas dinner; she asks whoever needs inviting the most, whether they have kids for us to play with or not; we don't have any say. But we are feeling full of Christmas spirit today. And in the end, it's Dad's stories that are the best Christmas presents of all.

Grandma Eva's New Year's Cookies
From Aunt Mary (Rafuse) Goertzen

1 tbsp. yeast
1 tsp. sugar
½ cup warm water
⅔ cup warm milk
½ cup soft butter
2 eggs, slightly beaten
½ cup sugar
½ tsp. salt
2 cups flour
½ cup raisins
½ cup chopped apple

Soften yeast in ½ cup warm water with 1 tsp. sugar in a small bowl. Melt the butter in the warm milk. Add eggs. Stir in yeast mixture, sugar and salt. Add flour to make a soft dough. Add fruit with the flour. Let rise a bit. Dip out by heaping tablespoons and drop into deep, hot fat (360 – 375°F). Turn. Fry 'til golden on both sides. Serve with powdered sugar.

CHAPTER 56

HAIR

O n Friday nights, the torment of the curlers begins. The pulling, tugging, rolling, the comb dipping in a cup of water, sometimes even some spit on the fingers to smooth the ends, the pile of spongy pink rollers on the table getting smaller ever so slowly. Is there some kind of law saying "Thou shalt have thy hair frizzed all up in order to go to church"? Or any important event of any kind, even the arrival of an airplane? The mothers think so.

Mom has three girls to labour over, plus herself, every Friday night after the busiest workday of the week. Aunt Gloria has only Helen and herself, but she feels it her duty to curl any girl's hair that is within arm's reach on a Friday night. When poor Rosemary stays with her, she regularly gives her a Toni! Helen got one, too, and it's terrible. Aunt Gloria even admits that it's terrible! A Toni's purpose is to keep your hair frizzed night and day for months so that you don't have to curl it every Friday night. But they can go very wrong.

I may hate the curling most of anyone. I whine and moan, beg to go last and entreat Dad on my behalf.

"Do you think we should have our hair curled, Dad? Why do we have to curl our hair?"

And Dad, from his armchair, admits in his diplomatic way, "Well, I think it looks pretty nice straight too."

And Mom says, "Louie!" as she dips and combs and rolls.

It isn't worth it. I truly believe I look worse.

The ladies give themselves Tonis, too, and pin curl their hair, leaving a little "kiss curl" on their forehead. They don't use spongy pink rollers for themselves, they use bobby pins—two bobby pins crisscrossed over each piece of twisted hair. They want curly hair all week, which means their heads are often covered in little round twists of hair with the criss-crosses on top, scalp showing between. They try to hide this with a triangled scarf tied at the back of their neck. Their attempt at constantly beautiful hair backfires all the time, though, when an airplane or boat shows up unexpectedly. As soon as the pin-curled lady hears the buzz of a plane or the hum of a boat, she clutches her head and cries, "My hair, my hair!"

And then one day, Mom takes me to see Aunt Gloria.

"NITS!" declares Aunt Gloria, picking through my hair. "Hard to see because her hair is so white, but they're there! Believe me, I should know, I've seen my share! The good news is, if there's lice, you'll be able to see them real easy—they'll stand out against the white."

Helen has them too. We are horrified and obedient. So there we sit, side by side, watching our hair fall to the floor as Aunt Gloria cuts it all off. Then we get the kerosene treatment. The kerosene burns, and we whimper and cry, holding towels over our faces. When we can't stand it any longer, our moms wash our hair in the bathtub. Then they clean everything with disinfectant and do loads of laundry, and Helen and I, shorn and sad, are mollified with sandwiches and cookies.

And now Aunt Dorothy is in camp. I love Aunt Dorothy. She is always smoothing things out between everybody, and she is so nice to me. When she says something, you know it's true because she is so wise and logical. But Aunt Dorothy loves short hair or hates long hair, I'm not sure which, and this turns out to be a problem for me. She would like to help out my mom by eliminating the stringy long hair issue.

"I could just cut it up to here," she says, levelling her hand in a chopping pose just below my ears. "It would be so cute, and it would grow back thicker. Like Donna's. You like Donna's hair, don't you?"

With Mom and Aunt Dorothy hovering and practically begging to cut my hair because it will be so "cute," I submit, watching sorrowfully as my locks fall to the floor. And there I am, shorn again, with my stick-straight hair. It's not like Donna's at all! Donna's hair bounces around her face and has a slight upward curl at the ends. Mine is just straight and square, bulging a little over the ears, bangs high on the forehead with a cowlick on the right. Mom still thinks she should curl it on Friday nights too. So for church, I have a *bumpy* square on my head.

When it starts to grow out, "Oops those bangs! I'll just get my scissors and fix that right up for you." All free of charge too. It's just what one mother does to help another mom with her poor daughter's hair.

I beg and finally insist on growing my hair out. I mean seriously grow it out—bangs and all. My hair hangs over my eyes and drives Aunt Dorothy crazy. Every time she sees me, she says, "Just a little snip here and here—it would fix those split ends right up and make it grow back thicker." Nope. Heard that before. Finally, "Just the bangs then, just a little trim." Nope. Stay away from the hair. I have to stay clear of Aunt Dorothy while my hair grows out or Mom might cave.

Finally, I have long hair again. Even the bangs. I wash it about once a week. By about the fourth day the colour is several shades darker and the strands separate into thin, greasy strings. I wash my hair at night before I go to bed and leave it wrapped in a towel so my head won't be cold—practical. In the morning, I have a matted twist of dirty-gold which detangles into a kinky mess with thin, ragged ends that I constantly toss out of my eyes. But it's not curled, it's not square and, most importantly, it is long!

CHAPTER 57

1966: A YEARFUL!

On the morning of Monday, April 11, 1966, a localized snowstorm at Actaeon Sound in Drury Inlet brings down a BC Airlines plane chartered by Nalos Lumber Company. Onboard are Joseph Haas, 55, president and managing director of Nalos Lumber Company; George McBryer, 50, director of logging operations for Nalos Lumber Company; Gerald G. Bell, 35, senior buyer from Domitar Chemical's Forest Products division; and Jim McClellan, 25, pilot.

A search party of three BC Airlines planes and three RCAF planes is sent out Tuesday morning. One of them stops in at GMG to ask if anyone heard a plane overhead the day before. The charter was meant to tour Nalos's four logging camps up the coast but didn't arrive at any of them. The plane is found around 9 a.m., nose down, its smashed cabin submerged in the waters of Creasey Bay. There are no survivors. When the announcement is made on the radiophone, Aunt Gloria and Aunt Dorothy are visiting the ladies at Nalos Landing. Everyone is in horrified shock. What will happen to Nalos now?

Two days after the crash, the forestry boat arrives at GMG to discuss quota. Aunt Gloria records in her diary: "The forestry men came in after supper, Louis came over, also Don [Kaufman].

They talked about quota, and it doesn't look good for either Don or us."

At a time when the GMG community is at its height for population, civilization and programming, GMG Logging has overcut their measly quota—the quota that is measly because they logged the Burnt Harbour claim for Nalos Lumber Company in 1957. Forestry laws have been changing, and buying more quota is beyond the reach of small operations like us—logging will now be a game only for the big logging companies. GMG will have just enough quota to support a summer logging show to help the kids through school. Alvin and Louis begin serious discussions about what to do next, and Hazel and Gloria begin scheming locations of where to do it.

The time period is a mix of planning for leaving and planning for staying. Mom and Dad are looking for just the right place to build a house up the road while looking for just the right place to live elsewhere near a school. We kids are oblivious and having the time of our lives.

Freddie and Donnie Anderson and Cousin Donalda and her new husband Frank are living at Kaufman's camp beside us. At GMG, the Nimmos are gone, the Betts are gone, and now we have Joe and Shirley Deucey. They have a little girl named Susie for Tammy to play with, and a baby boy. Sherman and Betty McCormick are new too. And Aunt Gloria is so happy to have all her children home again. Lance and Frankie married over a year ago, and they live in their own float house here with baby Roger, and Lloyd is going to marry Eileen soon and live here too.

All the moms have sons approaching the eighth grade.

"Went down to see Hazel and talked for a long time about what to do with our eighth graders," says Aunt Gloria in her diary. "Then Dorothy came and we discussed it some more, then Alma came in to ask if she could hang wash in Hazel's shed, and we discussed it some more."

The adults are planning ahead, but no one acts like we're leaving anytime soon. We are clearing a playground on the hill behind us. On Sundays, the Kaufmans come over and we all go up the hill; the loggers fall trees and cut brush, and the rest of us drag it to a pile. We make an enormous bonfire, sparks flying skyward into the night like a fireworks display, and on its edges, we roast marshmallows. The adults teach us how to play badminton in the flattest cleared area, just above the newly-built ramp to the beach and just below the newly installed one-thousand-gallon oil tank that gravity-feeds to supply the camp.

Uncle Roy builds the "twirly gig," the funnest swing in the world. It's on a tree growing out of a small cliff. He cut the top of the tree off and attached a round metal thing on the sawed top, with four knotted ropes hanging down that allow us to grab on and swing round and round the tree. We run on the higher bit and swing out over the cliff bit. Run and fly, run and fly. It's absolutely thrilling!

Someone ties a rope to a tall tree that hangs out over the hill dropping down to the rocky beach. We hang onto the rope, run along a log heading straight out towards the beach, jump onto the knot, swing out over the water, swing back and land with a thump at the base of the tree. The dads also put up a traditional set of swings between the trees; two swings with ropes and board seats that you can pump up high then jump off onto the springy earth.

Uncle Alvin builds teeter-totters on stumps high over the water—we can see the roofs of our houses while we teeter-totter—and there are trails between everything up and down the hill. On the north side of the hill is the "Queen's Throne," a rotting stump mounded with soft red moss, each frond like a little red star. There are earthy holes under trees to crawl into and hide when we play cops and robbers on a summer Saturday night, and if we're feeling adventurous, we can climb down the far side of the hill to a tiny cove and see the Kaufmans' camp. Uncle Alvin and Aunt Gloria make a garden on the hill right behind their house, but mostly it's our hill, and we spend hours on it. We feel like lucky ducks!

We're getting our exercise on the hill, but the moms get their exercise by walking up the road. They complain about being too fat, so when they don't have time to walk up the road, they run laps around their house while we're at school. When I go to my piano lesson, Aunt Gloria tells me she ran twenty-two laps this morning!

On a Sunday, Aunt Gloria takes all the ladies and kids to Boswell on the *Surf Isle* to meet the freight boat. It's like a party! While the ladies visit, we buy candy at the store, run up and down the huge water pipes, shimmy ropes in the net-loft and sit on the high edge of the wharf watching for the freight boat. When Aunt Gloria pulls the *Surf Isle* up beside the freight boat so they can unload the gas tanks onto her deck, I think, *When I grow up, I will drive the* Surf Isle *just like Aunt Gloria.*

On another Sunday, all the girls row to Zero Cove for a picnic, and we find treasure—two old coins in a tiny tidepool in the rocks. We take them home, and Dad says, "Wow! These are ancient Spanish coins!" Mr. McCormick wonders if Jacinto Caamaño stopped by in 1792. We make up several stories about how Jacinto Caamaño could have ended up in our Zero Cove. Perhaps he was searching for huckleberries to prevent scurvy in his sailors and while scrambling over the rocks, the coins fell out of his pockets. But because we can't agree on who spotted them first (though I'm pretty sure it was Brenda), and we all want them, with great ceremony we commit an act of sacrifice and solidarity and throw them into the chuck and watch them sink out of sight.

For the good of all. No one approves of our foolish solution, which imbues it with even more meaning.

Mr. McCormick is our new teacher. He's a pretty good sport and takes a lot of the boys' tricks with patience. Some of the boys make it a favourite pastime to invent ways of tormenting the teacher just to the point of getting into trouble. One time, the boys pour water on the floats at the schoolhouse door so that when Mr. McCormick comes to school in the morning he would slip on the ice and, with any luck, into the chuck. Mr. McCormick slips, as planned, arms windmilling, and lands—kathunk—just short of the chuck.

Then one day the class is playing Go Go Stop. The idea is to trust the person leading and keep your eyes shut. Dennis is the leader and yells, "Stop!" just as Mr. McCormick reaches the edge of the float. Mr. McCormick opens his eyes and sees that his toes are hanging over the edge. His arms start windmilling again, and when he realises he isn't going to succeed, he leaps out into the chuck. It is always so hilarious to watch an adult fall in the chuck— dignity lost, thrashing, hair in their eyes, clothes billowing, shoes falling off while they try to haul themselves out onto the float. But Mr. McCormick comes out angry, and Dennis sees that he is going to get in trouble, so he immediately stops laughing and says in a whiney voice, "Well, I told you to stop."

Sometimes Mrs. McCormick teaches class, and she has no problems with discipline. She has the gift of a special stare; one smiling stare from her pretty face and we all stop in our tracks and say, "Yes ma'am."

Mr. and Mrs. McCormick are very energetic, and they do their best to bring us out of the dark ages of the "just run off and play" days. Mr. McCormick teaches trumpet and trombone lessons and forms a little band. He drags us outside for callisthenics and sit-ups and push-ups and deep knee bends. He and his wife start a

Pathfinder program, with badges to earn: shells, birds, sewing, knots—there is a long list to choose from. And they start Friday night vespers programs and "tumbling" in the empty bunkhouse in the evenings.

When school gets out, we take a trip to Vancouver in the *Surf Isle* to pick up Marcia, back from school in Hawaii, and go to Lloyd and Eileen's wedding. We leave at midnight, so at bedtime all of us kids go to bed in the hatch. The men drive all night, all day and all the next night. Thirty-one hours we are on the boat, then we wobble off on our sea legs, smelling of diesel, our heads full of the sound of the absence of the motor, to pick up Marcia at the airport.

Marcia is like a *National Geographic* explorer! Every time she comes home, she brings new foods, music, clothes and hairdos. She wore slingbacks and told us about pizza last time she came home. This time she is wearing a bright blue muumuu, and her hair is poufed on the top with a little bow between the pouf and the bangs. She carries a ukulele on her back and sweet-smelling leis on her arm, which she puts around our necks.

After Lloyd and Eileen's wedding, Cousin Rosalie comes home with us. I love Rosalie. (Later Rosalie uses her middle name, Ann.) When I was little, she took me camping when my sister wouldn't. The big kids had a campout by a beautiful waterfall with round pools, like pearls, stringing out below it. Rosalie helped me up the steep rocks and let me sit beside her at the campfire with all the big kids. She took me to pee in the night and fed me breakfast in the morning, and I have adored her ever since.

This summer I tag along with the big girls as much as I can. Marcia and Rosalie are painting a house. They dance the hula and sing "Pearly Shells" with the ukulele, and they listen to all the Connie Francis records Frankie loans them. In the evenings, they go over to Donalda's or Aunt Gloria's to practise trios and play games. Or they go for boat rides in the dark with the boys. I am sent to bed, and I hear footsteps running by, talking and laughing outside my window, boats speeding in and out. I wish I was big too. In the mornings, I watch them rat their hair into the pouf and put the bow in front. If only my hair were as pretty. I'm trying to be like Marcia, but all that ratting would be such a waste because it all goes flat when you're swimming.

I swim with Helen every day—it's just Helen and me because our friends are away visiting family and Tammy doesn't swim yet. Sometimes we sleep on the island. We pull the rowboat up high, tie it to a cedar limb and throw our sleeping bags onto the soft moss in the centre of the island.

Dennis and Roland go all the way to Ethel Cove sand beach to go camping, and when they come back, Mom takes Marcia, Rosalie, Tammy and me to Ethel Cove and drops us off. Probably Marcia and Rosalie would rather go by themselves, so Tammy and I feel pretty lucky to be going camping with the big girls. The boys left the tent up for us—our big green canvas tent with the front porch that smells musty and smoky-salty. We put our things inside and collect driftwood for a fire. Rosalie and Marcia dig potatoes into the sand by the fire to bake for supper, and at bedtime Tammy and I crawl inside our tent and listen to an evening concert of "Pearly Shells" to the accompaniment of the ukulele and the surf.

In the morning there is a loud ziiiiiiip as the first person gets up and opens the tent, and the sound of the surf comes in. The sand has been smoothed in the night, ready for new footprints. But when I get up a sharp pain shoots through my neck. If I move my head too far to the right, the pain. Marcia is annoyed with my complaints, so I keep quiet even though I'm worried I might die of some kind of terrible, unknown neck disease.

Marcia and Rosalie suntan all day, shiny with oil, while Tammy and I play in the water and dig in the sand—though it's not as much fun as usual with the knife jabbing me in the neck all the time. But by the time Mom comes back to get us, there are bigger things to worry about than my neck.

"Heavens!" Mom says when she sees us. "You're all as red as beets!"

Rosalie is the reddest of all; she is so sick, she gets the whole bed to herself for days! She moans and gasps when she moves, and Mom puts wet sheets on her body, cool cloths on her head and gives her pills. When the blisters pop and ooze, the sheets stick to Rosalie. I feel like it's so unfair that my beloved Rosalie should be in such pain, and the knife in my neck feels like nothing in comparison.

Cousin Bruce, Aunt Mary and Uncle Paul's son, is working here this summer too. Once, long ago in the Saskatchewan days, Uncle Paul saved Dad's teenager neck, and now Dad is happy to give a job to his teenage nephew. Bruce lives in the bunkhouse, but he's at our house a lot. He is very smart and kind, like Aunt Mary. In the evenings after I'm in bed, he paints our kitchen cupboards turquoise. I ask Mom to leave my door open so I can watch him painting. It's fun to see the cupboards turn from wood brown to shiny turquoise. Cousin Bruce has baggy jeans that sag down and show his underwear. Good thing Mom doesn't see, cuz she would tell him to do something about that! She is always telling me to keep my legs together so my panties don't show. She tells my friends too.

"Ladies, what do I see?" she says to us as we all sit on the porch step.

And we know what she sees because she always says this.

"I see your underwear, ladies!"

"Mine? No, not mine! Not mine!"

Our knees snap shut.

"Yes, *everyone's*! It's time to start acting like ladies, girls!"

When school starts again, it's the same as usual, except Dennis takes his grade eight by correspondence and Lloyd and Eileen get the caretaking job at Boswell. So now on Saturday nights we can go to Boswell and play in the net-loft. Frankie, Eileen and Donalda are planning a big Halloween surprise for us in the net-loft, and we talk about it for weeks ahead of time.

Halloween arrives dark and stormy with great gusts of wind. All of our moms have been making costumes for us, and at dark, we go out to see what everyone looks like. "Boo!" A ghost, an old lady, a pirate, a princess, a girl dressed like a boy; costumed friends jump out at every corner, and the wind whips the shrieks right out of our mouths. We load into the boats and pound the waves to Boswell.

At the net-loft there is a witch dressed all in black wearing a tall, pointy hat.

"Enter, if you dare," she cackles, pointing at the haunted house.

It's Frankie, I'm sure of it. I turn the corner, and all is quiet. I see a sign: "Touch this," so I do, and a hand grabs my hand, pulls it.

"Eeeeeek!"

Another room is full of eyeballs and blood soup and a cauldron of something bubbling.

"Ooooooooo."

Each corner brings a new creepy surprise. It's so delightfully horrible, I come out the other side with a huge grin on my face to join an excited group of the previously horrified.

"How was it? Did the hand grab you? Did you feel the gushy eyeball? Hahaha."

Then somebody turns the lights on, and we have a big party with apple bobbing and party games and popcorn balls and juice. Lastly, Don Kaufman has a fireworks display on the wharf. It's an epic, unforgettable party.

While we are thinking that life will go on forever just like this, the adults are steadily preparing to change it forever. And as for Nalos Lumber Company—they are unable to manage without their managers and cannot recover from their terrible loss. A coroner's jury rules that no person can be blamed for the crash, but Rita Haas, Joseph Haas's wife, sues both the pilot's family and BC Airlines. In 1968, she receives a settlement out of court for $137,278—one of the largest settlements ever made in BC at the time according to the newspapers. Nalos Lumber Company's assets are sold for two million dollars, and the only company that was big enough to be a long-lasting presence in the inlet is the first to leave. We find their abandoned houses freely floating in the inlet, full of furniture and discarded belongings, and it feels disturbing and weird and sad.

CHAPTER 58

THE EXODUS

Some of the floats are getting very old—too old and too low to survive a tow across the sound—so in January, the men start building new ones for the Roy McGill house, the cookhouse and the Knopp house, and they help Don Kaufman build one for his house. It is the beginning of the mass exodus from Smith Inlet.

The first to leave—soon after the epic Halloween party—are Frank and Donalda. When school lets out for summer, the Kaufmans leave for Vancouver; Don stays to finish things up, and he'll soon be a full-time fisherman. The McCormicks leave to teach somewhere less isolated. Camps up the inlet shut down and tow out or abandon their houses to the fury of Queen Charlotte Sound. Randall Logging leaves—the Baders buy land on Salt Spring Island. Saying goodbye to old and good friends is so hard. As we pull away on our final visit, the water grows wider between us for the last time.

And then one day in July, my family loads most of our belongings onto the *Surf Isle* and we leave too. GMG is considering investing in something in Sidney; the community has good weather, a good school and opportunity. Our family goes now so that Roland doesn't have to be sent away to school for grade eight. Dad comes with us to help us move then returns to camp to keep logging.

In one year, GMG changes from its fullest and most civilized to the emptiest it has been since the beginning. There is no teacher and so few students left that Alvin is worried the school district will close the school. But Ron and Katie (Crooks) Lambert move to camp so Katie can teach, and the Wilfrid Michaels family, from Randall Log, move to GMG in December. Katie, the last teacher at Avalon, teaches students Helen, Gary, Doug, Donna, Laverne, Barbara, and Karen and Sam Michaels. Murray and Dennis are sent away to school, and Ken takes his grade eight by correspondence. When the school inspector visits in the spring, he says the school should be closed, but Alvin asks him to turn a blind eye for the remainder of the year.

Logging goes on much the same as before, but now the men spend all their spare time at the mill, sawing lumber. Dad trades our house with the Roy McGill house—they could use the space, he says, and it seems foolish for him to rattle around in it when somebody else needs it. He visits us in Sidney whenever he can, and when we come back for the summer, we live in the Roy McGill house.

But then Uncle Alvin and Dad hear about the big copper mine starting up in Port Hardy and decide that Port Hardy is the place to be. It is the closest town to Smith Inlet, and they can go back and forth to log in the summers until the quota is gone, so it makes sense to them.

On April 25, 1967, Gloria writes in her diary: "Alvin, Ernie, Don and Roy came home tonight. They were all full of stories of the auction. Alvin got a lot, Don and Ernie both got a lot, Andy Waterman got one too. Someday maybe we will all be neighbours in Port Hardy."

In June of 1968, GMG buys a huge piece of land near Storey's Beach for a trailer park and housing development. Alvin will develop the land in Port Hardy, Dad will log the remaining quota in Smith Inlet, and they'll help each other out as needed.

Mom hates living apart from Dad, and now that GMG has decided on Port Hardy instead of Sidney, we leave Roland in Sidney with friends to finish his ninth-grade year and come back to camp. I join the other kids at Avalon again, where the moms are teaching using the government correspondence lessons.

In April 1969, Uncle Paul and Aunt Mary Rafuse and Clyde visit camp to talk about building a school in Port Hardy. Soon, bargeloads of lumber are towed out of Smith Inlet to build new houses, a school and a church in Port Hardy. Andy Waterman, James Walkus and Bruce Rafuse start building two identical houses flipped backwards from each other for Alvin and Louis at the end of Storey's Beach. Later, Ernie will build his own right beside ours, and Laverne and I will be next-door neighbours again!

With full time work at GMG a thing of the past, the exodus continues. Joe and Shirley Deucey leave, Lance goes to work for Greenings (Frankie's Dad) in Rivers, and Lloyd goes fishing. The Michaels will leave last, near the end of summer. Now Fred and Don Anderson work for GMG when they're not fishing, and Ewan Sheard comes to work and brings his wife Irene (Charlie G.'s daughter) and baby June.

Still, camp life goes on. We go to school, do our correspondence lessons, play with our friends and attend church as usual. Gary and Doug finish their correspondence lessons in April and join the logging crew full time. They're only fourteen, but they go falling, and they chase and set chokers with their dads. In June, all the boys are back from school and working, which allows Alvin and Roy to spend more time at the mill cutting lumber for our new houses.

After years of discussion and preparation, the big day finally arrives in August 1969. All the float building is done, and Mom and Aunt Gloria have stocked the houses that will be left behind with their extra furniture, and the cookhouse and bunkhouse with extra bedding and kitchen supplies. We will be the first two houses to leave. The ladies fill their bathtubs, sinks and containers with water. The men separate Alvin's float and the Roy McGill float, where we are living, from the rest of camp and lash them together. We hook up to the *Surf Isle*.

Uncle Alvin pulls us away ever so slowly, out and around our little island and down the inlet towards Queen Charlotte Sound. It's really happening! But the great adventure of it is lost in sadness. We know nothing will ever be the same again. Aunt Gloria has been crying on and off for days. She has lived in Smith Inlet since 1937, and on the floats since she was born in 1922—forty-seven years! We stand outside watching camp disappear house by house as we pass the rocks. Mom is crying now too.

"We'll be back in the summers, don't worry," Mom says. "Just think of it as going away to school. And we will have a nice new house by the beach and you'll each have a bedroom all to yourselves. What colour do you want your new bedroom to be?"

But in my heart, there is no better house than my old house, and no better place to live than where we are. I cry too.

Aunt Gloria writes about our move in her diary that night:

> Sunday, August 24, 1969: Got up as usual and made a lunch for Fred. Alvin and Dennis went to work on lacing Roy's float. They were finished about 2 p.m. And then they cut us loose and started towing. I tried to think of everything. It was a sunny day today. It would sunshine and shower and so on all day. It is beautiful out here towing. I took several pictures. Got our freight when we were going by

Boswell. Got lots of fresh stuff. Helen thought she had lost her cat, but it finally showed up. Helen ate supper with Gayle over at Hazel's, and Roland ate supper here. We had fresh corn. Dennis and Roland are on *Surf Isle* with Alvin tonight. After work, Louis, Roy, Murray and Gary came out to see us. They have gone back now. I have a gas light going.

Monday, August 25, 1969: This was my sister's (Claire's) birthday. Also my dad's and Donnie's. We woke up (Helen and I) in my bed with the floats rocking and the house creaking and the sun shining in our windows. It was beautiful. We were just off Storm Island. I could see Pine too. It was all so lovely. We made good time, got to Port Hardy at 8:30 p.m. Daddy and the boys tied up the camp in Bear Cove and hooked up the water.

Tuesday, August 26, 1969: Hazel and I and the kids went to Port Hardy. [A boat ride across the bay.] We did a little shopping for groceries for Alma. Alvin and Dennis and Roland finished tying up camp, then at noon Alvin left for Smiths again to get Roy.

Two days later, the *Surf Isle* is back, towing our old house with the Roy McGill family in it. Our house will become the Roy McGill house for good and is eventually pulled up onto the beach at Seaview Drive next to Alvin and Gloria's house. Side by side they face Smith Inlet like monuments to their birthplace.

But the houses stay in Bear Cove until just before Christmas, and Gary, Helen, Donna and I take the speed-boat across the bay to go to Robert Scott School every day. Tamara will start grade one at the Fort Rupert School. Most people would think Robert Scott and Fort Rupert Elementary are small schools, but we think they are scary-enormous!

The Knopps stay behind for one more winter to take care of camp. When their house is finally pulled up onto land, a piece of coastal history is added to 5885 Carlton Street. It's the house that Miles Everett from Fish Egg Inlet built in 1952 for his bride, which became the Avalon schoolhouse and dormitory for a year before it was the McGill house. It served a decade as Alvin and Gloria's home, housing or entertaining the whole of Smith Inlet and nearly every visitor at one point or another before finally becoming the Knopp family home until its arrival in Port Hardy in 1970.

The Avalon schoolhouse and the Roy McGill house, both built by Roy, are pulled onto the beach in the Kwakiutl community at Tsaxis (Fort Rupert). And the church, one sad day, is towed to Rivers Inlet to become part of a sports fishing lodge.

Remaining in Smith Inlet, tucked behind the rocks and the little island at Boswell narrows, is the bunkhouse and teacherage, the old, salvaged house the Michaels lived in, the cookhouse with next-door shop, and the original home Dad bought for Mom in 1945 when they were newlyweds. GMG camp is back to its 1945 – 1950 size when it was the only gyppo logging camp in Smith Inlet. And now, two decades later, GMG is again the only gyppo logging camp in Smith Inlet.

PART III
THE SUMMER YEARS

CHAPTER 59

SMITH INLET SUMMER CAMP

School is out for the summer, and I meet the *SeaDoo* at the dock in Port Hardy. It's a sunny evening with a blue, blue sky, hardly a tickle of wind and glassy water. On the boat are Uncle Alvin and Aunt Gloria, Dennis, Helen, Tammy and I. While the sun drops, we nip through the islands and speed down Queen Charlotte Strait past the Cape Caution beach and around the corner into Smith Sound. Just as we pass Watcher Isle, the sun touches the horizon and I think that somebody has lit a match and melted the sky to the water. The flames flicker on our boat and our faces—we are inside the sunset! In awe, we watch the orange ball sink below the molten mass of Queen Charlotte Sound.

In this moment of magic, we come back home.

Camp, what's left of it, broke in half last winter in a violent windstorm, so Uncle Alvin strung it crosswise at the end of the bay, facing Coho Creek. It might be tired and worn, but it looks heavenly to me—home, home, home again!

Every morning when I go out on the porch to fetch bread from the bread can, I see the sun's first rays in the V of the mountains at Coho Creek and the glow of the morning mist on the water.

"The morning sky is an ocean of misty cloud-billows, and treetops are lonely masts of sunken and forgotten ships," Mom writes in her wilderness stories.

We kids used to think Mom's stories were too "flowery" with not enough action. But now, coming back to Smith Inlet from a world of too much action, things are looking more and more how Mom saw them.

It is so quiet here now. Camp was rarely quiet before, with all the kids and dogs and the boys spinning doughnuts in front of camp. Now, after the men go to work, there is complete silence. This must be how it was in the beginning before anyone came to live here. So quiet. We can scream as loud as we like, and only Boswell Mountain hears us and yells right back. When I sing, the melody floats and echoes off the mountain in a single thread, clear and alone.

These summers of the seventies with the GMG boys logging and we sisters cooking for them are a new chapter for GMG—a sort of unique summer camp! A summer camp of hard work, problem-solving and resourcefulness. But we were born for this! These summers are ours—we own them! I call them The Summer Years.

GMG logging truck. Left to right on roof: Gary, Trooper, Dennis. On the front: Ken, Roland and Louis (standing)

Chapter 60

Lou and the Boys

The boys call Dad "Uncle Louie" or "Uncle Lou." Sometimes, behind his back, simply "Lou." In the summers of the seventies, May through September, every day except Saturday, Uncle Louie drives the boys up the road in the crummy and depends on them to do a man's job.

The crummy ride is an experience unto itself. GMG has already worn out one crummy by now, and the road is well on its way to beating up the second. Among many other things that no longer work on the second crummy are the brakes. It hasn't had brakes for years, and only Uncle Louie drives it to work. He has learned the cranky personality quirks of the crummy and knows just when to downshift for the corners and hills.

"One morning, as the crummy rounded the corner by the first bridge, we encountered a big black wolf sitting as pretty as one of Auntie Alma's paintings in the middle of the bridge," says Dennis. "So Uncle Louie thought he'd have a little fun. He revved up the crummy, which only did about thirty miles an hour anyway on that road, and we went bumping along the road at full speed with the wolf easily loping ahead of us. But suddenly the wolf decided to sit down and take a good look at his pursuer. And of course the crummy had no brakes, so Uncle Louie ran over the wolf with a thump. He felt terrible.

'Awe! I didn't mean to kill him!' he says.

"But that didn't stop Uncle Louie from chasing things. When a grizzly was on the road in front of us one morning, Uncle Louie downshifted, the crummy roared, and the bear began to lumber ahead. The grizzly was a mama with two cubs, however, and seemed to remember she was also boss of the woods. She stopped and turned around, stood up and snarled. Uncle Louie downshifted as fast as he could and tried to get the crummy into reverse. Nobody wanted to run into that wall of brown fur or be stalled in her territory!"

At work, the boys pretty much know what to do. All the dads have been training the boys since they were young, some as early as nine, and by now they are real loggers. They've been taught how to fall trees, buck, hook chokers, chase, boom, run a donkey, rig and raise a spar tree, build road, run the loader, drive a logging truck. And of course, carry a knife. Louis waited for the right situation to teach this lesson.

Murray says, "When a knife was needed to cut or trim something, Uncle Louie would ask, 'Who's got a knife?' He was the only one who ever had one, and after gazing at each person and giving sufficient time for silent contemplation, he would say, 'A man with a knife is worth fifty cents more an hour.'"

Choking a log: Dennis, Gary, Kenny McGill (a.k.a. Trooper)

If a boy shows an interest or an aptitude for a particular job, it's given to them. Ken Knopp writes the story of when he was given the job of donkey puncher:

> I always had a desire to learn new things, and when I was fifteen years old that curiosity was rewarded in a big way. Uncle Alvin walked over to where I was preparing to go up the hill and set chokers, and what came next had a huge impact on my life. "Ken, we don't have a donkey puncher today. You are going to run the donkey." My excitement grew as I climbed up to the operator's position and assessed the task at hand; this couldn't be so hard.
>
> The first job of the day was to change roads, and that meant hooking up a small-diameter light cable to the haulback cable and pulling it out to the crew so they could restring it and move the tail-hold blocks to a new position to access more logs. It seemed easy enough, and under the watchful eye of Uncle Alvin I confidently started the operation. Everything went like clockwork right up to when I had to stop the lines where the crew wanted them.
>
> We could move rigging and chokers back and forth by pulling on one line (cable) or the other to either pull the logs to the landing or run the chokers back out to the crew. [Similar to a clothesline, as Roland has described earlier.] But when done incorrectly, as I was about to learn, this can end very badly. When the whistle signal came to stop, I closed down the throttle and applied the brakes.
>
> There was a loud cracking noise like a whip, and immediately everything dropped to the ground. I had stopped the machine incorrectly and it snapped

the strawline like a piece of thread. I figured that I would be fired or at least demoted—I had just broken a cable and caused the crew a whole lot of extra work. The next thing that happened was a life lesson. Uncle Alvin got one of his almost unnoticeable grins on his face and said, "Well, I guess you'll never do *that* again."

There are teaching moments in life that happen at the oddest times, ones that you remember for the rest of your life. Instead of getting angry, he saw this as a learning experience, and he was right. I never wanted to do that ever again. And I suddenly realized the responsibility that came with this job. Not only did I need to learn to be a skilled operator, but the well-being and even the lives of the rigging crew were my responsibility. One mistake could result in someone getting hurt or killed. A very sobering thought.

Raising a spar tree was a unique challenge. It took days of preparation. To get the tree to lift we had to pull from a point near the ground and lift up at the same time. By the time we were ready to lift, we had cables strung around the ground like a psycho spider web. It was zero hour on D-Day for the tree, and I fully expected Uncle Louie to take over the operation when he climbed up on the machine. I stepped back in anticipation of watching a pro lift the tree. To my surprise and shock, Uncle Louie said, "I am not going to lift the tree. It's your job."

What I needed to do was a perfect job of something I had never seen done before. I stepped up to the machine, not bristling with confidence like my first experience but rather very humble and focused. As the slack was taken up and the tree was nudged off the ground, I followed Uncle Louie's calm instructions. Very slowly the tree lifted off the ground and began to rise—all 130 feet of it. The trick was to slack off the two guy-wires just right as the tree lifted so it ended up in a standing position and not landing on the ground, and preferably not on the donkey. As it came up, Uncle Louie coached my actions—which line to pull on, which line to slack off and which line to hold in place.

Then I learned slacklining. There were five different configurations of blocks and lines that we could choose from to move logs from where they were felled to the landing where they were loaded onto the truck. The first was highlead—a simple clothesline set-up. Next a scabline, then a north bend skyline followed by a south bend skyline and last a slackline, which was by far the most complicated but very productive.

It was time to start logging in a new location, and Uncle Louie was silently surveying the setting.

"It's time we tried a slackline," he said.

His words brought both excitement and a bit of nervous anticipation. We were young and ignorant enough to meet every new challenge cheerfully, with confidence, and this was a completely new experience for our young crew. Once again, we strung lines out in a pattern unfamiliar to all of us except Uncle Louie, and once again he oversaw the operation with his usual calm and rational approach.

My job was to control this roaring, hissing machine and operate it with complete precision. There were three friction levers, three brake pedals, a gear shift and a throttle to control. It was somewhat like playing a pipe organ with your feet while directing an orchestra with your hands. The patience and understanding of our Smith Inlet dads while teaching us to be men has been a strong example that has molded my attitudes and my whole life.

Lunch at the donkey: Ken and Dennis

The boys can get a hard hat and caulk boots—required safety gear—at the GMG commissary. They can also buy all kinds of necessities from the GMG commissary, at cost. The commissary was once in the office, but now everything is just stored in a spare bedroom. There are gloves and socks, suspenders, hard hats and more. The price list looks like this: caulk boots $39. each; wool Stanfields, tops or bottoms $3.50 each; striped work shirt $2.75 each; denim work pants $4. each and briefs for 97 cents—tax included.

The boys have been trying on their dad's hardhats and caulk boots since they were toddlers, and it's a like a rite of passage to start wearing them. Safety is second nature to the boys by now; they have always taken it seriously. When Gary started working, he re-created the highlead scenario on his mother's kitchen floor so he could visualize. He built a donkey using his mother's thread spools for drums and thread for the lines, a stick for a spar, and doorknobs for tail-holds. And when he went logging for real, he knew where all the lines were going, what they were for and where not to be.

Greenhorns are a safety hazard. Every summer since 1954, GMG has been giving summer jobs to students to help them through school. Alvin and Louie missed out on a university-educated career due to the war, but they are determined to give that opportunity to anyone else who is hardworking enough to accomplish it. It is a risk to take on greenhorns, and each student has to be taught safety. Disregard for safety, above all the problems and rookie mistakes they encounter on a regular basis as the owners of a logging company, is the one thing they will not tolerate.

"When we were tightening the guy-lines one time," says Dennis, "my cousin Kenny, or Trooper as we called him, was working with us. He was standing in a bight. Uncle Louie told him, patiently at first, to move and get out of the way. But Trooper made a joke about it and jumped over the line like a skipping rope. Well, Uncle Louie stopped and confronted Trooper with the loudest, firmest voice anyone had ever heard. He said, 'I've been logging for thirty-six years, and in all those years nobody has ever died on my watch. And YOU will NOT be the first! Get out of the bight!' Well, we boys looked at each other and thought, *So that's what you had to do to make Uncle Lou mad.*"

Hand signals are taught too. These are done holding the hardhat so the signals are more visible at distances of up to a quarter of a mile away. STOP—swinging the arms back and forth in a horizontal plane like you are warming cold fingers—being the most important. Uncle Louie tells the crew, with a nod towards the donkey puncher, "Don't be swatting flies when you're out on the rigging. Keep your hands in your pockets. You start waving them around, that guy's gonna go ahead on 'er."

Roland says, "If I had to give a new logger safety advice, it would be 'Stay out of the bight!' A logger with any experience knows that the bight is a dangerous place to be, and when logging with cables there are always bights to avoid. A cable under tension wants to be straight; anything that keeps that cable from being straight creates a bulge in the path of the cable, and anywhere and everywhere in this bulge is the 'bight.'

"Trees, branches, rocks—any number of objects can obstruct the cable to create a bight. When the cable is tightened, tremendous pressure is applied to the obstruction. If the obstruction breaks loose, it becomes a projectile, and the cable snaps sideways quicker than you can see it happen. If it hits a logger, he is injured or killed.

"Some bights are necessary. For example, when the haulback circles around the back of the logging claim, it creates a bight. But even this one can be dangerous, as we will see, and when you must remain in a bight for some reason it is wise to get behind a stump or in a hole. A bight obstruction can even be a fire hazard, such as when the haulback is caught behind a log. As it runs back and forth during the course of the day it can generate enough heat from friction to start a fire.

"I don't remember when or how I learned how dangerous the bight is; it seems I always knew it. My dad probably drilled it into me from a young age. One summer I was training a greenhorn, and we had to move something fairly simple. I don't remember what it was, but I do remember that several men could have done it with simple manpower alone. I thought it would be easier to pull it into place with the strawline, so the strawline was pulled off the drum and attached to the object. As nearly always happens, the strawline was not pulled out perfectly straight, and it was obvious, at least to me, that when the engineer tightened the line it was going to create a bight, probably stuck behind a limb or something. It was also obvious the greenhorn was standing smack in the middle of the bight. Our conversation went something like this:

'Get out of the bight.'

'What?'

'When that line straightens, it will fly over and hit you. Get out of the bight.'

'If that little cable comes towards me, I will jump out of the way.'

"Well, in retrospect I should have practised some of my budding logger vocabulary and yelled something like, 'Get the @#$%& out of the &*%$# bight!' But I assessed the situation and thought even if the cable whacked him, it shouldn't be too dangerous because of the light duty job we were doing, so I signalled the engineer to go ahead. When the cable tightened, it slipped off the obstruction and, in less time than it takes to blink, it whacked the greenhorn in his midsection and threw him about fifteen feet. He was left with a bruise about the size and shape of a zucchini and a new respect for the dangers of the bight. For my part, if that cable had hit him in the neck or head, the outcome could have been a disaster.

"Several years earlier when I was pretty much just a kid, I was working on a crew setting chokers when the 'bug' quit working. Without that whistle, the only way we could continue logging was to send hand signals to the engineer, and this could only be done by someone in a place where he could see the rigging crew and the engineer at the same time.

"It was determined that the place had to be this stump high on the steep hillside, inside the haulback bight, and it was also determined that the kid on the crew—me—would be the one to do it. The hooktender would tell me what he needed done, and I would signal the engineer with the correct hand signal. The obstructions creating this particular bight in the haulback are blocks; they are there on purpose, and the bight is intended. The dangers are still there, however, and the forces put on those tail-hold 'obstructions' are tremendous; thus, they are always as strong as possible. Large stumps are the best. Sometimes there is no stump, as in this case, and a tree was being used for the tail-hold.

"My perch was a typical stump for a steep hillside, probably four feet in diameter, ground level on the uphill side and eight or ten feet above the ground on the downhill side. I was watching the donkey pulling in a turn of logs when I thought I heard yelling over the roar of the donkey. I glanced at the rigging crew, and they were all yelling and screaming at the top of their lungs and pointing at me. The tremendous force put on the haulback block, which was attached to the tree tail-hold, had torn the tree out by its roots and the tree was falling right towards me. In a situation like that there is really no time to think. I remember looking up, seeing this tree falling towards me, about ready to hit me. I remember leaping into space off the downhill side of that stump, and I remember flying through the air for a long time before I hit terra firma. Fortunately, the hillside was so steep that when I landed, I slowly skidded to a stop. With shaking knees, I climbed back up to have a look, and sure enough that tree had landed on my stump."

The boys learn a lot about life while learning to log. Especially in these "summer years." Uncle Louie teaches hard work by example, but he also teaches the art of napping. "Work hard, rest when you can," might be his motto. And he likes to joke about it.

"I don't mind work at all," says Uncle Louie. "I just don't like working between meals."

Polite chuckles every time.

"Work doesn't scare me a bit. I can lay down right beside it and go to sleep."

And he does. He likes to have a little snooze after lunch. He becomes famous for his snoozes. He snoozes on a pile of logs, under the loader, on the gravel road, pretty much anywhere.

Back in the crummy at the end of the day, Uncle Louie keeps his eye open for salmon berries—especially the yellow ones. The yellow ones are the sweetest, he says.

"On the way home after work, Uncle Louie would look at the salmon berries along the road and remark that we probably weren't getting enough vitamin C," says Murray. "Most of the other guys just wanted to get home and didn't care about vitamin C. Someone might say that you had to watch out for the worms. And he would usually snort, 'Watch out for the worms? They have to watch out for themselves!'"

Louie and Roland

CHAPTER 61

SASQUATCHES ANONYMOUS

Louie always says, "Believe nothing you hear and only half of what you see." But what if a person—you—were in a boat, speeding around the corner into Sea Lion Bay to show your friend a weird cave you'd found that had an old woollen coat laid out beside a long cold fire, and the boat motor stopped suddenly for no reason?

And then in the silence, what if you heard a bone-chilling scream/ maniacal laugh, and then you saw a creature—tall, covered in dirty-white hair or fur, you're not sure which—and it walked on two legs into the bay, and it swam across the bay and walked out into the woods on the other side, water streaming off it as it emerged?

And you felt freaked out, and your hair stood on end, and goose bumps rose all over your skin. And then when you pulled on the outboard to get out of that freaky place, it started immediately and easily, and you revved it up and got out of there at high speed and you never said a word about it to anyone because no one would believe you. And neither did your friend who was with you and saw the same thing.

What then? Do you believe nothing of what you heard and half of what you saw? Does the rule apply to what you feel? And what if you feel like there's still no scientific explanation for what you heard and saw but the remembrance of it gives you the chills and makes your heart race?

CHAPTER 62

A SMITH INLET ADVENTURE

S mith Inlet is nearly empty—the Gwa'sala are gone, and all the gyppo logging camps are gone but us. Of the canneries, only a small piece of Boswell remains, and it's only open for a month or two in summer. There's no longer any reason, besides touring, for anyone to venture into Smith Inlet's lengths. The inlet feels like our world—we can go anywhere and never see a soul. This is how it would have been for the Gwa'sala before the sockeye of Long Lake (Tse?la) attracted the first cannery in 1883, then the fishermen and then the loggers.

The GMG boys want to explore historical Long Lake all the way to the source of those coveted sockeye at Halowis, or Smokehouse Creek. Harry Walkus tells a story of how the Gwa'sala found Tse?la by following a merganser, and now Roland writes his story of finding Long Lake:

> It seemed like the adventures of the GMG kids were always time compressed. We had only one day off, working six days a week and taking Saturdays off. Sometimes we stretched an adventure by starting it after work on Friday, taking advantage of the long summer days.

Our teenage adventures took several different directions, this one being an exploration adventure. We often talked about exploring Long Lake, a lake that was twenty miles long and hadn't seen a human for probably years. There was a serious problem with this exploration, though. It would involve a long boat trip down Boswell Inlet, up Smith Inlet, passing through a tidal rapids into Wyclese Lagoon, across the lagoon to a deserted and overgrown logging road, ending with a portage up that road alongside the Docee river to the lake. All that before we even got on the lake. A canoe, the normal portaging craft, wouldn't work because our time frame wouldn't allow time to paddle down the lake and back and be at work on Sunday morning.

It was Murray and Ken who finally came up with the solution. Murray had access to the lightest boat in camp, a small tin rowboat probably ten feet long and possibly rated for something like a six-horse Evinrude outboard. Ken had access to a twenty-horse Merc outboard that he claimed he could carry up to the lake. It turned out that the twenty-horse motor would make that little boat leap out of the water like a panicked sockeye. I'm sure every rivet was stressed to the max, and it's a sure bet that any adult would have questioned our sanity. As you might imagine, space and weight were limited. I think I was invited as an afterthought, kind of with the idea of being a Sherpa, those brave men who carry gear for adventurers into far corners of the earth.

That Friday was sunny and warm, and after work we went on a quick raid of the cookhouse so we would have something to eat. We threw our sleeping bags and a minimal amount of gear in the boat and off we went. Down Boswell Inlet, around Olive Point, past Margaret Bay, up Smiths, up the tidal rapids into the lagoon, and down the lagoon to the portage location alongside the outflow river to Long Lake. Our little bit of gear was looking larger all the time, and I had some concerns about Ken packing that heavy motor up to the lake. Ken is solidly built, and I have seen him grab a two-hundred-pound moving block and muscle it around like a normal logger would move an eighty-pound haulback block. Sure enough, he put that motor over his shoulder and started walking up the road leaving Murray and myself to stagger along behind with the boat and gear.

By the time we reached Long Lake, we had put in a pretty long day, but there was still some daylight we couldn't waste. We hooked up the motor, threw everything back in the boat and off we went. The lake at that point was almost surrounded by high mountains and cliffs. Within minutes it was dark, then it began to drizzle, then it began to rain, then it began to pour, then it rained cats and dogs, then it was cataclysmic, then it really started to get bad. The pinging on the aluminum boat became a deafening roar. Ken was navigating the boat as best he could, which meant seeing the mountains against the sky on both sides of the lake and trying to stay somewhere in the middle, keeping water under the keel. Murray and I bailed water and tried to find a camping spot by looking at the shoreline, which we couldn't even begin to see in the dark and rain. Murray was the only one smart enough to throw rain gear in, but in rain like that he was probably only slightly drier than Ken and I.

Around midnight, we knew we had to stop and so turned the boat towards the bank and slowed to a crawl. We literally could not see the bank until we bumped into it. We were grateful there was a spot flat enough to spread out our bags. We threw a tarp over ourselves and tried to get some sleep, but the bear tromping around and snuffling didn't help much. Ken kept his trusty 303 Lee Enfield ($29 from the Sears catalogue) loaded and ready. Between the rain and the bear, quite possibly a grizzly (no, we didn't see it, but on a salmon lake like Long Lake it was almost for sure a bear), we finally dozed off about the time we needed to get up, waking to a pounding rain.

Gathering firewood, we were unable to see tracks of the mystery animal because they were all washed away. I now think we probably camped right in his living room and were fortunate he didn't decide to bite us. This was also the first time we got to see where we spent the night. It turns out we were fortunate in the extreme to have grounded our boat in the only flat spot for miles, being surrounded by steep banks and cliffs for as far as we could see.

Building a fire on the coast and in any condition is an art form, and Uncle Alvin and my dad were masters of the art form. I remember on another adventure I had fallen in the chuck on a trip to the west coast beaches (a story for another time), and it was colder than I imagined it would be. Uncle Alvin gathered some wood together, made a few motions with his hands and fingers, and all of a sudden there was a roaring fire. Having learned from the best, we had a roaring fire in no time, a little too roaring. I think it felt so good we kept feeding it, and before we knew it the fire was so big we couldn't get close enough to get warm. One side was freezing cold and the other side felt like the fires of hell. I actually burned my jacket, or rather melted it, as it was nylon.

In those days it took more than bears and a little rain to chase us back to the bunkhouse, so we tossed our soggy sleeping bags in the boat and took off. When we got to the middle of the lake, we sat awestruck. All that drizzling, pouring, cats and dogs, cataclysmic and pounding rain had resulted in something miraculous. Every freshet, gully, stream and creek was overflowing its banks, resulting in dozens of waterfalls cascading over many of the cliffs surrounding the lake. We felt we were probably the only three people in the history of the world to see that sight from that spot.

As the end of the lake approached, we saw salmon jumping everywhere and something I had never seen before in a freshwater lake: Seals, dozens of them, had apparently swam up the river, navigated the twenty miles of lake and were enjoying quite an all-you-can-eat seafood buffet.

The trip back was uneventful until we got to the portage site. My mother used to say: "One boy, one brain. Two boys, one half brain. Three or more boys, no brain," and we were set on proving her right. Someone had the bright idea to shoot the rapids so we wouldn't have to carry the boat back down to the lagoon. The rest of us thought it was a wonderful idea. We still had about a tenth of a brain left, though, because it was decided to take the motor off; that way, in the unlikely event that taking the little tin rowboat down the rapids didn't turn out well, we wouldn't have ruined the motor. So we did.

It turns out there is a little more to this white-water stuff than one would think. About a hundred yards in, we went over a small waterfall, maybe two feet high. The boat made it over just dandy, but some strange current backed it up to the waterfall and a thousand gallons rushed into that little boat in less than a second.

There was no one within many miles to see us, but I wonder what we would have looked like, three forlorn looking teenage boys drifting down the river sitting in a sunken boat. The good news was even though we were immersed in water up to our necks, we were no wetter than we had been for the last twenty-four hours.

Now all we had left to do was hike back up to the lake, retrieve the motor, and boat all the way home through a driving rain in the dark and try to get a few hours of sleep before work.

Boating adventure: Ken and Roland in
front, Doug and Murray in back

CHAPTER 63

THE SUMMER YEARS IN WINTER

In the fall, all the GMG students go back to school, and an ever-changing set of crew, including Marcia's new husband Don, fill in until everything is wrapped up for the winter— usually well into November. Then somebody has to stick around and take care of camp. Mom writes me letters from Smith Inlet. Or rather, she types them on her beloved old typewriter, the capital Ds and Hs soaring out of sight above the lines. It's November 1971.

> Here I am sitting at the big yellow table with a candle lit beside me writing you a letter. And it isn't late at night either, like the olden days when they had to write by candle. The men aren't home from work yet, and none of us gals know how to start the light plant.

> Marcia and Don got a lantern from Boswell last night, and Donnie (Anderson) and Marion got some groceries. They were getting pretty low. I had given them some and told her she could get cabbages and carrots from us. They seem to be getting along fine. Her brother Sonny is learning the ropes. They were all over Sabbath night playing games. We ladies played Yahtzee while the men were yelling and hollering over the crokinole

board. Daddy likes Donnie to work for him. He doesn't wait around to be told to do things…. Oh, here's the men, so I'll get this off. Don and Marcia and Eskil are coming over for supper. I have a big thing of soybeans and Linkettes in the oven, potatoes and carrots on. Marcia is bringing the dessert and salad.

Her next letter tells of Eno leaving Smith Inlet for the last time. Eno rowed into our lives in about 1965, all the way from Vancouver. He said he was trying to get away from the "rays." He set up camp at the end of our little cove, and all we could see of him was the smoke rising from his fire. Dad went over and introduced himself, and the ladies gave him loaves of bread, but he would only accept an invitation to dinner on extreme occasions, such as Christmas, and only at Louie's house. Sometimes he would leave his campsite and row to Boswell for grub.

Eno, with his hunched back and his strange ways, was a mystery man and this intrigued the boys. A couple of times, they went over and sat around his fire, silently. Eno was a man of very few words. When Dad asked him to watch camp and invited him to stay in our house, he never did. Instead, he slept outside on the floats behind our house in his tent. He must have needed to feel that people were around, however, because he could have lived anywhere, and he camped right beside us. And when we left for Port Hardy, he went too. Mom says in her letter:

Maybe you heard that we had to tow a clunky old boat of Eno's over with us last Friday, but we never got it here. The rope broke twice before we even got to Christie Pass. The waves were so big, and the swell jerked the rope, and it was old and frazzled already and, of course, it broke. Then broke again later on. But way out by Storm Islands, it broke the third time. It was pretty big waves there, and

Dad couldn't get near it to put a rope around it. So finally, after wallowing around in the waves and bouncing around and stuff flying about the cabin awhile, Eno suggested we leave it. Was hard enough for him because it's all he had. As long as he had his boat, he could at least still get about without asking someone all the time. Worse still, he had his stuff on board. Wasn't much, but all he owned, I guess.

Tamara, or Tammy as we call her when she is little, is the youngest GMG child by several years and the last kid left at GMG in the winters. Lance is forever the oldest sibling of the GMG family and Tammy is forever the baby. She was the cutest camp baby, with her white hair in a halo about her head or tucked into her fuzzy blue hat. It was hard to say no to such cuteness. "Treat, Auntie Alma, treat?" she would say, and Auntie Alma would give her a walnut stuffed inside a marshmallow, even though she got in trouble for it from Mom.

Now she is here at camp after everyone is gone. No kid wants to be the last and only kid left, stuck with their parents, but if it has to happen, what a wonderful place of many freedoms. Tamara writes about it:

> I had the best backyard in the entire world. Mountainsides of mossy trees, winding woodsy trails, sunlit, dappled glens—magical things. Even more special, although I didn't realise it at the time, I had a pet deer to share it with. One summer Specky didn't have a fawn of her own, so she adopted me. I roamed the hills behind camp with Specky following me like a puppy. Whenever I went home, she would become terribly distraught because the ramp was no longer there for her to access camp. She would swim back and forth

trying to reach me until I was in tears. But the next day we would play again. Much to my distress, when I brought my new little kitten Ginger up the hill to play, Specky fiercely attacked and stomped at Ginger. Mom explained to me later that Specky thought of me as her kid and was simply trying to protect me.

Often, I encountered bears, but I had almost no fear of them. The bears are more afraid of you than you are of them, Dad told me, and I believed him.

I explored my ocean yard too; the islands and tide pools were a constant source of entertainment and discovery. I made aquariums out of Mom's big aluminum washtubs and filled them with all manner of interesting fish, crustaceans and shells. Puggles were a large portion of my cats' diet, so I fished for them daily and kept the washtub stocked.

Nearly every day I piled my two cats in the rowboat and headed out to find adventure. Often we would get caught struggling to return home against the wind and tide; I had to row with all my might to make headway and not end up on the rocks. One glorious, sunny afternoon begged for adventure, and I went a little farther than usual—down the inlet towards Boswell. In the distance I saw a pod of killer whales moving fast. Before I could blink, they had surrounded my thin little rowboat, their huge bodies bumping and jostling me up and down. My heart gave a strange blip of awe and fear. I wanted to reach over and touch one of their massive shining black backs, scattered with patches of barnacles. Before I could decide, they gave the boat a final bump, and were gone. I sat with the wind blowing through my hair and the sun on my face, filled with a sense of wonder. How lucky was I to be a child of the wilderness!

Tammy with her rowboat and her lucky cats

But no matter how beautiful, wild and free, Smith Inlet winters are rainy and grey, sometimes snowy, and the moisture seeps right into your bones. When camp was full of people, it seemed warmer. Now when it snows, all the snowy quiet can make a person feel very cold and isolated. I can hear it in the next letters I get from Mom.

> January 11, 1972: Right now I'm sitting on the bed writing on that chocolate box against my knees— the only place there is light! Daddy doesn't like starting the plant just for us. It takes so much fuel, and the oil boat still hasn't been in.
>
> We had a good trip back. I stayed up all the way even when it got a bit bumpy. Still was nothing

compared to last time! Had quite a bit of snow when we got home. It's been cold and windy. Cold in the house too. I finally put on an old pair of Daddy's Stanfield underwear, and I was the warmest today I've been in weeks!

I'm working on my wilderness stories, and Tam is doing fine with her studies. It's easy for her, it seems. Tam and I get outside for some exercise every day if possible. Helps clear our brain. I shovel snow, and we trot back and forth on the airplane float, which is shovelled off most. Of course, our water is frozen up. Gets a little tiresome. Daddy will have to get water again for baths tomorrow.

March 3: We're fine over here, just wish it didn't keep on snowing so much all the time. When we came back from Hardy last Wednesday, it was lovely and almost spring-like. There wasn't one speck of snow on the floats. We were sure surprised because there was so much when we left. The day after, it began to snow, and all our ideas of spring went out the window fast. It snowed and snowed and snowed, with just short recesses in between. Soon we had over a foot and a half of the stuff. I don't even like the looks of it anymore.

Mom, who waxes eloquently about the beauty of snow in the Wilderness Diaries series she is writing, has had enough of it. The remainder of her letter plans a trip to Mexico next winter!

The next September when the summer crew leaves for school again, Dad and Uncle Alvin scrounge up another fall crew to finish up. Dad writes me a letter for my birthday while I'm away at school, and Marcia writes a lot of letters—a historically familiar pastime for ladies at camp. And this fall there is a momentous event to write about: the end of Boswell.

Boswell is the last remaining cannery of all the canneries that were built in Smith Inlet, the last evidence of the busy cannery era that started with the Smith's Inlet Cannery built by Quashella Packing Company in 1883. Boswell was built in 1926 by Gosse Packing Company, but soon after, in one of the great mergers to save the canneries, it became a BC Packers Ltd. cannery. It operated as a cannery until 1936, then was used as a camp, which is the only way any of us has ever known it. Only Margaret Bay outlasted Boswell as an operating cannery, running its canning lines every summer from 1916 to 1945 under Canadian Fishing Company. But Margaret Bay has been abandoned for nearly a decade now, leaving Boswell as the last bit of "civilization" in Smith Inlet. Until now.

Dad's letter is dated October 1, 1972: "Boswell went up in smoke Friday [September 29, 1972]. No more Boswell. It seemed a shame to burn up all those buildings, but I guess they didn't want them standing there if they weren't going to be used. We are really isolated here now."

I look up from Dad's letter and see my dormitory room and my school friends projected over the bustling docks at Boswell on boat day. Then I read Marcia's letters, which come all in a bundle:

> October 1, 1972: We're at camp again! Don and I are in the cookhouse, Aunt Gloria and Uncle Alvin are in Knopp's old house [Mom and Dad's original 1945 home]. Aunt Gloria has the old blue couch from Freddy Anderson and stacks of stuff we looted from Boswell, so they're set up pretty fair. I am cooking. She helps me once in a while—made bread Friday, which was a big help, and always

washes supper dishes, which is the job I hate most of all!

Last Tuesday we went to Boswell and took whatever was any good. There wasn't much. John Moore [the man hired to burn it] got most of it. The main houses were burnt down already. Some "Chuck" is staying with Daddy—maybe you met him when you were up here. Uncle Roy comes tomorrow, then he'll be in that house too. All the guys without wives here, except Eskil, are in Daddy's house. Eskil needs a house of his own to contain his messes.

I haven't seen Specky at all, but Yenta [Marcia's dog] is always chasing Oscar around. And eating Eskil's honeybees! Eskil gives himself "shots" with his bees and jumps in the chuck every morning and night, figures it'll keep him healthy so he'll live long enough to build his city. He's all hopped up on his city.

Aunt Gloria and I have been going over to the road in Uncle Roy's little aluminum boat every day and walking up to where the men are and back. They're just a ways past the first bridge, so it's a good walk. The sun doesn't shine back there at all, all day! It gets real frigid as soon as you stop moving! Camp still gets four hours of nice warm sunny Mexico-type climate every day. Can walk around in shirtsleeves. By the way, "Jason Louis" or "Caralee Dawn" is coming along just fine! [Marcia is pregnant.] Such a masculine name, Jason.

October 15: Lloyd and Eileen were here this weekend. Our weather is still fantastic, and yesterday we all went to the sand beach in Lloyd's beautiful new boat. It was lovely and warm, no wind even. We had dinner there and had a great time.

Compensation Joes came in—made out a repair/replace list five pages long! Thirty-three items! The men had a fit! I guess Compensation wasn't even sure if anyone was still logging here. Aunt Gloria kept telling the guys we've always been loggers and we love logging and we're gonna always be loggers, and Dad was trying to tell them that we were finishing up, hoping they'd go easy on us because we'd soon be done. [These men from the Workers' Compensation Board were responsible for ensuring occupational health and safety but sometimes carried things too far, in our loggers' opinions.]

November 26: Well here it is Thursday night. I guess the barge is coming in Wednesday next week to take the logs, so we'll probably be leaving sometime around then.

Eskil stays to watch camp for the winter. In April, Mom and Dad, freshly back from Mexico, return with Roy to start working on the thirty-three-item to-do list before the Compensation "Joes" come back. And Mom writes my favourite Smith Inlet letter.

CHAPTER 64

A LETTER FROM SMITH INLET

Mom's letter is dated May 7, 1973.

This is Tuesday evening. We just turned back our watches last night, so it's light out still, and about eight o'clock. Missed out on an hour's sleep last night, we did.

We've had really rainy, windy weather lately. Real squally. I had a quart jar filled with water, and daffodils in it (that we picked at Margaret Bay) out on the porch rail, and the wind blew that off today, as well as my half-filled milk carton I thawed out last night. And the clothes really whip about on the line in this little shed here by Daddy's house. The shed Mr. McCormick built. I fixed it up with lines and hauled out any engine parts and oil cans, etc. and nailed up a sign that reads like this:

NOTICE

Please be
advised that this
is now a drying
shed, and not
a workshop!
By Order D.O.T.

I did it in crayon on a piece of lined paper this size. The D.O.T., as you may remember, stands for Department of Transport. Daddy said, "I guess that means Dame of Tomorrow."

The reason I did this sign is because the boys in the bunkhouse always have their old kicker parts and oil cans, etc. in there. And that just doesn't go along with clean clothes.

The beavers have been busy as usual. They have the road flooded most of the time. When it gets too deep, Daddy pulls some of the sticks out and lets the lake rush out to its proper level. The other day, or evening after work, I went along with him to get some fresh air. You know how I love walking up the road. Well, since I was there watching him, he suggested maybe I could also pull out some sticks. And do they ever plug those sticks in there tight. And rocks and moss and limbs. Wow. They're hard to pull out. They surely are well called nature's engineers.

Anyhow I left then, after a while, and walked on a bit up the road. Daddy came up to turn the jeep around and lay down on the road for a rest. He has a sore leg. I walked up to where the donkey sits and discovered a bike, so went farther. Then came sailing back down. Very exhilarating indeed. Daddy was cleaning all the garbage out of the jeep. Expecting the Forestry and Compensation men any day. The last one left a list about a mile long of things they were to do to make the place safer. Rails up the ramp to the road and along the walk! Daddy said he told him, "Well, the women would sure like that anyway."

Right now, Daddy got out of the tub and shouted, "It's all yours!" So I guess I'll go and have a soak. He usually has it so hot I can hardly stand it even after it cools awhile. So I'll finish this epistle likely tomorrow. Goodnight dearie!

Hello. This is Tuesday morning at ten o'clock. I think I need a new typewriter ribbon. This one is getting feeble. Well, we plan to go to Port Hardy this coming weekend, so I'll pick one up there—and maybe phone you too.

It seems to me I was telling you something about beavers when Daddy called me last night for the bath. Well, I rode this bike on down the road while Daddy finished cleaning out the jeep. As I got to the lake, I heard a great splash, then a WHACK of a beaver tail. I stopped quickly, then another splash and whack. I watched silently and saw a couple beaver swimming. It was just about dusk. Soon I heard the jeep roaring down towards me. I motioned Daddy to stop, and he got out and sat down on a log and we watched the beavers. Two of them swam fairly close about. One huge one got out on a little island hummock and started chomping grass and feeding himself with his front feet. Sure looked interesting. Then I saw two more down farther, also eating. We could hear them chomping with their big beaver teeth. No wonder the dam gets built back so quickly when we yank sticks out of it. There are four of them to fix it up. First time I've seen the beavers up here.

We really had a South Easter last night. The wind blew and blew and did it rain! And it was really quite raw and cold outside. The barometer went down, down. I see it's going up again now.

Oh yes, I must bring you up to date on Eskil's antics. Lloyd McGill calls him Oscar … can't remember his name. And Uncle Alvin mentioned him in a note to Daddy and called him Esco. Guess one name's as good as another. I suppose you saw the house he made last summer? That A-frame sort of a deal? Did you also see the boat thing he got together? Sort of propelled by paddlewheels powered by an old engine. Well, one day he came in and said to me, "I'm taking the boat out on its maiden voyage, I don't suppose you'd like to come along?" Well, I told him since it was Friday, I was quite busy so I wouldn't go. When I told this to Daddy he grinned and said, "Well, I guess you'd have been the maiden."

Anyhow, he took off, slowly by our house here and the *Surf Isle*, and out, the paddles churning away grandly. I waited for him to round the point and start the trip out. He was going to Boswell to scrounge around a bit. After a while I looked out and he hadn't got very far at all. In about two hours he slowly came back in again. Later I asked him what was the matter, why he never got any farther. He said he'd had a bit of trouble. When he wanted to go backwards, he went forwards and couldn't turn properly. Seems he discovered he'd put the transmission in backwards. He felt a bit blue about that but fixed it best he could. Couldn't reverse it though, that is, completely change it without tearing the whole engine out and putting it in right. He didn't want to do that so he learned to work it the way it was.

Anyhow, he decided he was going to set off for Draney Inlet. Daddy had thought of towing him around, over the sound, because he thought it would never stand up to going all that way on its own power. Anyhow, we were up the road after work, Daddy and I, that night we saw the beavers. And here Eskil was getting all ready to go. He'd been packing all his junk on his house for days. Was very surprised he had so much stuff! So he cast off about 9 p.m. Wanted to go out on the tide. Well, the tide wasn't high 'til midnight, so he had to buck it going through the narrows here, and nearly stood still for ages.

Daddy went with the speed boat and gave him a little push, but it pushed crooked, so he came back. Finally he got by the rocks and out of sight, and we, with Uncle Roy, breathed a sigh of relief. And wondered what the RCMP would say if they saw that creation coming around at them someplace! And what indeed would the people in Rivers and Draney say when that contraption came bearing down upon them?

That was a Tuesday night he left. And oh, how we breathed freely all day Wednesday. We are to help our fellow men when we can, you realize that dear. Always. But there comes a time, sometimes, when your fellow man, though he gladly asks for and accepts handouts of gas and oil and this or that, doesn't want to take any advice anyhow and wants to be left alone to fulfill his dream. So we let him do it and wished him bon voyage! He is in fact somewhat of a sponger. Doesn't want much to work hard but dreams of building a city in Draney Inlet.

So all day Wednesday we wondered how Eskil was doing and where he'd be about now, and etc. We intended to check up on him to see how he was going. We went to bed Wednesday night, and it was raining and miserable out. I heard a noise outside and went out in my nightgown to see if it was kitty—got another one—and lo and behold a voice nearly scared me to death.

It said—a man's voice— "Have you gone to bed Louie?"

I said, "Is that you Roy?"

"No, it's Eskil."

Oh my heart sank to my boots.

"Whatever happened to you?"

And his stupid dog jigging about all around chasing the cat—just a pup but homely and gangly. Well, he got to the other side of the sand beach when something went in the gears and some gear chewed all up or some such. He'd been rowing for five hours! And if you could see the rowboat he'd built himself, you'd be sympathetic to realize he had to row THAT in the rain for five hours! Well, he was a bit deflated, I tell you. He'd finally managed to get his rig close enough to the beach to tie it up.

So I asked him in and warmed up some food for him. He's been on a raw diet and wouldn't even eat raw oatmeal for breakfast the last morning he ate with us, in case it was partly cooked! But he didn't worry about it too much now! Felt sorry for him, really. Sent him into the bathroom and gave him some dry clothes of Daddy's to put on. Hung his over the rack above the stove to dry. Put him to bed between the clean white sheets of the bed in the little bedroom where Tam sleeps when she's here. I had just spent five hours cleaning up his hogpen of a house and wasn't about to put him back in there. Told him I had, too. Was quite angrily muttering all the time I was cleaning, in fact. How could any human being be so filthy? Ugh. But Daddy said he saw him pick up his dog's job with his hand and throw it overboard. And he doesn't much believe in washing, as you know, either.

Gayle, you should have seen that house! You just couldn't imagine it, not in your wildest dreams. Oh dear, it'll take me a long time to get over that. It looks nice now. Put some curtains in there even. You'll likely sleep there in summer, with maybe some of the girls, don't know yet. Aunt Gloria thinks since it might be the last summer here, everyone should take turns cooking and helping with the work. No one will want to be tied down to the job all the time. Will want some fun too. Maybe she's right at that. Was Uncle Alvin's thought also.

Anyhow, Daddy towed Eskil across the sound next morning. So he's over there safely now at least, and Daddy feels he did his part for him. We must help fellow travellers along life's way even though they may not think just the way we do, or how we think they ought to think. Right? Jesus always did that.

A Helen and Gayle adventure

CHAPTER 65

MOMS AND GIRLS

When the Worker's Compensation "Joes" fly in, the first thing they want is a toilet. We show Compensation Joe One to the bathroom in the cookhouse and hope it's in at least some condition of cleanliness. But no! When he leaves, we check the toilet and it's filthy! Did he do that or us? We'll never know. There are two of them; they always arrive in pairs like they're afraid to face the loggers all by themselves. It might be a valid fear.

Should we offer them a sandwich or cookies or something? Butter them up? Our moms aren't here; they would know what to do. We just don't know. But they want to borrow our boat and go over to the road and check their five-page, thirty-three-item list. We don't like that they borrow our boat to go torment Dad, but we let them take the twenty-horse, and the airplane pilot says he'll be back and roars off.

At the road, the Compensation Joes get a ride up the road in the logging truck, and Dad gives Roland the job of showing them around. Which might have been a mistake because Roland can get pretty sassy!

"They saw a ladder with the bottom rung missing, and one Joe was pretty panicked about it," Roland tells us at supper that night.

"I told them it was a test. If a logger had trouble with that ladder they weren't allowed in the woods where they had to step over things bigger than that a hundred times a day."

We are logging with a raised spar, its web of lines spread out as complicated as a spider's web, and the Compensation Joes are clearly puzzled. They're neatly dressed, Joe One and Joe Two, with bright, shiny hardhats, and they each have a pair of spanking-new white cotton gloves tucked into their belts.

"Probably neither of them had seen a traditional spar tree before," Roland says. "Probably they didn't know a bull block from a buckle guy."

"You don't see too many wooden trees anymore," says Joe One.

Roland knows the guy is talking about steel towers, but against his better judgment, he smart alecks back.

"Really? What are trees made of where you come from?"

Dennis asks, "Well, does it look OK to you?"

And Compensation Joe One and Two, still puzzled, say "Oh yes, ya, it looks OK," though everyone knows neither of them have any idea what they are looking at.

At the end of the day, Dad drives them back down in the crummy and one of them says, "My, the muffler's a little loud, don't you think?" And later, around the supper table, Dad chuckles and says, "If only he knew it was from all the downshifting because there's no brakes!"

There is much laughter at the supper table. There are comments on the lily-white cotton gloves tucked in the pants and the shiny hardhats.

"And can you believe he wanted a handrail on the trail? Hahaha! If a logger can't cross the trail to work, he's sure not gonna make it up the hill. Hahaha!"

We girls aren't sure we want to share our toilet story.

We started out the summer as our moms suggested. We girls— Helen, Donna, Laverne, Tammy and I—taking turns cooking, our moms helping out if needed. We are all enjoying what we think could be our last summer in Smith Inlet. Our mothers were here hanging about, vacationing and supervising for a couple of weeks. They ate what we cooked and gave us advice.

Probably because they were here, we weren't always taking things as seriously as we should have; it's true that we're having more fun than our moms expected. Helen says her goal is to kiss every boy by the end of the summer! Excluding her brother, naturally. (You can believe I won't be following Helen on *that* adventure!) But we do cook breakfast, lunch and dinner seven days a week and make eight loaves of bread every other day.

One evening after supper, when Aunt Gloria was still here, we did a quick clean-up and ran over to the road for a walk. When we got back, Aunt Gloria was busily cleaning the cookhouse.

"Why, I wouldn't be caught dead leaving my kitchen like this!" she scolded. "You never know when somebody might pop in for a visit, and then wouldn't you feel ashamed!"

No, we wouldn't, actually. Aunt Gloria has a higher standard of cleanliness than we do.

Uncle Alvin eventually sent all the moms home because he probably knew we would never learn responsibility with our mothers around. And now the camp is ours! We leave the kitchen dirty if we feel like it, eat cookie dough and cake batter, swim nude, and on starry nights, we lay our blankets on the floats and sleep outside, the moon wobbling across the water and dancing on the floats. We lay on our backs and gaze at the endless stars and call out when we see one shooting across the sky. Then we flip over on our tummies to see the stars in the water, banging our feet on the floats to see the little fish and tiny skittering things all aglow with phosphorescence.

Summer Years girls

We get up early to make breakfast: oatmeal—always oatmeal—plus eggs and potatoes and toast toasted in the oven, or pancakes cooked on the middle section of the stovetop, sometimes cinnamon rolls or muffins, canned fruit. At the same time, we make stacks of sandwiches and wrap them in wax paper like little presents. We fill the tin lunch kits with two sandwiches each, fruit or veggie sticks, cake or cookies and sometimes a thermos.

Then the guys go to work. They look so cute in the boat, hardhats bobbing orange, white, yellow and silver above their plaid shirts and those huge, suspendered logger pants. Like a handful of lollipops. When they're gone, we bake bread, cakes, cookies, pies, and plan dinner. On wash-day we do all the bunkhouse laundry in the wringer washer, hang it out to dry in the drying shed and change all the beds. It's an all-day procedure. We fill the oil barrels for the stoves and fill the fridge with coal oil.

It seems I spend a lot of summer baking bread, doing dishes, and peeling potatoes on the edge of the float, watching the fish dart at the peelings as they sink. Our logger brothers can eat a lot of spuds and a lot of bread. And their girlfriends and future wives keep coming to visit, so we feed them too.

It's fun hanging out with our brothers. They're so much nicer than they used to be. Sometimes on a Saturday, they take us to the big sand beach, Cape Caution beach or hiking up the mountain to slide in the snow. Once, they took us to Calvert Island where the beaches stretch on forever, white and soft. Sometimes in the evening, Ken comes into the cookhouse while we do the supper dishes and plays his guitar for us. Dad does his own thing; he chats with us at supper then he tinkers on things in the shop and reads or does office work in his house and leaves us be.

The music is different now too. No more musical "get-ups" of trios and instrumental "specials." There's not even a piano here anymore. The boys have an 8-track player in the bunkhouse, and every evening after they get home from work, we hear "One is the Loneliest Number," "Jeremiah Was a Bullfrog" and "Never Been to Spain," "Eli's Coming" and "Joy to the World" (not the Christmas version), accompanied by our brother's voices in the shower. The concert continues, echoing off the beach 'til we ring the dinner bell, which is a big rusty shackle hanging from the eaves that we loudly bang with an equally rusty wrench to be heard over the music. On wash-day (or just any rainy day) when we make the guy's beds, we play Three Dog Night in the bunkhouse and dance. But the guys don't know this.

Three Dog Night seems to be the favourite, but the boys have other albums too: The Guess Who with "No Sugar Tonight," "No Time" and "These Eyes," and Supertramp's "The Logical Song" and "Take the Long Way Home." And sometimes Harry Nilsson's soaring, gut-wrenching "Without You" floats out over the water, making me want to cry for I don't even know what—intergenerational loss and sorrow, maybe. Smith Inlet has probably never heard such sounds before.

One day there is a morning so beautiful we have to meet it where we see it rise—in the direction of Coho Creek. Helen says she is sure Ken won't mind if we use his boat. I am sure he will mind. Laverne probably would stop us if she were still here, but—oh well, here we go following Helen again! We leave the breakfast dishes and speed through the mist into the sunrise and don't stop 'til we get all the way to the head of Boswell Inlet. Helen turns off the motor so we can feel the quiet and float with the sun on our faces. It's so beautiful.

But we have lots of work to do, so Helen pulls on the motor. It won't start. Over and over she pulls, then Donna gives it a try, then me. Helen takes the cover off the motor and looks inside, trying to remember what our dads do when a kicker won't start. But it's no use. There's one oar, so we paddle to shore and assess the situation. We know we'll be here at least all day, maybe even all night. When the guys come home from work, they will find the breakfast dishes still on the table, with us and Ken's boat missing, and they will come out looking for us. But no one ever boats to the head of Boswell Inlet. They will look everywhere else.

We get hungry. Donna finds a place to make a bed just inside the woods, and when evening comes, we figure that if we have to, we could sleep here, huddled together to keep warm. Maybe in the morning we'll have to paddle the boat around the bay and see if we can find some water to drink—Helen says we will die of dehydration before we die of starvation. As the sky begins to darken, we see a boat roaring around the distant corner. It slows down then turns around to leave. No! Come back! We wave and jump and scream and pray—Donna literally kneels down on the rocks and prays—and finally the boat turns back around and heads our way. Ken jumps into his boat, flicks something inside the motor and it starts on the first pull.

At the end of the summer when we all go back to school, Mom writes a letter to the Ministry of Forests on GMG's behalf. For years, GMG had been logging about five million board feet over their annual quota, and now they are required to shut down until the quota catches up to the years. But Uncle Alvin and Dad just want to log the rest of their quota and be done. I don't know what Mom said in the letter, but we end up logging another three summers! We girls are the cooks. I have been designated the full time cook because Helen has found a more permanent job elsewhere, and Donna, Laverne and Tammy work portions of the summers.

Tammy writes in her diary:

> It's so beautiful here, words cannot describe. Yesterday I went and fed Specky and her fawns. One is from last year and one from this year. The little one is so cute! He still has his spots on! Right now, we are washing clothes in the old wringer washer and wondering what we should make for supper.

Wash-day: Donna wringing clothes, Tamara eating a popsicle

She continues:

> I'm so tired I could drop. But let me describe the
> scene. Gayle is sitting at the desk writing to her
> love in Hawaii by the light of a coal-oil lamp. How
> romantic. Donna is sitting on the bed reading a
> novel. The radio is playing, and I am lying on my
> stomach on the floor, writing. Just now Donna
> suddenly drops to the floor beside me at eye level.
> She was getting changed into her nightgown just
> as Kenny and Laura [visiting girlfriend] walked by!
> We all crack up laughing.
>
> We are having so much fun here. We went to the
> beach yesterday. There are hundreds of them
> with not a soul on any of them. I got a peach of a
> sunburn. Today it's foggy and rainy and dismal,
> but yet in a way, fascinating. It's easy to imagine
> all sorts of intriguing things such as mermaids
> or sea monsters or fairies whose reflection is the
> phosphorous in the water.

The boys often go on their own adventures, and we girls feel a
bit put-out because we have to cook every day of the week. So
one Friday, we tell the guys we're taking the twenty and going
to the big sand beach (Dsulish Bay) for an overnight campout.
Laverne, Tammy and I make enough food for the guys to get by
for a day and load the boat with a couple of gas tanks, a box of
food and utensils and an old canvas mailbag full of blankets, and
we pound our way down the inlet against the westerly.

We build a fire above the tideline and whittle some limbs into
forks to toast our cheese sandwiches. When the colours fade out
of the sky and the stars come out, we go skinny dipping in the
cold surf. Our brothers said they might come visit us, so we have
our ears open for a motor. Tammy's diary says:

It was so funny! Whenever we thought we heard
a boat, we would swim like mad back to shore,
laughing so hard we would sink, spluttering,
under the waves.

We make our beds by the fire and look for shooting stars and
tell stories. We keep the fire stoked. If there are bears or wolves
or cougars in the night, we will whack them with a fiery stick.
The next day we beachcomb and swim and lay about and get as
sunburned as possible. Float planes fly over, and we wonder if
they can see us in our bikinis—Laverne's purple velvet with gold
rings, Tam's blue and white flowers, mine hot pink—far below on
the golden sand, out here in the middle of nowhere. When a plane
turns around and flies low, we are terrified that it will actually
land, and then what will we do?

In the late afternoon, we load the boat and head for home. Just
past the point, the motor dies. These outboards are our weakness;
we haven't learned to fix motors like the boys have. We pull
and pull on that motor, and fiddle with the choke, but nothing
happens. We're floating in the middle of Blackney Channel.
We know our brothers will come looking for us but maybe not
until morning. There are a couple of oars in the boat; if it was a
rowboat, I suppose we could take turns rowing all the way home.
I remember Mom saying it took Eskil five hours to row from the
sand beach when his boathouse affair broke down here. But we
can't row without oarlocks.

The westerly is going with us, so we rig an oar as a mast in the
middle of the boat and tie a wool bunkhouse blanket onto it for a
sail. We'll sail close to the beach, then after dark we can stay on
the beach if we have to. We use the other oar to steer. The wind
catches our woollen sail, puffs it out and makes the slightest
wake behind us. We feel as clever as Captain Vancouver sailing
the HMS *Discovery*, which could have been in our stern view if it
were 182 years ago.

Just before the sun slides into Queen Charlotte Sound behind us, we see our brothers in the distance off our bow coming to our rescue. But we've blown part-way home by then with our woollen sail!

Camp Bread

The moms teach us to make bread by eye and feel. They pour the water into the bowl until it looks right, then add oil—glug, glug—two handfuls of salt and a spoonful of brown sugar. Then they add the softened yeast and flour "'til it feels right." Here is my translation, guaranteed to make good, old-fashioned logging camp bread.

Soften 2 rounded tablespoons traditional yeast in ½ cup warm water in a small bowl for about ten minutes. In a large bowl put 7 cups of warm water, ¼ cup brown sugar, ⅔ cup vegetable oil, and two handfuls of salt (about 4 tablespoons). Add some brown flour to make a sort of thick sauce. Add in the yeast and beat with a wooden spoon. Add about a 60/40 ratio brown to white flour to make a soft dough. Knead 'til it feels right—elasticy! Let rise, covered with a tea towel, in an oiled bowl until double. Punch it down. You can let it rise twice if you're busy. Then divide into 8 loaves and fill the bread pans about halfway up. Poke fork holes in it—maybe 6 times. Let rise again 'til the dough begins to mound above the pan. Bake at 350°F until there's a sort of hollow sound when you knock on it, about 40 minutes. Dump it out of the bread pans and let cool on a rack. Oil the tops to make them shiny.

CHAPTER 66

MOM

I always feel like my mom deserves an explanation. Like I might be the only one who understands her. It's true, she's not perfect. First of all, I think her expectations are too high. I never appreciated her spankings, and afterwards I would hide in the closet and tell her I hated her. And she wouldn't let me read Nancy Drew mysteries. (What silly nonsense—do I want to turn my brain into a sieve?) So I had to read them under the covers with a flashlight at night or she would take them away in a great huff and I'd never find out who did it.

But she is also fun. Mom gives marvelous birthday parties and plays crazy, silly games, like the one where you look up into a tube (Do you want to see the stars?) and she pours water down into your eye. And then she laughs so hard she snorts! She reads us hundreds of books, a chapter a night—or two or three if we beg. She loves "nature walks" up our logging road.

"Breathe a little deeper, kids, now a little more, a little bit more, get that oxygen into your lungs."

She does high kicks in the hall in her turquoise pedal pushers. She is the only mom with pedal pushers. She takes us camping at the big sand beach for a week each summer. She tappity-taps and riiiiips on her typewriter late into the night by the light of the smoky coal-oil lamp—tappity-tap, riiiiip, scrunch, toss. In the morning there is a pile of scrunched paper balls on the floor around the table, and we know that later we'll get to read "by Hazel I. Goertzen" in a magazine and feel proud.

Mom loves adventure, like hiking, boating, camping, exploring and travelling to new places. She is obsessed with flowers and trees and plants, wild creatures and beautiful sunsets—nature in general. She writes about nature. She wrote four stories on the seasons for a magazine. She wrote things like:

> The tide sets her table twice daily on yonder flats. As the tide recedes there gathers a motley crowd of feathered folk. The eagle from his stronghold as master of ceremonies, the raven as preacher in his jet-black suit, with crows, gulls and a few ducks as willing participants. All join in a sort of solemn but haggling coroner's inquest and funeral service combined, and without ado have a very ghoulish feast of fish carcasses.

Only Mom could think that stuff up. Some might even call it silly nonsense.

Sometimes I hear bits of conversations about Mom from the other moms in camp.

"Hazel should not go gallivanting off like that! Louie needs her. Poor Louie."

One summer we are visiting an uncle and auntie on my dad's side, and Mom whispers for me to come outside. I follow her out into the yard and behind a tree. She pulls out two pairs of flowered bell-bottomed pants from a bag.

"Here, try these on," she says. "But don't tell anyone about them."

I feel the spell of secrecy.

"Why not?" I whisper. I would like to show them off to my cousin—they are really "neat" and they fit fine!

"Dad's family thinks I spend too much money," says Mom. "So we'll just pack these up 'til we get home, OK?"

"OK, Mom."

I sure don't think Mom spends too much money. Not on me anyway. But I am enlightened. My friends' moms think my mom gallivants off too much, and my cousins' moms think she spends too much of "poor Louie's" money.

But I know that Dad is proud of Mom. I hear him brag about her adventurous spirit and her willingness to try new things—beginning with her steamer ride to Ocean Falls to marry him!

And Mom and Dad share the same goals—educating us kids so we can be "of service in the Lord's work" (doctor, nurse, teacher strongly encouraged), then finding a piece of land (preferably with a little creek) and growing things—especially cherry trees! Dad says his dream is to sit under a cherry tree and let ripe cherries fall into his mouth. So I feel sad that people say things about Mom, but I think my parents are happy the way they are.

One summer day when we girls are cooking for the loggers (earning money for those educations), I suddenly realize my mom and dad will die. I'm with Helen in front of the cookhouse, bouncing on the big black logging-truck inner tube, soft and warm from the sun, eating a chocolate chip cookie gooey from the oven.

"What are you gonna do when your mom and dad die?" asks Helen.

"What?" I am horrified. This is a typical Helen question—disturbing. My moment of bouncing, gooey-cookie-eating serenity is ruined. "What do you mean? They're not gonna die!"

"Of course they are! They are older than you and they will die before you. What are you gonna do?"

I try to imagine life without my mom, but I can't imagine it.

"Well, ya, but that will be forever away! So long away I don't even have to think about it."

"You never know," says Helen, bouncing and eating her cookie nonchalantly beside me.

I hate that Helen seems always and irritatingly right, and I try to imagine life without my dad. I feel like I know my dad will never die—he's too good. God wouldn't let him die. But I feel uneasy just the same, and when I see Mom and Dad next, I look at them differently. Dad looks the same as always—he still has grey hair combed over his bald head. But Mom has a few wrinkles around her eyes and some grey hair too. Suddenly I feel badly about all the things I have done to pain her, and about saying I hated her when she spanked me. Suddenly I know that she has always done the best she could. And I love her with an intenseness that burns my eyes.

Chapter 67

Killer Whale Summer

On the first day of the last summer GMG Logging Company is in Smith Inlet, the killer whales come to visit. Their great bulky backs rise and fall, black and white, as they round our little island and circle the bay. Slowly, they pass the floats, eyeing us, before continuing their way up the inlet.

If Chief George had become a blackfish as he said he would, he would have seen how big we had all grown. And he would have wondered where his people were. We can only breathe "Wow," in awe of their enormity gliding by our feet.

They have probably come for the fish; there seems to be an abundance of salmon this summer. Dennis cans salmon on the stove in the spare house so it won't stink up the cookhouse. There are tommy cod too—Uncle Ernie and Trooper fish tommy cod in front of camp and feed them to the eagles. A dozen or so eagles perch in the trees, waiting for someone to throw them a fish. Then they all make a dash for the same fish, and there is a big shrieking scrabble on the rocks in front of us.

Fishing is so good that Gary and Murray and Donna have become fishermen. They visit camp in their new seine boat, and we watch them mend their net on the airplane float. Lloyd stops in to visit too; he has a troller. Even the sports fishermen are stopping in this summer. One sporty came while the guys were at work and gave us two sockeye—said Snuffy Ladret (family friend from the old days) told him we were here and to come see us. We served the fish for dinner that night and told the guys we caught them ourselves, to impress them.

The Fisheries boat stops in too. Our guys catch their guys looking at us girls through the cookhouse window with their binoculars!

Our crew is Dennis and his cousins Dave Anderson and Kenny McGill (Trooper), Roland and his friend Rob, and Uncle Ernie. Dad and Mom have found their cherry trees and sunshine home by now, so Uncle Ernie is the adult this summer. Laverne and Tammy and I are the cooks until Laverne and Tammy leave to get ready for school, then there is only me.

Because we know it's our last summer, Tammy and I keep diaries to remember it forever. My little sister is five years younger than I, and her entries tell the stories of DB the cat and her kittens, Rover eating the roast off the table and her encounter with the grizzly bear standing on two legs in the road. (Back-up slowly until you're out of sight, then run like mad.) She writes about the time we ran out of food, the terrible cake I made for Laverne's birthday, and the phosphorescence dripping like liquid gold off her oars when she goes for a rowboat ride on a starry night.

My entries talk about boys. One boy in particular. Rob and I fish for puggles for the cat, play cards at the kitchen table and eat onion and cheese sandwiches late at night while he points out the constellations. Rob helps do the dishes, Rob and I stay up late talking every night—Rob said this, Rob said that, Rob, Rob, Rob. I even like to watch his name transferring from the end of my pen onto the paper.

When I am alone in the last half of the summer, Rob twists his ankle and has to stay home from work. Then Rob and I suntan on

441

the floats, Rob fixes the fridge and makes steaks for dinner, and one day we take the *SeaDoo* and visit a beautiful red sand beach on the south side of Smith Inlet that I've never been to before or since.

Ernie brings home a bear. Left to right: Dennis, Rob, Trooper, Ernie holding the bear on a rope

Meanwhile, Laverne's hair gets caught in the wringer and nearly tears her scalp off, the light plant comes to a shuddering, sputtering halt in the middle of wash-day, and the stove quits working and soots all over the house. My future sister-in-law, Elaine, visits Roland—Tammy and I think she's really cool—and Dennis's wife, who has just asked for a divorce, comes to see him and I don't want to be nice to her.

I do occasionally record the things I want to remember about the inlet—I describe the moon and its path across the water to the floats, and I wonder where I'll be looking at the moon from next summer, and all the summers. The days shorten, it's nearly time to leave, and I write:

> September 7, 1976: I have to get up earlier now I'm by myself, to get everything done. When I get up it's really dark and clear out—a sharp breeze whipping leaves up against the floats, blowing the clouds around, stars and moon bright and clear, a musky salty smell like autumn—reminds me of when I was a kid. I used to go to school when it was like this. In the mornings now I go out on the porch to get the bread out of the bread can and just stand there feeling it. I don't want to go back in. But I light the lamp and turn on the radio and start the lunches. Just the lamp, the radio and me.

> September 12, 1976: Foggy today. Made my last breakfast, my last meal actually, for camp forever and ever. Had potatoes and eggs and cinnamon rolls. And oatmeal, of course. Uncle Ernie always has to have his mush. Some of the guys will be here until everything's wrapped up; Auntie Alma is going to take over the cooking. Then in spring, Dad and Uncle Alvin will start dismantling camp, and we're done. So weird.

> *Phhhh-aaaawe-g—muffled awe.* That's what I think when I sit on the step of the front porch after breakfast, listening to the strange silence of a thick fog. Space and time are smudged, disappearing. Men emerge out of the grey nowhere, hard-hatted shapes like bulky mushrooms, caulk boots quietly crunching, shuffling into the workboat. The roar of the kicker is swallowed up with the departing boat. The wake slaps against the logs, smaller and softer, until I am very alone, sitting on the step.

Now other men appear through the film, in canoes, paddles dipping smoothly, quiet and ghost-like. One has long black hair, he smiles and nods his head, fades towards Coho Creek. Then a Spanish galleon drifts by on its way to drop Spanish coins in Zero Cove for Brenda to find. A lone man in a misty double-ended gill netter crosses the galleon's fog path, probably headed for Wyclese to load his boat with sockeye.

The cry of an eagle is absorbed, wobbling into the same white that settles on me like a strangely cold comforter. I smell the low tide and sense the predators and prey, huddled. I feel the fear of a boater in the foggy inlet, going in circles over his own wake, killing his motor to listen for the movement of water against solid, watching for looming rock.

I am beginning to sound like my mother—she saw these things. But it's all gone now—the Gwa'sala, the galleons, the big years of the canneries and fishermen and loggers. We are the only gyppo loggers left and we are almost gone. My parents are gone, and their friends, even my friends. Tonight, I will be gone, in the *SeaDoo*, watching the inlet speed away behind me. On the step, the fog settles colder around me, and only I am there to hug myself for a little warmth. Somewhere, a loon mourns.

And the loon still mourns—calling us back. Always calling us back.

Epilogue

I have thought about going back. We all have—even the Gwa'sala. Maybe especially the Gwa'sala. But let's face it, things are different. Now, in 2022, we all have cell phones and Wi-Fi, a grocery store and a hospital just down the street.

If we didn't care about any of that, could we even do it? I couldn't. (Though I'm about ready to give it a go, if this planet gets much crazier!) I would have to buy a house already on a float because how could I ever build my own? It would take me years to fall and prepare enough trees just to build either a float or a house. And then what? Maybe if all of us combined our knowledge, effort and resources it could happen. A commune of sorts.

There has been no community there since we left. A big logging company based itself out of Security Bay for several years, with loggers two weeks in, two weeks out, clearing off the hills. A few hand-loggers came in and took patches off the beach in sail-shaped patterns, and most recently, large companies are flying in to heli-log ragged chunks off the tops of the hills. There is a couple presently living in Security Bay, salvaging logs mostly.

Progress, greed and politics have eliminated the gyppo logging communities and devastated the fish stocks in Smith Inlet, leaving few job opportunities. And there is no internet. Without work, a community would have to live survival-style. If I came back with my old GMG family, we would have to arrive with everything we needed. We would build houses on top of floats or on land. We would need to build a greenhouse to try and grow something. (We learned how well food does not grow here from our parents!) We would install plumbing and run a hose up the creek, go out and buy appliances, tools, oil, kerosene, furniture, food, soap—literally everything from somewhere else—and buy it again whenever we ran out. And bring it in on a boat we already owned (hopefully one we didn't have to paddle or sail). When we ran out of money, we would have to rely on our Gwa'sala neighbours' survival knowledge.

If our Gwa'sala neighbours came back with us, together could we remember enough to survive on our own? We'd need to know how to build a permanent shelter from the trees that is adequate for winter and maybe even the tools to build it with. We would have to catch and preserve every kind of seafood, hunt, kill and prepare animals for food, blankets and clothing, and start a fire with sticks and stones. And when we ran out of familiar necessities, we'd have to fabricate our own utensils, clothing and boats from a cedar tree, concoct medicine from herbs and even create a social system—hopefully not a potlatch system, but still one with a lot of giving in it. Is all that even possible in a lifetime? Perhaps in our grandchildren's lifetimes—barring an ice age or worse.

The closest any of us has got to going back is John Henderson, who spent a few years hand-logging (which is no longer an option due to politics), and Lance and Lloyd, who built Great Bear Lodge at the mouth of the Nekite. But Great Bear Lodge relies on wealthy looky-loos from all over the world, which is only conditionally sustainable, as a pandemic has taught them. In the future, Elon Musk and his Starlink could make the internet available, so online jobs might support someone living in Smith Inlet someday; a strong and hardy, resourceful someone, as they would still be subject to the factors of isolation and weather.

Recently, fish farms have been looking at the inlet with interest. But because we don't yet know the extent of their possible effects on the environment, just as we once didn't know the environmental affects of logging, the establishment of fish farms in the inlet would make me sad.

If we did go back, what about our children and grandchildren—would they hate it? Could they live a life without cell phones and internet? Or restaurants, concerts, and Amazon?

"Horrors be!" as my mom would say of the unthinkable. "Hopefully we haven't 'civilized' ourselves to death!"

Probably that's what old Chief George would say too.

Every generation has a better way than the last, or so it seems to them. The wise learn what to keep and what to leave behind, to make the best present and future possible. I think that applies to long-held traditions as well. Just because our parents and ancestors did something certainly doesn't make it always and forever the best course of action. No, I don't think our grandchildren would choose to live in Smith Inlet.

But just say I *do* know a way to go back—Wi-Fi, hospitals and all—and take everyone with me who wants to go. What is worth going back for? Why should I take us back?

For the soft mists on the water and the soul-stopping call of the loon and the wolf. To feel the power of whales breaching, their spray on your face. To see the waters bubbling with fish at the foot of forests dense with enormous trees—the resources that sustained us. To remember the examples of the people before us: their love, tenacity and hard work, and their faith through painful losses. To forgive and be forgiven. To learn the meaning of "enough."

Or simply for the sockeye-coloured sunsets and wild beaches. To make footprints around a fire, listening to the stories of our ancestors, roasting salmon on cedar strips and toasting cheese sandwiches on forked sticks. And to re-learn the connection of gratefulness to the Creator. Then to tell our children—and everyone's children—all of this, to pass down a legacy of beauty, strength, courage and hope.

So I built a little boat to take us there.

Appendices

Sources and Further Reading:
(Note: much of Part I and II is based on interviews and unpublished sources as indicated in the text)

Chapter 2
W. Kaye Lamb & Tomas Bartroli, "James Hanna & John Henrey Cox: The First Maritime Fur Trader and His Sponsor" (B.C. Studies no 84, Winter 1989-98)

Ed. W. Kaye Lamb, *The Voyage of George Vancouver 1791-1795, Volume II,* (p. 641-655) Hakluyt Society, Cambridge: University Press, 1984

Robert Galois, *Kwakwaka'wakw Settlements, 1775-1920*: A Geographical Analysis and Gazetteer. Vancouver, UBC Press, 2015

Franz Boas, *The Social Organization and the Secret Societies of the Kwkiutl Indians*

Clellan S. Ford, *Smoke From Their Fires:* The Life of a Kwakiutl Chief. Illinois: Waveland Press, Inc, 1996

James R. Gibson, *Otter Skins, Boston Ships, and China Goods:* Maritime Fur Trade of the Northwest Coast, 1785-1841. Univ of Washington Pr, 1999 (p.168 - the incident of the *Belle Savage*)

Wikipedia List of Historical Ships in British Columbia (the incident of the *Belle Savage*)

Chapter 3
Alvin McGill, Helen McGill, interviews by author

Albert L. Hendrickson, "Home on the Deep," unpublished manuscript from interviews with Gloria McGill

Chapter 4
Heather Gildersleeve, Darby Gildersleeve, Email interviews by author

Chapter 5
Frank E. Wall and Ava C. Wall, *Uncertain Journey,* Washington DC: Review and Herald Publishing Association, 1974 (chapters 1 and 9)

Marilyn Pond, *Never Say Whoa in a Bad Place:* Amazing Adventures of an Unassuming Man. Teach Services, Inc., 2010

Greg Kier, "Gumboot Navy: Securing or Sundering British Columbia," (Thesis, University of Victoria, 2015)

Chapter 6
R. Brian McDaniel, *Ocean Falls, After the Whistle,* 2018

Bruce Ramsey, *Rain People: The Story of Ocean Falls,* Wells Gray Tours, Limited, 1997
www.oceanfallsmuseum.com/Recollections/R-F-Patterson.htm (steamship ride)

Chapter 7
Edward Higginbottom, "The Changing Geography of Salmon Canning in British Columbia, 1870-1931" (Thesis, Simon Fraser University, 1988) summit.sfu.ca/item/5427

K. Mack Campbell, *Cannery Village: Company Town*, Victoria: Trafford Publishing, 2004

Chapter 11
Donald Graham, *Lights of the Inside Passage*, Madeira Park, Harbour Publishing, 1986

Dennis Wilkins, "The True Story of the Egg Island Lighthouse Disaster," *Lighthouse Digest*, December 2001

Lighthouse Friends.com Egg Island BC

Lighthouse Memories.ca, BC lighthouse keeper database

Lance McGill, Lloyd McGill, Louis Goertzen, Author interviews

Chapter 14
Ada Johnson, "Green Point," unpublished manuscript

Albert L. Hendrickson, "Home on the Deep," unpublished manuscript

Frank Johnson, *Jesus Is There All the Time:* A Canadian Story of Life and Ministry. ForwardMoving Publishing, 2014

Chapter 15
Robert Galois, *Kwakwaka'wakw Settlements, 1775-1920*: A Geographical Analysis and Gazetteer. Vancouver, UBC Press, 2015

Franz Boas, *The Social Organization and the Secret Societies of the Kwkiutl Indians*

Franz Boas, "Social Divisions of the Kwakiutl" and "The Wail of L!a!Eqwasila, A Gwa'sela Woman," (p. 835-886)

Clellan S. Ford, *Smoke from Their Fires:* The Life of a Kwakiutl Chief. Illinois: Waveland Press, Inc, 1996

Ed. James P. Spradley, *Guests Never Leave Hungry*: The Autobiography of James Sewid, a Kwakiutl Indian. Yale University Press, 1969

Jim McDowell, *Hamatsa*: The Enigma of Cannibalism on the Pacific Northwest Coast. Vancouver, Ronsdale Press, 1997

Agnes Alfred, Qwiqwasutinuxs Noblewoman, *Paddling to Where I Stand*, Edited by Martine J. Reid and Daisy Sewid-Smith. UBC Press, 2004

Chapter 47
Ada F. Johnson, "Green Point," Unpublished Manuscript

Alan Fry, *How a People Die*. Toronto: Doubleday & Company, 1970

How a People Live. Directed by Lisa Jackson. Produced by Bliss Pictures Inc., 2013

Louis Goertzen, logbook, 1964

Other Sources:

Gertrude Reimche Machan, *Frontier Footsteps.* Caldwell: Griffith Marketing and Publishing, 1989

Murray McGill, *Dead Birds Don't Sing But Witching Rods Talk.* Teach Services, Inc., 2010

ADA'S BIRTHDAY LIST

Please note that this is not a historical document, just the typed list of a schoolteacher. Though it has some idiosyncrasies, it is still a valuable list. If a child had married, Ada listed them separately and did not include them in the list of children who were still at home. I have tried to place each name under their parents. Also, if family members had moved away or died, they may not have been included in her list.

Walkus: The ancestors of the Walkus genealogy come from five siblings: Chief George (eldest son), William (Gooje) and Edward. The sisters are Mary (who married Tom George) and Maggie.

Walkus	**Chief George (Wyulth)**	June 15, 1882
		(d May 1960)
	Charlie G., Harry, Louis, Lily	
Walkus	**William (Gooje)**	1884
	George James	Dec. 26, 1915
	Mary	July 1, 1927
	William	Oct. 12, 1933
	(Winnie?)	July 9, 1931
Walkus	**Edward**	July 10, 1897
	Sally (George) Walkus (wife)	Feb. 15, 1902
	Edward John	July 9, 1934

	Simon	Mar. 20, 1936
	Alex David	Nov. 1, 1937
	Moses	Nov. 22, 1938
	Marian	Feb. 27, 1943
	Sarah (Hunt)	
Walkus	George James	Dec. 26, 1915
	Eliza Walkus (wife)	Dec. 19, 1915
	James	Feb. 23, 1939
	Alec Clyde	Sept. 22, 1940
	Robert	Feb. 7, 1942
	Archie George	Nov. 24, 1943
	Andrew Weldon	July 12, 1945
	Alvin David	Dec. 25, 1946
	Clara Agnes	Apr. 22, 1949
	Lloyd Herbert	June 14, 1951
	Nancy Doris	Nov. 8, 1953
	Wayne	Jan. 21, 1955
	Gordon	Sept. 1957
	Walter Frank	Nov. 17, 1958
	Louisa Lena	Sept. 30, 1961
Walkus	Charlie George (chief's eldest son)	June 7, 1907
	Jean (Johnny) Walkus (wife)	Mar. 20, 1917
	Robert	Aug. 25, 1932
	Janet	Aug. 19, 1934
	Johnny Wesley	Oct. 17, 1936
	Margaret	Feb. 9, 1938
	Edith Helen	Sept. 1, 1939
	Isabelle	Feb. 13, 1944
	Irene Jean	Mar. 29, 1948
	Clara (Ruby)	July 2, 1949
	Julia	Dec. 14, 1950

	Hazel	June 22, 1953
	Clarence Henry	June 23, 1955 (died)
Walkus	Robert	Aug. 25, 1932
	Violet Walkus (Married Oct 30, 1960)	Apr. 13, 1929
	Leslie	July 16, 1953
	Beatrice	July 24, 1954
	Lawrence	Oct. 28, 1955
	Willis	Oct. 20, 1956 (died)
	Mildred	June 4, 1958
	Roberta	July 4, 1959
	Victor	Aug. 15, 1960
Paul	Vivian	
	Janet (Walkus) Paul (wife)	Aug. 19, 1934
	Agnes Gloria	Oct. 17, 1955
	Rose Marie	Aug. 6, 1956
	Dorothy Lily	May 8, 1958
	Linda Rebecca	Sept. 7, 1959
	Helen Isabelle	Jan. 4, 1961
	Sandra	Jan. 30, 1962
Walkus	Simon	Mar. 20, 1936
	Margaret (Walkus) Walkus (wife)	Feb. 9, 1938
	Simon	Feb. 11, 1956
	Stanley Elvis	Jan. 31, 1957
	Dolores	Apr. 1958
	Susan Stella	Dec. 26, 1961
Walkus	Johnny Wesley	Oct. 17, 1936
	Mary Walkus (wife)	Mar. 1938
	Daniel	Aug. 1955

	Clyde	June 28, 1956
	Doreen	Nov. 17, 1957
	Clarence	Jan. 14, 1960
	Bruce	Mar. 23, 1961
	Brenda Lynn	June 24, 1962
Walkus	Harry George (chief's son)	Nov. 19, 1920
	Mary (Walkus) Walkus (wife)	July 1, 1927
	Albert	June 21, 1941
	Mabel Louise	Aug. 14, 1942
	Willie Johnson	June 13, 1945
	Mary Virginia	May 22, 1948
	Tommy Lloyd	Aug. 8, 1949
	Gloria Elizabeth	Feb. 19, 1951
	Fred Allan	June 25, 1954
	Shirley Laura	June 26, 1955
	Joseph Henry	Mar. 21, 1957
Walkus	Louis George (chief's son)	May 20, 1924
	Elizabeth (Boone) Walkus (Happy's daughter)	Aug. 27, 1932
	Martin Sampson	June 26, 1949
	Paddy Gary	Oct. 2, 1950
	Caroline Jessie	Oct. 14, 1951
	Christine Lydia	Oct. 7, 1952
	Catherine Alice	Mar. 21, 1957
	Louis Jacky	Apr. 29, 1958
	Oliver Victor	July 16, 1959
	Ronald Harvey	Aug. 22, 1960
	Ethel Lowena	Feb. 6, 1962
Walkus	James (Jimmie, Edward's son)	Jan. 20, 1920
	Winnie (Walkus) Walkus (Gooje's daughter)	July 9, 1931

	Cecelia (Florence)	Oct. 1, 1949
	Nellie	Feb. 24, 1951
	Daniel John	Dec. 31, 1952
	Matthew	Sept. 20, 1954
	Darlene Ethel	Mar. 27, 1956
	Mona	Apr. 3, 1960
	Alfred Donald	Sept. 27, 1961
Johnny	Mrs. Chief Johnnie	Dec. 3, 1874
Johnny	Joe	Oct. 1909
	Jane (wife)	
Johnny	David	1911
Johnny	Alfred (Chief Johnny's son)	Dec. 1920
	Lily (Walkus, Chief George's daughter)	Mar. 21,1928
	Geraldine Eva	July 3, 1944
	Alfred Eugene	Dec. 13, 1945
	Douglas Arthur	July 5, 1948
	Judith Lillian	Nov. 21, 1949
	Morris Jonathan	Oct. 27, 1952
	Arlene Rose	July 10, 1956
	Ricky Erwin	Nov. 8, 1958
	Joseph David	Nov. 18, 1960
Boone	Charlie	1889
Boone	Happy	1895
	Elizabeth (daughter)	Aug. 27, 1932
	(The Boones lost many family members to TB)	

George	Annie	Oct. 7, 1940
George	Charlie Walkus (Charlie T, son of Mary Walkus and Tom George)	Oct. 6, 1903
	Rachel (wife)	June 18, 1927 (died)
	Frances Elizabeth	Sept. 29, 1944
	Mary	Jan. 19, 1947
	Raymond	Sept. 19, 1955
Dick	Abel	
	Ada (wife)	July 19, 1927
	Aster Jennie	Jan. 13, 1944
	Mary Violet	Nov. 19, 1947
	Martha	Feb. 27, 1952
	Simon Richard	1955
	Gertie	born 1955, died 1957
	Nora Annie	Mar. 7, 1957
	Sally Helen	Mar. 27, 1958
	Roseanne Melinda	Feb. 10, 1960
	James Moses or Timothy	Apr. 30, 1961
Hunt	Annie (Gladys)	May 28, 1942
	Barbara (Annie and Barbara; grandpa is Edward)	Jan. 21, 1944
Walkus	William (Bill, Gooje's son)	Oct. 12, 1933
Jones	Ida	Sept. 19, 1941
	Heather Marilyn	Aug. 8, 1960
	Joyce Flora	June 2, 1961

Walkus	David (Edward's son)	Nov. 1, 1937
	Annie (George) Walkus (wife)	Oct. 7, 1940
	Gilbert Willie	Nov. 4, 1959
	David Charles	Jan. 12, 1961
	Rachel Annie	Jan. 12, 1962
Walkus	Edward John (Edward's son)	July 9, 1934
	Gertrude (Henderson) Walkus (wife)	Oct. 7, 1941
	Kenneth Sam	Mar. 11, 1960
	Edith	Dec. 2, 1961

Darylee Ann (Nollie) (Sarah's)   May 2, 1962

Chronological
List of Events

1200s: Gwa'sala in the inlet traced back this far in "Wail of a Gwa'sela Woman"

1575–1600: Gwa'sala receive rights to Hamatsa (see "Wail of a Gwa'sela Woman")

1786: Hanna visits and names Smiths Inlet

1792: Vancouver charts Smith's Inlet

1801: Visit of the *Belle Savage*

1833: Hudson's Bay Company builds fort at Bella Bella (Fort McLoughlin)

1848: Fort Rupert is built

1850s: The Heiltsuk from Bella Bella raid the Gwa'sala at Wyclese

1862: Smallpox epidemic

1873: Israel Powell Wood (BC's first superintendent of Indian Affairs) visits the Gwa'sala, first photographs taken (BC archives)

1882: Chief George born

1883: Smith's Inlet Cannery (Quashella Packing Co.) built near Wyclese

1885–1930: Franz Boas researches Kwakwaka'wakw people

1891: Twenty-five canneries in Rivers and Smiths

1890s: The Gwa'sala move from Wyclese to Takush

1916: George Hunt records "Wail of a Gwa'sela Woman"

1937: Gildersleeves tow their logging camp to Smith Inlet

1939 –1945: World War II, Alvin and Goertzen Brothers arrive Smith Inlet

1946: GMG is formed (Security Bay)

1948-ish: Clyde leaves, Roy replaces him, *Stewart K* burns up

1950: Don and Claire, Frank and Ada tow their house to Takush, school begins

1951: GMG tows to Moses Inlet

1952: Don and Ethel die, Roy tows camp to Fly Basin, Alvin and Louie leave Smith Inlet

1953: Alvin family, Claire family back to Smith Inlet in May, Louis in fall

1954: Avalon School begins, Nancy Gildersleeve first teacher

1955: Roy McGill family leaves

1956: Ms. Baker Avalon schoolteacher

1957: Mrs. Thorn Avalon schoolteacher, Joyce Egolf replaces Ada at Takush School, GMG moves to Burnt Island and logs for Nalos, Harold dies

1958: GMG to McBride Bay, Nov. 3

1959: GMG to Boswell Mar. 24, build A-frame, Goertzen house

1960: *Surf Isle* arrives May 15, Chief George funeral May 27, GMG to McBride Bay June 29, Crooks leave

1961: GMG tows to Klak Sept., Knopps arrive, Ada replaces Joyce Egolf at Takush

1962: GMG to Boswell, church dedication Sept. 15, Joyce Egolf teacher at Avalon, Bob Betts arrives

1963: Truck logging preparations in Coho Valley, Katie Lambert replaces Ada at Takush

1964: GMG moves to final location, truck logging begins, Miss Schneider teacher at Avalon, Roy McGill family arrives, Johnsons leave Smith Inlet, the Gwa'sala move to Port Hardy

1965: Sherman McCormick teacher at Avalon, Joe and Shirley Deucey, Frank and Donalda arrive

1967: Katie Lambert teacher at Avalon

1967 – 1969: Everybody leaving the inlet, GMG tows houses to Port Hardy 1969

1970 – 1976: GMG logs summers only, last gyppo logger out

Manufactured by Amazon.ca
Bolton, ON

25910949R00265